Classic
Pennsylvania Dutch
Cooking

With Illustrations
by Heather Saunders
& Nancy Murphy Griffith

Classic
Pennsylvania Dutch Cooking

Printed March 2011

Copyright© 1990 by Betty Groff

International Standard Book Number: 978-1-931294-66-9

Library of Congress Control Number: 2004110912

Edited, Designed and Published in the United States of America
and Manufactured in China by
Cookbook Resources, LLC
541 Doubletree Drive
Highland Village, Texas 75077
Toll free 866-229-2665

www.cookbookresources.com

*cookbook
resources* LLC
Bringing Family and Friends to the Table

ACKNOWLEDGMENTS

Thank You:

Barbara J. Adams, for always being a friend and for the joy of working together on this book. The long hours of research and testing were fun because of your energy and excitement at every turn. Your sensitivity, artistic presentation, and willingness to help in any situation have lightened each responsibility. The mutual enjoyment of rediscovering our roots through the preparation of our regional foods has been so stimulating—it seems we've only scratched the surface. May it open many new doors into the future.

Pam Hoenig, for being a super editor with a keen understanding of my desire to preserve our heritage through food.

Bob and Betty Shirk, for sharing your family cookbooks and insight into other areas of Pennsylvania Dutch foods and folklore.

Saranna Brown Miller, whose illustrations of family heirlooms are the bases of those in this book.

Diane Stoneback for the many hours of late-night inquiries and interviews to search the inner recesses of my mind. The many memories and customs, often taken for granted by all of us, come alive through your ability to ask the right questions. Your sense of humor, warmth, and understanding in writing my story are deeply appreciated.

My husband, Abe, for having faith in me and "pushing" when necessary. Our son, Charlie, and his wife, Cindy, grandsons, Matt and Travis Groff, our son, Bob, and his wife, Janice, and granddaughters, Susan and Sherry, and my Dad and Hazel Herr, for understanding and loving me when the "days were long and patience short." Words cannot express my pride in the strength and commitment of my family.

Contents

THE SEASONS OF THE PENNSYLVANIA DUTCH

❧ SPRING ❧

My ancestors, who settled in Lancaster County, Pennsylvania in 1710, thought they'd found paradise. Ten generations later, I can safely say they did, or we wouldn't still be here! Their enthusiasm was evident in a letter they sent back to family members in their homeland: "This is a rich, limestone country, beautifully adorned with sugar maple, hickory and black and white walnut, on the border of a delightful stream, abounding in the finest trout. The water of the creeks is clear and cold; grapevines and clematis intertwining among the lofty branches of the majestic buttonwood form a pleasant retreat from the noon beams of the summer sun."

William Penn was also a convincing salesman when he described the abundance of his land: "Of living creatures, fish, fowl and the beasts of the wood, here are divers sorts, some for food and profit including the elk, as big as a small ox; deer, bigger than ours in England; beaver; raccoon; rabbits; squirrels...some eat young bear. Of fowl of the land, there is the turkey (40 to 50 pounds weight) which is very great; pheasants; heath birds; pigeons and partridges in abundance...Of fish: sturgeon, herring, shad, catshead, eel, trout and salmon. The fruits which I find in the woods are the black and white mulberry, chestnut, walnut, plums, strawberries, cranberries, burtleberrieis and grapes of divers sorts."

To this day, the variety of top-quality vegetables, fruits, and flowers grown here annually reaffirms the richness of the soil. And nowhere is it more evident than on the farms of our Amish neighbors here in South Central Pennsylvania. Their vegetable and flower gardens are so lush and immaculate that they could be mistaken for a horticultural college's test plots.

Of course, they are not the only residents to take planting seriously. January and February, the bleakest months on our farm, were brightened largely by the arrival of seed catalogs that offered us a glimmer of hope. Many a spare moment was spent studying the pages for new varieties and totally new crops, though evenings were still given to skating and sledding. The picture brightened considerably a few weeks later when my aunt opened her potting shed and planted the flower and vegetable seeds which sprouted into seedlings on the window sills of the farmhouse.

April 1 isn't just April Fool's Day in Lancaster County. It's the day farmers begin their new year with the first of the spring planting and yearly contracts.

Because life was slow and easy until spring planting began, we had plenty of energy to expend on the holiday preparations. While New Orleanians celebrate the day before Lent with the Mardi Gras, we observe "Fat Tuesday" as Fastnacht Day. Some say it's the best part of Lent because the day's main event is the making of a special kind of doughnut—the fastnacht. What better way to spend the day before a fast day than gorging on doughnuts?

The doughnut-making custom began as a good way to use up the household's old lard. But if you're picturing Pennsylvania cooks turning out the usual, run-of-the-mill doughnut shop products drizzled with anything from pink icing to chocolate cream and flaked coconut, erase those images. Fastnachts are never round; they're always square. And there are no holes that will become "Munchkins."

To be the real thing, fastnachts have to be made with yeast, eggs, milk, flour, mashed potatoes, and potato water and must be fried in lard. The fried squares are then rolled in powdered or granulated sugar. I'm told that in the days when sugar wasn't as easy to come by, many people simply cut the fastnachts in half and spread them with molasses.

The last person to rise on the morning the fastnachts are made becomes the family "fastnacht" and endures some teasing between bites of rich, moist doughnut.

Our Easter preparations always centered around food and family, with very little emphasis on new spring wardrobes. Whenever my mother had some spare time during the year, she turned hand-blown eggs into bejeweled works of art. We also created molded sugar eggs with cutout scenes, to say nothing of the chocolate-covered fruit, and coconut and peanut butter eggs which were Easter basket highlights.

Often, women would get together and turn candy-making into a social occasion. In our family, however, my father or I did the writing and borders on the eggs while mother did the flowers. That is, that's the way we did it until I took a decorating course and mother and dad eagerly turned all decorating chores over to me.

Easter eggs, the hardboiled ones that the Easter Bunny hid on the lawn, once were colored with golden or red onion skins. But that custom had died out by the time I was a child. We used Hinkle Easter Egg Dyes, made in nearby Columbia. The rich colors that stained our hands (as well as the eggs) and the distinctive aroma of the dyes were as much a part of the holiday as the fresh ham and snowy white coconut cake that were Easter dinner traditions.

Although the Moravians in the eastern part of the state love their saffron cake, the coconut cake is a Lancaster County specialty for Christmas and Easter. The cake trimmed with freshly grated coconut was very special in a day when coconuts weren't so readily available. The round cake has four lofty layers that are piled high with fluffy seven-minute icing. Spread into peaks that resembled whitecaps, the icing always sinks a bit under the heavy layer of freshly-grated coconut that tops off the cake.

Early spring was also the time for suckers (known to early settlers as a form of trout) to spawn in the smaller streams. They came up the runs by the hundreds, to lay their eggs before returning to larger streams. I remember going by the stream on our property at night and shining a flashlight into the water. Hundreds of fish were in one cove—so crowded that I could have reached in and pulled them out with my hands. Although the fish wardens said they shouldn't be caught, many a sucker landed in the frying pan for breakfast.

The Pennsylvania Dutch have a reputation for eating a boring meat and potatoes diet. That's as much of a false stereotype as the idea that Scotsmen are tightfisted with their money. We always ate plenty of fish and more vegetables than some people see in a lifetime. When it came to fish, what we couldn't catch was delivered to the door by a fisherman who called at the farm each week. The vegetables we couldn't raise were available at the farmers' market stalls.

Our local streams are full of brown trout—a legacy from old Simon Cameron, former Secretary of War under President Lincoln. A Scotsman, Cameron imported stock from his native land to fill the stream on his estate that's now our Cameron Estate Inn. We keep the stream at the inn, and the pond at our farm, well-stocked with trout as a tribute to him and because there's nothing I like better than a fresh trout cooked with the head and tail intact and then filleted tableside. The flavor is unbeatable.

Each spring, when shad come upstream to spawn, we're responsible for preventing a few from making the trip back downstream. Shad or shad roe, parsleyed new potatoes, and fresh asparagus are a dinner-salute to the season. I always think of my grandfather, Newton, when I have some roe because that delicacy was always reserved for the older men, especially him.

Oysters, expensive and highly coveted, were for special people and special occasions. That's why Lancaster County cooks spent so much time finding substitutes for oysters like salsify or deep-frying blossoms of dandelion, squash, or pumpkins. Although my mother managed to buy oysters weekly when times were good, the large oysters were breaded and pan fried for my father or grandfather. We children were given the broth and ate some of the small ones in stews and casseroles. We never fussed or complained. That's because we realized quickly that while we liked the taste of the broth, we didn't like the mouth-feel of those plump, squishy oysters on our tongues.

Fish and holiday foods helped make spring special, but the season's contributions to the salad bowl made it particularly memorable. While the farmers sterilized the raised beds in the field closest to the house to ready them for their biggest cash crop—the tobacco used for cigars—their wives coaxed them out of a little space in that rich soil for the household's vegetable garden.

It was no different at our farm. The first foods I remember planting were radishes and tender leaf lettuce. Although we can buy all kinds of greens today, I am still partial to the earliest leaf lettuce, tossed with a very light dressing.

Even if you live in the city and can't plant a garden, you can raise oak leaf lettuce in a long window box. If you try it, make some of our dressing to go with it. Just combine 2 cups sugar with 1 cup vinegar and 1 cup water, a pinch of salt, and some celery seed. "Fancy it up" with some slices of hardboiled eggs, if you like.

Although it's a well-kept secret, the little town of Mount Joy is the watercress capital of the world. During the peak season four tractor-trailer loads a week are taken out of Donegal Springs which starts near our inn. But I have a personal supply that's closer than that. Whenever I have some freshly baked homemade bread that's still warm, I dash to the pond and cut some watercress. Practically before the kitchen door has closed behind me, I have bread buttered, sprinkled with salt, spread with cream cheese, and buried under a mound of watercress. Now, that's living!

Spinach and asparagus, two of the earliest vegetables to be planted, were not among my favorites when I was young. (Asparagus and I were on particularly bad terms because one of my jobs as a child was picking the tender asparagus spears each morning. And the reason it was my task—I was the closest to the ground, even when I was standing "tall".) When Abe and I were first married, one of my earliest shocks was learning that these were his favorite vegetables. I looked at him and said, "You must be kidding, I hate both of them." But I've mellowed and have learned to savor them both. My change of heart has a lot to do with making sure they're prepared properly, but it might have something to do with love, too.

At our house, the asparagus is stir-fried quickly and served with a bit of brown butter rather than being cooked to death and then being served in cream and butter over toast points, as my family used to prepare it. Our favorite way to have spinach is the simplest way—in a salad with crumbled bacon and hardboiled egg.

Sugar peas, a delicacy we've enjoyed in Lancaster County since the days of the earliest settlers, are some of the most delicate and most misunderstood vegetables we grow. They look like snow peas but are smaller, sweeter, and tenderer. I know of some people who have moved into the area and were given a quart of sugar peas as a welcoming gift. They tried to shell them, thereby throwing the best part away.

As soon as the plants are three inches tall, a fence or some brush is placed along the row to give the vines something to cling to. Accomplished gardeners say to get the very best crop; the sugar peas should be planted on St. Patrick's Day. But that's sometimes hard to do because we often get an "onion snow" (the last light snow) late in March. It doesn't hurt the young growth, but it often discourages the gardener.

Green onions or scallions were another springtime treat, though consuming them was a bit tricky. Because I grew up in a minister's family, eating onions was only allowed on days when there were no scheduled church events. That ruled out Tuesdays and Wednesday as well as weekends. Mondays and Thursdays were my days to hit them hard as a snack with bread and butter or on fried potatoes.

Not all the coveted spring greens here in Pennsylvania are specially planted. One of our favorites is regarded elsewhere as a plague to be obliterated with a bevy of lawn chemicals. In our part of the state, however, dandelions never get out of hand until after they bloom. That's because we love eating the tender young leaves long before the plants ever flower. Even if they get beyond the early stages, we have happier ways of dealing with them than spraying them with poison.

In the old days, thoroughly cooked dandelion was considered a spring tonic. All I know is that it certainly got you going—as fast as you could go in another direction. There's nothing more bitter than dandelion that has been cooked for any length of time. When we make it, the hot bacon dressing that's poured over the uncooked greens wilts the salad without making it mushy or bitter. If you do want to use dandelion in a cooked dish, saute it very briefly or fold it into the other cooked vegetables. The flavor is pungent but less bitter than endive.

There's a joke we tell on ourselves that will give you an idea of how much we love dandelion greens. It goes like this: "Do you know a simple way to kill a Pennsylvania Dutchman?" When answered "No," deliver this punch line: "Just tell him there's dandelion growing in the center of the nearest interstate highway."

The plants that have escaped the careful eyes of the greens hunters and manage to flower sometimes have their blossoms plucked and batter-fried. I prefer to allow the yellow flowers to ferment with oranges, lemons, and raisins for a smooth, fruity wine. I always say, "Dandelion wine is a sure cure for a cold or cough but even if it isn't, it'll make you forget your troubles while it's going down."

SUMMER

In Lancaster County, we never used a calendar to tell when summer began. That's because our busiest season of the year always began long before the solstice. The date changed from year to year, however, depending on the number of snowstorms we had. Sound strange? It really isn't any more curious than our Pennsylvania custom of depending on a groundhog's shadow to forecast the severity of the remaining winter months or at arrival of an early spring. For us, summer started with the last-day-of-school picnic at our one-room schoolhouse. If severe winter storms forced the closing of school numerous times, the picnic wasn't scheduled until the first week of June. After a mild winter, we could count on the end of May for the picnic. It was a day children looked forward to almost as eagerly as Christmas or Easter. Every last minute was planned to the smallest detail. Although our parents often went to school with us the day of the picnic, there was never any dread. It was a day for games and good eating. Of course, the teacher always had the good sense to wait until the end of the day to distribute our grades.

Today, when I pass an Amish school and see the children tossing a ball over the roof to see how many times they can get it back and forth without the ball falling to the ground, I remember those picnics vividly. Collee-over, as they call it, was one of our favorite games in a repertoire that included other amusements like baseball, rope-jumping matches, and tug-of-war.

Appetites were huge after a morning of play, but the spread of picnic food our parents prepared was even bigger. Crispy fried chicken was stacked on platters with the same kind of precision early settlers used to build log cabins. The bowls of potato salad and light-tasting homemade potato chips must have required at least half the county's potatoes (little did I know how plentiful they were). There were stacks of chicken and ham salad sandwiches and pickled red beet eggs whose bright color matched the day's mood.

Desserts topped the day by providing an ending almost as sweet as a "straight A" report card. Chocolate-covered pretzels, caramel corn, homemade pull taffy, whoopee pies (sweetened whipped cream sandwiched between two chocolate cake-like cookies), and cupcakes (each with enough icing to cover a small cake) were just a sampling of the temptations that passed among us.

At the end of the day, we headed for home and a season of hard work that still allowed time enough for swimming in the creek, hunting arrowheads, and playing lookout from the top of the silo. In early summer, we watched almost as eagerly for the first bumblebees as our parents did for the first spring robins. That's because my mother and dad always said that when the bumblebees appeared, it was warm enough for us to go barefoot. From then on, of course, it behooved us to watch where we stepped to avoid unwanted encounters with those same bees.

My mother, an avid gardener, tested her skills annually by attempting to have the first new potatoes and garden peas in time for my parents' June 12 anniversary. She succeeded at least 80 percent of the time. The peas, in a day when fat and cholesterol weren't such concerns, were served in cream and butter. And the potatoes had to be scraped rather than peeled. We're fussy about our potatoes and the care we lavish on the new potatoes is just one example. When you're new to the task, scraping enough potatoes for six people will take an hour. But the taste will be worth it because scraping preserves the part of the potato that contains the most nutrients and the bulk of the flavor. After they're scraped and cooked, they crack, providing enough nooks and crannies to retain the brown butter that's poured over them.

Potatoes for mashing are always peeled after they've been boiled because the skins lock in the flavor. Potatoes for homemade chips must never have been stored at a temperature below 52 degrees or they won't stay crisp after they're fried. Potatoes for old-fashioned potato salad are peeled when they're hot and are coated with dressing while they're still warm. Because the dressing permeates the warm potatoes more evenly, less is needed to achieve the final flavor.

When I think about it, however, I guess my family was always rather fanatic about the foods we raised. The garden peas and lima beans were picked when they were young, not when the pods were completely filled. Tomato varieties producing fewer seeds were chosen for planting and each one of the stalks had to be staked so there would be no ugly spots on the tomatoes. Straw was carefully placed in the strawberry beds to keep the berries and the pickers clean.

Those luscious strawberries, the first real treats of the summer, sent our kitchen into full-scale production. We savored plenty of them plain or in the thick fresh cream we always had on the farm. But as the season progressed, we raced to keep ahead of the crop with such treats as shortcakes and pies as well as whole berry jams for special occasions and crushed berry jams for everyday use.

Berry picking wasn't over when the last of the strawberries were picked. We often made a party out of our searches along meadow fence rows or in the woods for wine berries, blackberries, blueberries, raspberries, and mulberries. Naturally, we asked permission to pick if we found any of these treasures on someone else's property. And we always went on these expeditions armed with an ample supply of bug spray and bee-sting medicine because we knew we weren't the only creatures who liked the berries' sweetness.

A friend raised in north central Pennsylvania mentioned another precaution her family took on forays to mountainside patches of wild huckleberries. Before women and children started picking the tiny blue berries from the low bushes, several men in the crowd beat on the ground with walking sticks to scare rattlesnakes away. She was never certain, however, if the rattlesnake ritual served any real purpose other than displaying a bit of bravado.

The summer berries, particularly the strawberries and raspberries, were grand atop dishes of our homemade vanilla ice cream—a summer treat we had at least three times a week. For the ultimate splurge, we sometimes were allowed to spoon on the fresh berries as well as some of my mother's homemade chocolate syrup. The ice cream was an evening treat, particularly if other families came to visit or to buy some of our special Persian melons. My brother or cousin would crank the eight-quart freezer until the batch was smooth and creamy. When the ice cream was ready, my mother or aunt always counted noses before deciding on the size serving bowls to use. Naturally, we children always hoped for fewer visitors and bigger bowls.

Close to the Fourth of July, Mother Nature stages her own fireworks display in certain parts of Pennsylvania. That's when lightning bugs or "fire bugs," as we call them, appear and add a special sparkle to lazy summer evenings. When the first frontiersmen settled the area, they were amazed to see something flashing in the air above the meadows at dusk or even later. They wondered if those twinkling lights were the sparks from Indian campfires or were they the wood fairies? Today, we know the lightning bugs are the adult stage of the "glowworm"—beneficial insects that feed on other small pests. Interestingly, no one has been able to breed these insects in captivity so they can't be brought and established in areas where they don't exist. They're so highly treasured that they were made Pennsylvania's state insect in 1974!

We'd even hurry to finish our ice cream so we could catch a few lightning bugs. Our "captives" were put in jars with breathing holes poked in the lids. For a few fleeting minutes before we released them again, the lightning bugs made splendid lanterns. It was a good thing the lightning bugs came out at night because there wasn't time for such frivolousness during the days of mid and late summer. That's when we spent much of our time working with all the fruits and vegetables the fertile soil produced. Although my husband, Abe, has always liked eating tomatoes while they're still in the field and warm from the sun, my family spent a lot of time making something more out of them. We made zesty tomato juice by adding watercress to it. We cooked up stewed tomatoes and served them over mashed potatoes. Green and red tomato slices, first dipped in flour, were pan-fried in a mix of butter and lard, then glazed with sugar. They didn't look great but the flavor was unbelievable. We also turned green tomatoes into pies and green tomato relish. Just before the first frost, my mother always wrapped the prettiest green tomatoes she could find in tissue paper and put them in the basement to ripen so there would be a few for the holidays. Corn on the cob picked fresh in the morning before the sun was too high, was a staple at our noon-time dinner, as long as it was in season. Chicken-corn soup, corn pie, and corn fritters used up still more of the crop. What we couldn't eat fresh was cut off the cobs and dried. The operation was something of a culinary ritual conducted carefully by my grandmother, mother, and aunt. As the corn dried on the stove in the corner of the farm kitchen, they took turns staying awake all night to make sure it didn't burn or get too brown. When done properly it turns golden and has a caramel flavor. I loved the taste of newly dried corn more than the taste of candy.

I've chuckled to myself as chefs have "discovered" cold fruit soups in recent years. My family was enjoying that summer treat more than forty years ago. In the days when milk had cream on it, my mother kept handy a pretty old crystal pitcher of sweetened milk. For dessert, we'd toss some of the season's first freshly sliced cling peaches with bread cubes and pour the sweetened milk over the top.

When the freestone peach crop ripened, we canned peaches of every variety we could buy. There were the big white Champion peaches as well as the smaller bright orange peaches with red centers. Because my hands were small, it was my job to arrange the peaches in the canning jars. Their centers had to be turned toward the outside of the jar so they'd look their prettiest. My mother-in-law also taught me to put one peach pit in each jar to help the peaches retain their color and give them a slight almond flavor. The peaches we didn't can became peach pies, peach sundae toppings, and peach ice cream. Still more of the fruit became peach wine.

Toward the end of summer, my thoughts always turn to smoking meats. It's the result of spending hot summer days playing with my dolls on the second floor of my family's smokehouse. Because we only smoked meats in the winter, the building was cool in summer and wonderfully scented with the aroma of hickory smoke. Though I'll never be able to re-create the scent that took years to impart, I get out my smoker and spend several late summer weekends working to impart a hint of the flavor I remember into turkeys, roasting chickens, pork, and fish.

Although the availability of fresh fruits and vegetables all year-round means it's no longer essential to can some of everything, I can't help myself. I still can some fruits and make pickles and relishes every year. When I look at the finished array of bright colors and shapes in the jars, I know what my mother meant when she said that food preparation and preservation is an art.

One evening when guests at the Groff's Farm Restaurant included an Amish neighbor, I said, "I hope you will come down to the basement and see my canned fruits and taste our homemade wines because I'm very interested in keeping the tradition." After dinner, when she and her friends descended the basement stairs, she commented as she surveyed my handiwork, "For you, it is a matter of preserving a tradition. For us, it is still a matter of survival."

🦋 FALL 🦋

The harvest of colors in the canning jars, from the scarlet red tomatoes and peppers and maroon beets and cherries, to the green beans, yellow corn, and golden peaches and apricots, painted the shelves of country fair exhibit halls with a brilliance that nearly matched nature's outdoor display of changing leaves. Each autumn, these country fairs marked the beginning of a social season that lasted at least until everyone had his good luck dinner of pork and sauerkraut on New Year's Day. Sometimes it lasted even longer if the family calendar included a visit to the grandest fair of them all, the Pennsylvania Farm Show in Harrisburg. Pennsylvania's answer to the state fair, the farm show has always been a test of the participants' ingenuity. After all, it's far easier to come up with fresh vegetables and canned goods in August than it is in midwinter.

Farm families planned and prepared for the fairs all summer long—putting aside the best-looking of the canned goods for possible blue ribbons. When we were at work, we remembered the subtle touches that made the preserved food look top notch—such as making sure the jars of Queen Anne cherries had no more than an inch of liquid at the top so the jars looked as if they were absolutely brimming with perfect fruit and arranging the plump, round apricots so their creases faced the outside of the jars. The fair competition was intense.

On the line were culinary reputations, including some established by earlier generations and carefully defended by later descendents.

In the week or two before the fair, my mother, aunt, and I sorted through our canned goods for our entries. Our kitchen went into full production a day or two before the fair to produce the cakes, pies, cookies, and candy that would be entered in the baking competition.

On opening day, while the men spent their time ogling the farm animals and new harvesting equipment and the children did their best to eat their way along midways lined with stands selling everything from French fries, caramel corn, and red candy apples to funnel cakes, the women sized up their competition in the exhibit halls. They studied the jars of jellies and jams, relishes, vegetables, and fruits with the precision of quality-control inspectors. They were their own judges as they decided whose canned and baked goods looked the best. Of course, the fun was seeing if the real judges had the good sense to make the right choices when it came time for the blue ribbons and their accompanying two-dollar cash prizes.

I loved the competition, particularly because a few blue ribbons gave me some extra spending money. The year I was thirteen was one I'll never forget. I managed to win both the fair's adult and youth divisions with a plate of chocolate chip cookies and a tall lemon chiffon cake made from my mother's recipe. I still make that chiffon cake, which is served plain or with an orange sauce. But try as I do, I can never make my modern cakes measure up to the height of the blue-ribbon cake of my memories. I have finally concluded that the ones I bake now seem smaller because I'm taller!

Barn raisings—when community members pitch in to help a young couple just starting out or to replace a barn destroyed by fire—have occurred whenever necessary. But most of those that are planned are finished by the time the brilliance of autumn has faded to winter grays and browns.

Going to a barn raising has always raised my spirits at least as high as the barn's main beams. There are the fellowship and the warm feelings that come from helping friends, to say nothing of the food that is unrivaled by any other social event. Wedding fare can't hold a candle to the groaning boards set out for barn raisings. After all, at a wedding there's usually just one meal and loads of people to eat it. At barn raisings, on the other hand, there's usually three or four times as much food and half as many people to eat it!

Barn raisings almost always begin at 6 A.M. and last until the roofing is nailed on a little after dusk. And food is served practically from the time the first hammer strikes the first nail. Hot and cold drinks and all kinds of cookies keep up the strength of the 150 (or more!) builders until break time when cold sliced meats and cheese platters are passed. But the main meal is the highlight of the day. There's a whole baked ham or fried ham slices, a rolled rib roast or brisket of beef, roast chicken, chicken pot pie or fried chicken, potatoes, three or four different vegetables, at least "two colors" of cake (white or yellow and chocolate or spice), any number of pies, two or three flavors of homemade ice cream, and at least three puddings. It's a wonder the men are able to climb back up on the beams after a meal like that!

But autumn meant more than a round of social events and good eating. Although the tobacco crop was usually in by fair time, there was often one more cutting of hay and the corn harvest still to be done.

And there was a large culinary task that was as sure a sign of autumn as the sight of birds flying south and the smell of burning leaves in the air. That was the morning each October when my father and uncle built the outdoor fire and set up the copper kettles for the women to make the annual supply of apple butter. When I was young, my mother and aunt never gave me a chance at stirring the apple butter with the big wooden paddle because it could scorch too easily, but I put in many a shift at the apple peeler.

Although our day of making apple butter wasn't as grand an event as the Adams County Apple Harvest Festival (where city folk still can see how apple butter is made), I savored every minute of it. The smell of the apples cooking over the smoky open fire gave me a taste for the butter that lasted all year.

Our family experts always selected tart Staymen and Smokehouse apples for their recipe and combined them with dried applies (schnitz), sugar, and spices to provide the depth of flavor and rich brown color we all loved. The mixture was stirred and stirred from early morning until late afternoon when all the excess moisture had cooked away. We stored it in crocks and jars till we needed it.

A dish of apple butter was always on the table, ready to be spread over fresh homemade bread at a moment's notice. But we also put it in half-moon pies or filled cookies, glazed ham loaves with it, ate it with scrapple, matched it with wild game, and even dared to serve it, rather than cranberry sauce, with turkey.

When the cooler weather brought an end to garden chores and made us all feel more like firing up the kitchen range, we made the seasonal adjustments. Heavy, hearty bran and wheat breads went into the oven (though we lightened up again around the holidays by making festive yeast breads and cookies like the ever-popular sandtarts). Homemade ice cream and shortcakes with fresh fruit gave way to warm puddings and gingerbread topped with hot lemon rum sauce.

We experimented with flavored vinegars long before they became trendy. I particularly love the old-fashioned celery and onion vinegars which go a long way when it comes to adding extra flavor without adding calories or chemical additives.

There was time for making fun foods, too. Cinnamon heart candies were turned into red coating for our own candy apples. Caramel corn was another treat that always had to be eaten quickly, before it became sticky and soggy. I've since discovered the candy shops' secret, that is, baking off the caramel corn for a little while in the oven to dry it out and keep it firm. Today, my caramel corn always cracks like the store-bought versions. Trouble is, I no longer have an excuse for eating so much of it so quickly.

Although I didn't enjoy fall cleaning nearly as much as autumn cooking it was a necessary evil to prepare the house for the much more formal winter entertaining which replaced the casual summer gatherings that consisted of bowls of ice cream on the front porch. Table linens were starched and pressed. The silver was polished, and the china closet's entire contents were freshly washed.

The weeks before Thanksgiving were also the time for making our holiday supply of mincemeat. Ours always contained meat, but the beef was ground so finely that you wouldn't have realized it was in there unless someone told you. We added the dark red wine, applies, raisins, and currants to the meat and let the mixture simmer on the coal stove for hours and hours. But the finished mincemeat was worth all the trouble for it truly made festive pies. Even people who made a point of saying they didn't drink couldn't resist a slice or two of pie which was loaded with the taste of the alcohol; in addition to the wine the meat was cooked with, the mincemeat in each pie was topped off with another half cup of spirits just before baking.

Thanksgiving, of course, was autumn's most festive meal and required the most advance planning. My mother ordered our holiday turkeys from a nearby farm. Because there was always fourteen around the family table, nothing smaller than a twenty-two-pound bird would do.

The day before Thanksgiving, the turkey was picked up and my mother and aunt busily baked the cakes, cooked the sweet potatoes, peeled the white potatoes, and soaked the dried corn in milk overnight.

After Thanksgiving morning church services, the men in our family went hunting for rabbits and pheasants in nearby fields while the women went back to work in the kitchen. Before long, the wonderful aroma of celery and parsley being sauteed with butter and a bit of saffron began building our appetites. The basis of our moist bread stuffing, the sauteed vegetables were blended with the bread cubes, eggs, milk, pepper, and salt. Although Berks County residents served their turkey with potato filling (a mix of mashed potatoes with bread cubes, onion, celery, parsley, and butter) and still other Pennsylvania cooks dared to fill their turkeys with a mixture of chestnuts and oysters, we never wavered from our plain and simple stuffing. Once the breast and neck cavities of the turkey were stuffed full, the bird went into the oven to be slow-roasted, breast-side down.

The work for our 1 P.M. dinner was far from done, however. Pies and puddings were baked. The giblets and neck meat were cooked with onions and celery for the gravy. The dried corn went onto the stove, to be further flavored with sugar, butter, salt, and pepper. Cranberries, apples, and walnuts were ground together for a festive relish. Sweet potatoes were fried in butter and then sprinkled with granulated sugar. A traditional green salad or Waldorf salad was tossed. Lima beans came out of the freezer and were cooked in butter and cream and potatoes were mashed and whipped till they formed the perfect peaks over which to pour cascades of browned butter.

It didn't take long for the hungry hunters to devour a feast of those proportions. I still marvel that there was never anything left of that twenty-two-pound turkey. I didn't even know what turkey hash was until after Abe and I were married and had moved away from home. Thankfully, Thomas Jefferson faced the left-over problem before I had to. It is a modified version of his turkey hash, served at Jefferson's White House breakfasts, that we use in our home.

Fully fortified after Thanksgiving dinner, the hunters walked the same fields once more—supposedly to bag their limit of game on the season's last day but also, effectively, to miss the major clean-up operations in kitchen and dining room.

When we finished washing up, we talked about our plans for the Christmas season—everything from the gifts we were making to the cookies we would bake. As the hours passed, we kept an eye out for the men and hoped we'd see them come home empty-handed. In those days, women usually cleaned the game. (Today, most men clean their own game—at least at our house.)

Fall breakfasts on the farm were always hearty, for it seemed with every degree the temperature dropped, our appetites increased a few notches. Sometimes the early morning fare included fresh sticky buns studded with newly harvested walnuts, buckwheat cakes, and sausage or heavy cornmeal waffles with golden molasses. (Please note that I'm talking about light molasses here and in my recipes. The darker blackstrap molasses, which is heavily sulfured, on the farm was reserved for women with headaches and for bulls that didn't perform properly in the barn!)

Although maple trees are tapped and syrup was made in early spring, pouring it over pancakes brings it to my mind during the autumn. And while most people think of Vermont or Quebec when it comes to maple syrup, nearby Somerset County producers turn out enough for a good many Pennsylvanians.

Barb Adams, my friend and assistant, said her family managed to turn out 350 gallons of maple syrup from their own sugar camp on the family farm in Somerset. Saving it only for pancakes meant eating pancakes three times a day for the year, inviting Paul Bunyan for breakfast each morning, or finding additional uses for the syrup. It wasn't long before family members were candying sweet potatoes with maple syrup, baking apples with butter, cinnamon, and syrup, and brown sugar came to mean maple sugar. Although Barb notes that spotza, maple candy made by pouring the syrup onto a cold plate or pouring it over snow and eating it like a snowball, is popular (particularly at Pennsylvania's Maple Festival in April in Meyersdale), her family wasn't impressed with it. She said, "My grandmother said the family worked too hard cooking the sap down to syrup to waste it by pouring it on snow." I'm inclined to agree when I hear about the wonderful maple fudge and the taffy Barb's family made. They had the usual pull taffy but they also had pans of taffy that sat around the house, tempting anyone who dared go near them. Barb explained, "All you did was dip a dull table knife into the taffy and twirl it until it was covered with the sticky candy. Then you simply sat there and sucked on your knife until the candy dissolved!"

Autumn meals were often simple in Huntingdon County, where Barb spent most of her early years. Her grandmother was a great one for one-pot meals (another "new idea" that's not so new). A meal of ham, green beans, and potatoes was popular. So were homemade pot pie, corned beef with cabbage, and beef pot roasts. Her grandmother also liked to fry off a piece of meat in a pan and then brown slices of cabbage in the drippings.

Just a week or two after the fancy dishes from Thanksgiving were safely stowed in the cupboard, we knew my father and uncle would be anxious to begin butchering. After we'd had several good freezes in a row—several nights and early mornings when the breath billowed from our mouths like clouds of smoke—the weather meant the meat could be cooled down quickly without benefit of a modern refrigeration system.

Butchering meant extra work for everyone, but no one complained. Thanks to dad's vocation, we lived fairly high off the hog. The only time we ate pork variety meats was right after butchering, because dad didn't sell them in the shop. We didn't even make much of the stuffed pig's stomachs which were so popular in Lehigh and Northampton counties. Even when we had it, my mother fancied it up a bit by calling it "French Goose." We bought the pork we turned into sausage, bacon, and hams. The rows of hams, top rounds that would become dried beef, the beef tongues, and bacon laid out on planks in the old arched cellar (ten or twelve feet below ground and chilly all year) were sights I'll never forget. The meats were rubbed with a thick coating of salt and sugar that would seep into the meat for several days. Then, they were dipped in a salt brine and carried up narrow, winding stairs to the second-floor smokehouse that was above the butcher shop.

Already brimming with the rings of freshly made sausage and bologna, the smokehouse was a supernatural place. In summer, when you could see the rafters, they literally sparkled under layers of shiny black soot. In winter, the hickory and apple smoke swirled so thickly in the huge room that you couldn't see your hand when you held it six inches from your face. Unless you were very familiar with the room, a collision with an ugly beef tongue or two was entirely possible.

The fresh bologna was a real treat for me when it was new, lightly smoked, and still soft. My grandfather, on the other hand, believed it was at its best when it was so smoky and dry that he could cut a quarter-inch slice and chew on it for an hour.

Paper-thin dried beef, the most expensive of all the smoked meats, was served in a milk gravy or went into sandwiches with cream cheese.

The flavor of the wonderful hams that came from the smokehouse is another taste I'll never forget. The hams were smoked and aged for nearly six months, the earliest ones in time for Easter. True fans, however, waited a year, rather than six months, for the special salty, smoky flavor that comes from a country ham.

Once the ham's rind is peeled and it has been soaked and baked in a small amount of water, it's shaved or served in very thin slices because a little of it goes a long way. Although the ham is half the weight it was the year before, it delivers at least twice the flavor.

Smokehouse delicacies like the smoked hams and dried beef were enjoyed on special occasions. But our daily diet also included plenty of fresh roasts, chops, and steaks as well as wonderful wild game, from pheasant and rabbit to venison.

Although farm families' diets often have been depicted as monotonous and bland, nothing could have been further from the truth in Pennsylvania, where each season heralded a new kind of feast.

Grains have always played an important role in history. Not only are we all dependent on them for our daily bread, but farmers count on the grain for income as well as straw for the cattle. It is difficult to imagine the physical work involved in harvesting this beautiful golden wheat crop since we live in a day of large automatic equipment.

While comparing our family's contributions to Pennsylvania Dutch cuisine, our friends Bob and Betty Shirk of Lancaster reminisced about Bob's distant relative, Michael Cromer, from Mercersburg, Pennsylvania, who on July 12, 1858, established a world's record—in one day, with only the aid of a grain cradle, he cut twelve-and-a-half acres of wheat. The illustration on the previous page, an imagined recreation of the event, is adapted from the original by Charles Stone.

🌺 WINTER 🌺
Moravian Christmas

Walk in Bethlehem's historic area on a December night when snow blankets streets, sidewalks, and trees like a freshly plumped down comforter.

Listen to the carolers who look for all the world like gilt figurines in the glow cast by an old-fashioned street lamp. Linger on Church Street to absorb nearly 250 years of history and watch as women who simply can't make fewer than four Moravian sugar cakes at a time deliver the extras to friends and neighbors. Breathe deeply to catch the aroma of paper-thin brown spice "cakes" baking in kitchens all over town. Longtime resident Alice Knouss declares it takes twelve of these cookies to make a single mouthful.

Have a thin Moravian mint and the crunch will recall the childhood sensation of biting into a wedge of crusted snow. It's moments like these that give visitors an insatiable appetite for Bethlehem and offer a taste of the reasons why eastern Pennsylvania cooks deserve recognition for their artistry. Although much of the activity in central Pennsylvania was devoted to agriculture and savoring the harvest, "Easterners" carefully nurtured bountiful gardens in their spare time and ate well from them, too.

Allentown, Bethlehem, and Easton cooks artfully prepare shad and its roe, thanks to the bounty in the nearby Delaware River. And they have become excellent bakers because area breweries have always kept them well-supplied with brewers' yeast.

From the earliest days, Bethlehem, in particular, gained a reputation for the hospitality extended to those who made the three-day horseback ride from Philadelphia to the frontier outpost.

Although the area's Moravians (Bethlehem's first settlers) were better known for their contributions in music and art, they also were teaching cookery in their seminary. Aided by the many cookbooks they had brought with them from southeastern Germany, they practiced a high standard of cookery in their homes. No wonder Ben Franklin, George Washington, John and Samuel Adams, John Hancock, and even Benedict Arnold enjoyed tarrying in Bethlehem!

Today, no matter what the occasion for celebration, food is a part of it. When the men of the central Moravian church are finished decorating the sanctuary for Christmas, they have a "schmaus." As Alice Knouss explains, it's a party that always includes oyster stew, Moravian sugar cake, and other hearty fare like ham, potatoes, and beans.

During love feasts, simple Moravian worship services with plenty of singing and very little talk, women dressed in white pass baskets of sweetened rolls resembling buttersemmels and men follow with trays of coffee (or chocolate milk, if it's a special children's love feast). No one partakes until everyone is served and the minister gives the signal to begin.

Between stirring Christmas Eve vigil services (which are highlighted by the glow of hundreds of beeswax candles held aloft by the Moravian congregations in their darkened churches), choir members often dash home for lentil soup and sugar cake or have snacks in the church.

Between Christmas and New Year's Day, putzing parties go from house to house to see the putzes, which are elaborate nativity scenes set up beneath Christmas trees. The revelers particularly relish stopping at the homes where hosts frequently pass well-stocked trays of brown and white cakes (actually cookies), sandtarts, and pfeffernusse.

Sugar pretzels—sweet rolls shaped like the familiar Pennsylvania Dutch snacks—glisten with melted butter and a sprinkling of granulated sugar. A New Year's Eve tradition, they add extra sparkle to the Watch Night church service that's climaxed by a burst of brass from the Central Church's trombone choir at the stroke of midnight.

Moravian sugar cake, though it is baked year round by Moravians living all over the Lehigh Valley, is particularly evident during holidays when hurried cooks still take the time to bake. Mrs. Lee Butterfield, who proclaims proudly that she was born and bred on Church Street within the shadow of the Central Church's belfry, commented, "There has been many a tooth-and-nail debate about whether sugar cake can be made with or without potato water." But Mrs. Pat Dimmick of Hellertown is convinced she knows the answer. She says, "Although my mother used mashed potatoes and potato water, I use instant mashed potatoes. I am convinced that if earlier Moravians had instant potatoes, they'd have used them, too!"

Cooks have definite opinions about the qualities of a good Moravian sugar cake. Explained Mrs. Butterfield, "It shouldn't' be a quarter of an inch thick, but it shouldn't be two inches high either. The right height is about one-and-a-half inches and it has to have lots of butter and sugar holes. The cake shouldn't be over moist but it shouldn't be dry, either. It shouldn't taste two days old when it isn't."

Eighty-eight-year-old Martha Luckenbach recalls how her mother's sugar cake was improved accidentally. "We mixed the dough as usual on Friday night, put it in cake pans and covered it with linen cloths so it would rise overnight. When we lifted the cloths in the morning, we discovered that the cat apparently had pranced across the tops of the cakes on the way to his window perch for bird watching. My mother simply filled the paw holes with extra butter and sugar and baked the cakes. When my father asked why the sugar cake was so much better and heard the story, he gently stroked the cat and suggested that she make a habit of walking on the rising sugar cakes."

The molasses cookies called brown spice cakes are probably the most pervasive of holiday treats, according to Mrs. Knouss. "We also had sandtarts and chocolate cookies which were cut in rounds, but the brown spice cakes had to be cut into all kinds of fancy shapes."

The dough for the brown spice cakes ages for three or four days in a cool place (but not the refrigerator) so the spices can work their way through the dough. Miss Luckenbach, who recalls learning the art when she was eight or nine, first used a six-inch rolling pin and a cat cookie cutter to make her own rolled cookies. "My mother and I always made the dough right after Thanksgiving and baked it at the start of December so the task was out of the way when it was time to begin work on the Christmas putz."

A well-seasoned expert on these cookies, Miss Luckenbach said the biggest challenge to these cookies was determining the proper baking time when all the gas ranges in Bethlehem were filled with baking goodies and the gas supply fluctuated wildly. Although it's not nearly as difficult to regulate temperatures today, she advises novices: "Grease your pans each time you're readying them for the oven. Rotate the top and bottom trays after five minutes. Don't take your eyes off them. And if the cookies blister, take a spatula and press them down lightly." She claims she manages to make about a thousand cookies from a single batch of dough so it's no wonder she says the cookies should be so thin that when you run the knife under them to pick them up, you should be able to see the knife clearly.

Mrs. Butterfield, whose family never opened their stash of brown spice cookies until Christmas Eve, noted it was something of a tradition to burn the last tray or two of cookies. It wasn't deliberate, however—just a matter of forgetting to watch them closely when there was so much cleaning up to do in the kitchen after a long day of baking.

Although the area's Christmas traditions are as varied as the many nationalities who eventually came to settle Bethlehem, there are a few culinary traditions that have been lost or are fading. Mrs. Knouss recalled a time when many a Bethlehem cook owned a "half-moon" cake pan specially made for baking half-moon" cakes for holiday time. Made from a pound cake recipe, the cake was sliced thinly and each half round slice was iced with half chocolate icing and half lemon icing. But today, the taste is a fading memory and most of the pans are museum pieces.

There are those who worry that Moravian mints will become extinct, like the two-layered chocolate caramels with vanilla cream centers that were made by a local confectioner. Today, the thin red, white, and green mints are made almost exclusively by a group of elderly Moravians in the nearby town of Nazareth. These enterprising seniors worry about who will carry on their work in a time when traditions often are sacrificed to the demands of the modern world.

But food is only part of the celebration in Bethlehem. It's not hard to see why lifelong residents absolutely refuse to leave home over the holidays and why thousands of visitors make pilgrimages to the city first named on Christmas Eve of 1741. From that first Christmas Eve, when a small group of Moravian settlers gathered to worship in a log house that sheltered both man and beast, the residents of the town that would be Bethlehem were charged with the keeping of the holiday.

That night, Count Ludwig von Zinzendorf, of Hernnhut, Germany, and patron of the Moravian, had just arrived and was leading the service. He began the hymn, "Not Jerusalem, lowly Bethlehem, 'twas that gave us Christ to save us: Not Jerusalem." Then, still singing, he led the group to the stable within the log house and continued, "Favored Bethlehem, honored is that name: Thence came Jesus to release us, Favored Bethlehem." With that Zinzendorf suggested that the town had been named. Christmas had created Bethlehem.

The holiday traditions that can be traced to that Christmas Eve live on in Bethlehem, no matter what happens. In fact, keeping the holiday just may have prevented a massacre. Legend has it that Indians were ready to attack in 1755 when they were frightened off by the sounds of the Moravians' brass trombone choir heralding Christmas Day from the roof of the Brethren's House (now Moravian College).

During two winters of the Revolution, the Moravians nursed the Continental Army's wounded soldiers in the Brethren's House and noted that all the officers and doctors attended their Christmas Eve vigils.

In 1941, just one week before Pearl Harbor, fire raged through the Central Moravian Church and explosions blew out the windows. Though the church was blackened, the celebration of the two-hundredth anniversary of the founding of Bethlehem went on as scheduled on Christmas Eve.

Most years, Christmases in Bethlehem are marked less dramatically. In contrast to Lancaster County where the plain folk sew quilts, do tole painting, make clear toy candy, dip chocolates, and plan traditional plates of goodies for the children, Bethlehem is vibrant with the celebration. Elaborate putzes and putzing parties, multipointed Moravian stars, hundreds of Christmas trees sparkling with thousands of lights, carolers, pageants, lantern-light tours, candles in the windows of homes and historic buildings, church vigils, and love feasts, as well as distinct culinary traditions, over shadow department-store Santas, tinsel and bows, and give this city a glow that shines as brightly as the Christmas star.

CHAPTER ONE

Appetizers and Beverages

GLAZED BACON

This is one of my favorite appetizers and one that will amaze every guest.

½ **pound bacon, sliced**
½ **cup lightly packed light brown sugar**
1 **tablespoon Dijon mustard**
2 **tablespoons red wine**

Preheat oven to 350°F.

Place bacon in large baking pan and bake for 10 minutes or until crisp. Drain fat off. Mix brown sugar, mustard, and wine together thoroughly, then pour over bacon. Bake until it bubbles, making sure the bacon glaze is covering both sides, approximately 10 minutes.

Remove bacon from pan and place on wax paper or aluminum foil. Cut bacon slices in half, if desired. Do not refrigerate or cover, but let sit at room temperature until ready to serve. It should be dry to touch, not sticky. If it is limp or sticky, bake a bit longer, about 2 minutes.

YIELD: 6 SERVINGS—PEOPLE REALLY LOVE TO EAT THIS, SO COUNT ON 5 POUNDS FOR 30 GUESTS.

🦃 TURKEY BITS 🦃

*A great way to use up leftover turkey, this recipe may be made into
turkey patties as a delicious substitute for hamburgers. Serve the
turkey bits with a hot sauce or sweet and sour sauce or both.*

4 cups minced turkey (roasted or cooked)
1 cup fresh bread crumbs
½ teaspoon salt
½ teaspoon ground white pepper
2 large eggs
½ cup cream cheese
2 scallions, with tops, chopped
½ cup salad olives
1 tablespoon vegetable oil or butter

Preheat oven to 200°F.

Blend first eight ingredients together thoroughly. Place large, heavy skillet
over medium heat and add oil or butter. Drop mixture by teaspoonsful into
heated skillet and fry until golden brown on each side, about 3 minutes per
side. Add more oil as necessary while frying. Serve immediately or remove
from skillet, place on baking sheet, and keep warm in oven until ready to
serve. These freeze well before or after frying.
YIELD: 10 PATTIES OR 24 BITS

Variation:

Substitute crushed crackers or potato chips for bread crumbs and roll
bits in an egg wash of 1 large egg beaten with 1 tablespoon milk or
water and then fresh bread crumbs. This will make them crunchier.

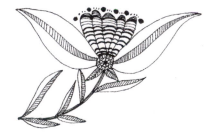

CHEESE STRAWS

This recipe is one of Barbara Hoerle's specialties. While researching old cookbooks, we found several cheese stix recipes, but I think this is the best one ever! A food processor works perfectly for this recipe, but you may use a heavy mixer or work it by hand.

½ **pound (2 sticks) butter**
3 **cups grated sharp cheese**
3 **cups all-purpose flour**
1 **teaspoon baking powder**
1 **teaspoon salt**
¼ **teaspoon paprika**
⅓ **teaspoon red (cayenne) pepper**
Few drops of Worcestershire sauce
2 **to 3 tablespoons water**

Preheat oven to 350°F.

Cream butter and grated cheese together in large mixing bowl till fluffy. Sift dry ingredients together, then add to butter-cheese mixture. Add Worcestershire and water, starting with 2 tablespoons, mixing until thoroughly blended. If dough is too dry, add rest of water—it must be pliable enough to press through cookie press. Place dough in star cookie press. Press it onto greased cookie sheets in long strips. Cut into 3-inch lengths and bake for 8 to 10 minutes or until golden brown. Cool and store in an airtight container.
YIELD: ABOUT 150 THREE-INCH LONG STRAWS. THESE ARE SO GOOD, YOU HAD
    BETTER COUNT ON AT LEAST 4 PER PERSON.

DEVILED EGGS

Parties are not complete without deviled eggs. They are easy to pick up and perfect for picnics.

12 **hardboiled eggs, cooled and peeled**
¾ **cup mayonnaise**
1 **tablespoon Dijon mustard**
½ **teaspoon salt**
1 **tablespoon mixed minced fresh herbs (parsley, chives, chervil, and
    oregano)**
¼ **cup sour cream**
Paprika or minced fresh parsley for garnish

Cut eggs in half, lengthwise. Remove yolks and place in mixing bowl. Add rest of ingredients and beat until smooth and creamy. Place in pastry tube and pipe yolk mixture into whites. If you do not have a pastry tube or cake decorator tube, spoon mixture into whites. Garnish with paprika or minced parsley and chill until ready to serve.
YIELD: 24 HALVES

 EASY SPICED PECANS

Pecans were much more plentiful in years gone by, but they are still grown in Pennsylvania.

10 tablespoons plus 2 teaspoons butter
2 large egg whites
½ teaspoon salt
½ teaspoon ground cinnamon
⅓ cup powdered sugar (superfine if possible)
1 teaspoon vanilla extract
1 pound pecan halves

Preheat oven at 300°F.

Melt butter in small, heavy saucepan over low heat and place in 9 x 13-inch baking pan. Beat egg whites until nearly stiff and slowly add in salt, cinnamon, sugar, and vanilla. Continue to beat until stiff peaks form and then fold in nuts. Pour mixture evenly into pan and bake for 40 minutes, stirring every few minutes to prevent the pecans from burning. Remove from oven and place on wire baking rack or slotted broiler pan top, then pour onto paper towels to remove excess butter. Store in an airtight container.
YIELD: ABOUT 1½ POUNDS

CANDIED WALNUTS

Nuts were candied for special holidays and important guests, but I suggest these year round.

1½ cups granulated sugar
½ cup water
½ teaspoon cider vinegar
½ teaspoon ground cinnamon (optional)
1 tablespoon butter
4 cups English walnut halves

Combine sugar, water, vinegar, cinnamon and butter in deep, heavy saucepan over high heat. Stir until dissolved, then boil till candy thermometer reaches 240° to 242°F, the hard ball stage, when you drop bit of mixture into ice water and it forms hard ball. Stir in nuts and then pour onto large sheet of wax paper. Break into pieces when cool.
YIELD: ABOUT 2 POUNDS

Variation:

Substitute any type of roasted nut.

OLD FASHIONED LEMONADE

Ice cold lemonade with sprigs of meadow tea (spearmint) brings back the best of every childhood memory. It was the highlight of all the threshing, haymaking, and summer work days. As a child, my family chose me to carry the bucket of lemonade to the fields, and I loved it. The funny thing was I didn't realize how special ours was and that not everyone had lemon slices floating on the top. The secret was pounding sugar into the lemon slices. This made the rind sweet and wonderful for keeping in the mouth long after the thirst was quenched. The nutmeg also gives it extra punch. Enjoy!

5 large or 6 medium-size lemons
1 cup granulated sugar
16 cups cold water
4 cups ice cubes
⅛ teaspoon freshly grated nutmeg
Several sprigs of fresh mint

Squeeze 4 of lemons and reserve juice. (If lemons are cold, place in microwave for 30 seconds or in bowl of hot water for 5 minutes. Warmed oils in rind will give extra flavor to juice.) On cutting board, cut remaining lemons into ¼-inch-thick slices, removing all seeds. Press ½ cup of sugar into slices with wooden mallet or potato masher. Place sugared slices and any resultant juice into container you plan to serve it in and let stand for at least 15 minutes. Add reserved lemon juice and sugar, and cold water. Stir in ice cubes, sprinkle with nutmeg, and garnish with fresh mint.
YIELD: 20 CUPS

Variation:

Add 2 cups of lime drink made from concentrate and
2 cups strong tea for a delightful summer cooler.

🜲 MULLED CIDER 🜲

*This heartwarming beverage is always served warm to hot and is best when
the weather is cold. Most important to remember when serving, always place
a silver spoon in a glass punch bowl before pouring in the hot liquid. This will
prevent the glass from cracking. If you prefer stirring the cider with teaspoons
instead of cinnamon sticks, just sprinkle the top with ground spices.*

1 cup lightly packed light brown sugar
6 cups apple cider, fresh or pasteurized
1 orange, seeded and sliced thin
1 lemon, seeded and sliced thin
**2 cups dry white, rose, or red table wine (cranberry juice may be used
    as a substitute)**
Cinnamon sticks (optional)

Place sugar and 2 cups of cider in large kettle. Stir until sugar is dissolved.
Place over medium heat and add orange and lemon. Bring to boil and simmer
at that heat approximately 6 minutes until rinds are clear. Add remaining
cider and wine. Heat but do not let boil. Serve with cinnamon sticks for
stirrers.
YIELD: 12 SERVINGS, ABOUT 10 CUPS

Variation:

Juice from mulberries, cherries, currants, or raspberries may be substituted.

🐦 WINEBERRY SHRUB 🐦

Wineberries grow, and look, like red raspberries. They grow wild in meadows and fence rows mainly in the middle Atlantic states. They are very tart, so you will need to use more sugar or sugar substitute than you will with other berries. Shrubs are prepared juices that are canned or frozen as a syrup and diluted before drinking. The formula for making a punch is always one third shrub to two thirds ice and water, though many added soda for variety. The undiluted syrup is excellent over sponge cake, ice cream, or fresh fruit.

4 cups wineberries
2 cups cider vinegar
2 cups granulated sugar
½ teaspoon ground nutmeg
Dash of ground cinnamon
Lemon slices or 2 tablespoons fresh lemon juice (optional)

Combine berries and vinegar and let stand overnight in glass or stainless steel container, covered. Next day, press through double thickness of cheesecloth or strain slowly. Add sugar and spices to taste, remembering that syrup will be considerably diluted before serving. Add lemon slices and let stand for at least 24 hours, then strain again and place in containers for freezing or can according to cold pack method (see pages 249-250).
YIELD: ABOUT 6 CUPS

Variations:

Use any kind of berry, such as strawberries—with or without rhubarb—blueberries, cranberries, blackberries, gooseberries, or raspberries. A combination of cranberries and apples or raspberries and sour cherries makes a very interesting drink. Try your favorites or experiment. Adjust amount of sugar according to sweetness of berries. To assure best tasting shrub, start with 1 cup sugar, stir until it is dissolved, then taste and add more sugar until you reach desired level of sweetness, again remembering that shrub will be diluted before serving. Add bit of orange or lime juice and rind for extra flavor.

🐾 DANDELION WINE 🐾

*It takes forever to pick the blossoms, but the end result is well worth
it. If made properly and you have enough patience to let it stand a year,
dandelion wine will be so smooth you'll want to make it every year.*

12 cups boiling water
12 cups dandelion flowers (without the stems)
3 oranges, sliced
3 lemons, sliced
1 pound seedless raisins
5 cups granulated sugar
6 cups water
1 teaspoon wine yeast (see note)

Pour boiling water over washed dandelion flowers. Let stand, covered,
overnight. Next day, strain mixture through doubled thickness of cheesecloth,
pressing out all liquid. Discard dandelions. Put strained liquid in plastic pail
and add oranges, lemons, and raisins. Combine 3 cups of sugar with 4 cups of
water in large saucepan. Bring to boil, stirring until sugar has dissolved. Let
syrup cool to lukewarm, then add to dandelion liquid. Add wine yeast and
stir well. Cover and ferment for 15 days, stirring mixture each day.

Combine remaining sugar and water in large saucepan and bring to boil,
stirring until sugar is dissolved. Let cool to lukewarm. Meanwhile, strain
dandelion mixture again, then add cooled syrup to dandelion liquid. Pour
into gallon jug fit with fermentation lock and leave in warm place until all
fermentation has ceased, approximately 6 to 8 weeks.
Yield: 1 Gallon

Note:
Wine yeast may be purchased from a home brewer's or winemaker's
shop. If unavailable, substitute an equal amount of baker's yeast.

CHAPTER TWO

Soups and Salads

🏺 POTATO-LEEK SOUP 🏺

Basic, but wonderful!

3 leeks
5 medium-size potatoes, peeled and diced
2 tablespoons (¼ stick) butter
3 cups chicken broth
½ teaspoon dried chervil
1 teaspoon chopped fresh parsley
½ teaspoon dry mustard
½ teaspoon chopped fresh tarragon
½ teaspoon ground white pepper
½ teaspoon salt
3 cups milk
½ cup heavy cream or evaporated milk
Chopped fresh parsley or a few slices of leek for garnish

Clean leeks, washing away all sand, trim course tops, saving as much of top as is tender, and slice thin. Save several slices of leek for garnish. Saute potatoes and leeks in butter over medium heat in 6-quart stock pot for 5 minutes or until edges are golden. Add chicken broth and bring to boil. Simmer over medium heat for 20 minutes. Add all seasonings and milk and continue simmering for at least another 30 minutes, stirring occasionally to prevent sticking. Add cream and check for salt, adding more if desired. Heat thoroughly. Garnish with parsley and or a few slices of leek on top of each bowl.

YIELD: 8 CUPS OR 4 SERVINGS

Variation:

Vichyssoise:
Puree potatoes and leeks, reduce milk to two cups
and chill thoroughly. Serve ice cold.

🐦 LENTIL SOUP 🐦

*See how many varieties of dried peas and beans you can
combine in this colorful and nutritious soup.*

2 cups dried lentils
14 cups water
1 large onion, chopped
2 stalks celery, chopped
2 pounds ham, veal hock, or beef short ribs
2 cups tomato or vegetable juice
½ teaspoon salt
½ teaspoon coarsely ground black pepper
½ teaspoon Tabasco sauce (optional)
Croutons for garnish

Wash lentils and soak them in 8 cups water overnight in 6-quart stock pot.
Drain and add 6 cups water, onion, celery, and meat. Cook until meat is
tender over medium heat, stirring every 10 minutes to prevent sticking.
Depending on thickness of meat and bone, it will take about 1½ hours.
Remove meat from broth and remove fat and bone. Dice meat and put it
back in soup. Add tomato juice, check for seasonings, and add salt and
pepper if desired. Add Tabasco carefully, few drops at time, till you achieve
right level of hotness. (Some folks like to add Tabasco at the table.) Simmer
over low heat for 15 minutes. Serve hot with croutons. Longer soup stands,
thicker it gets.
YIELD: 12 CUPS OR 6 SERVINGS

Variation:

Dried Bean or Split Pea Soup:
Use dried split peas or any combination of dried beans with
above recipe but substitute milk for tomato juice.

 SUNSHINE SQUASH SOUP

This will brighten up any meal and is a must for celebrating Halloween.

¼ **pound bacon (about 4 slices)**
1 **medium-size onion, chopped**
1 **stalk celery with leaves, chopped**
¼ **clove garlic, minced**
½ **teaspoon curry powder**
¼ **teaspoon ground nutmeg**
8 **cups water**
2 **pounds butternut squash or neck pumpkin, peeled, seeded, and cut
   into 2-inch chunks**
3 **large carrots, peeled and sliced**
1 **medium-size potato, peeled and sliced**
1 **medium-size rutabaga, peeled and sliced (if unavailable, use
   another potato)**
½ **teaspoon salt**
¼ **teaspoon ground white pepper**
¼ **teaspoon ground thyme**
¼ **cup rum**
2 **tablespoons fresh lemon juice**
1 **tablespoon granulated sugar**
Salt and freshly ground white pepper, if needed
Spiced Whipped Cream (page 213)
Fresh parsley sprigs for garnish

Fry bacon in heavy, 6-quart stock pot until crisp. Remove bacon, drain,
and crumble. Add onion, celery, garlic, curry powder, and nutmeg to bacon
fat and sauté over medium heat for 5 minutes. Add water, squash, carrots,
potato, rutabaga, salt, pepper, and thyme. Cook over medium heat, covered,
for 45 minutes. Cool slightly and pour by batches into food processor,
blender, or food mill. Puree thoroughly. Pour back into pot and stir in rum,
lemon juice, and sugar. Check for seasonings and add additional salt and
pepper as desired. Simmer slowly over low heat until bubbles appear on top,
about 10 minutes. Serve hot with dollop of spiced Whipped Cream. Garnish
with parsley sprigs.
YIELD: 8 CUPS OR 4 SERVINGS

 GERMAN TOMATO SOUP WITH DILL

I prefer most of my soups very hot, but this is excellent either cold or hot.

4 white onions, about 1 to 1½ cups chopped
1 carrot, scrubbed and chopped
1 stalk celery, scrubbed and chopped
½ green bell pepper, chopped (optional)
3 tablespoons butter
2 teaspoons salt, less if desired
1 teaspoon ground white pepper
2 cups water
5 cups tomato puree
¼ cup honey
1 tablespoon granulated sugar
2 tablespoons fresh lemon juice
2 cups tomato or vegetable juice
⅓ cup finely chopped fresh dill or 2 tablespoons dried
1 cup sour cream
Fresh dill or parsley sprigs for garnish

In 6-quart stock pot saute onions, carrot, celery, green pepper, and butter over medium-high heat until tender, about 3 minutes. Add salt, pepper, and water; reduce heat to low and simmer for 5 more minutes. Remove from heat and puree in food processor, blender, or food mill. Pour puree back into stock pot and add tomato puree, honey, sugar, lemon juice, and tomato or vegetable juice. Blend and simmer over medium-low heat for at least 15 minutes, stirring frequently. Add chopped dill and simmer another 5 minutes. Serve hot or cold with dollop of sour cream and sprig of fresh dill or parsley.
YIELD: 12 CUPS OR 6 SERVINGS

Variation:

Substitute watercress for dill and add 1 cup cooked rice.

Hint:
If tomatoes are high in acid, add pinch of baking soda.

 CORN-SPATZLE SOUP

This soup is a special treat any time and is hearty enough for a meal.

2 cups water
1 tablespoon butter or vegetable oil
1 cup cooked Spatzle (page 54)
2 cups corn kernels, fresh or frozen
1 tablespoon chopped fresh parsley
½ teaspoon coarsely ground black pepper
½ teaspoon salt
⅛ teaspoon dried marjoram
⅛ teaspoon dried basil
2 cups milk
½ cup evaporated milk or half and half
Celery seed or chopped fresh parsley for garnish

In 6-quart stock pot, bring water to boil and add butter. If you are using fresh spatzle, boil them until tender in boiling water. Once cooked, add corn, parsley, pepper, salt, marjoram, and basil. If using cooked spatzle, add it now. Simmer over medium heat for 15 minutes. Add whole milk and evaporated milk and heat thoroughly, about 5 minutes. Simmer until thickened, about 12 minutes, but be careful not to boil rapidly. Garnish with celery seeds or parsley.

CHICKEN-CORN SOUP

A meal in itself, this soup has helped many a volunteer fire company pay for a new engine or equipment in their sponsoring Chicken-Corn Soup Suppers.

4 to 6 pounds chicken (or 2 cups diced, cooked chicken and 6 cups chicken broth)
8 cups water
¼ teaspoon salt
¼ teaspoon coarsely ground black or white pepper
2 tablespoons chopped fresh parsley
2 cups corn kernels, fresh or frozen
1 cup chopped celery
1 cup Egg Noodles (page 53)

If you are starting with fresh chicken, remove giblets and place chicken in 6-quart stock pot. Add water, salt, pepper, and parsley. Cook over medium heat until tender, about 45 minutes. Remove and discard skin, debone, and dice chicken. Cool broth, skim off fat, and strain it through double thickness of cheesecloth. Bring 6 cups of broth to boil in large saucepan over high heat and add corn, celery, and noodles. Lower heat to medium and simmer, covered, for at least 1 hour. Add chicken and heat thoroughly. Serve in heated bowls.

⚜ OYSTER STEW OR SOUP ⚜

*When I was a child I loved this stew, but I always gave the oysters to my
parents. Now that I'm grown up I find many other children doing the same
but it is a great way to learn to appreciate the flavor of oysters.*

1 pint stewing oysters with liquor, approximately 3 dozen
2 tablespoons (¼ stick) butter
2 tablespoons all-purpose flour
½ teaspoon dried chopped chives
½ teaspoon chopped fresh or dried parsley
½ teaspoon dried chervil
¼ teaspoon paprika
½ teaspoon Old Bay (seafood) seasoning
½ teaspoon salt
¼ teaspoon ground white pepper
2 large eggs, well beaten
½ cup evaporated milk or heavy cream
4 cups milk
Fresh parsley sprigs or croutons for garnish

Check oysters for shells. Melt butter in a medium-size saucepan over
medium heat. Add flour and stir until smooth. Stir in seasonings and oyster
liquor. Heat thoroughly, but not to boiling. Blend beaten eggs into milk
and heat in heavy, 3-quart saucepan over medium heat until nearly boiling,
stirring constantly with wooden spoon. Blend oyster liquor mixture into milk
mixture with wire whisk. When slightly thickened, about 12 minutes, add
oysters and heat until oysters begin to curl around edges. Do not boil! If it
does boil and curdle, add pinch of baking soda. Serve immediately, garnished
with parsley sprigs or croutons. Serve with lots of oyster crackers or crusty
bread.

YIELD: 7 CUPS OR 4 TO 6 SERVINGS

⚜

Variation:

Mock Oyster Stew:
Substitute salsify (oyster plant) for oysters. Scrub 1 pound of salsify and
cook it in 2 cups of water, mild chicken broth, or veal stock over medium-
low heat until tender, about 15 minutes. When cool, peel, cut into slices
and use as oysters. Strain broth and substitute for oyster liquor.

🦉 PEACH BISQUE 🦉

So refreshing and tasty, this recipe may be adapted for many fruits.

1 pound fresh or frozen drained peaches, peeled
6 tablespoons light brown sugar
1 cup sour cream
1 quart half and half or milk
1 pint heavy cream
1 tablespoon ground cinnamon
1 teaspoon ground nutmeg
2 tablespoons brandy (optional)
Whipped Cream (page 213) or fresh peach slices for garnish

In blender or food processor puree peaches with sugar. Add sour cream, half and half, cream, and half of spices. Refrigerate for several hours to draw flavors. Stir in brandy just before serving. Sprinkle top of each serving with remaining spices, then top with dollop of whipped cream or sliced peaches. If you chill bowls before filling them, soup will stay cold longer.
YIELD: 6 SERVINGS

🦉 BEET SALAD 🦉

You can't "beet" this salad for color and flavor, especially on a hot day.

3 cups shredded beets with liquid (add enough water to make
      3¾ cups)
1 (6-ounce) package lemon gelatin
2 tablespoons prepared horseradish
½ teaspoon salt
1 tablespoon honey
Yogurt or sour cream for garnish

Heat beet juice in medium-size saucepan until nearly boiling over high heat. Dissolve gelatin in beet juice, then add shredded beets, horseradish, salt, and honey. Pour into 1½-quart mold or 8-inch square pan. Chill until set. Cut into serving and top with dollop of yogurt or sour cream.
YIELD: 6 SERVINGS

 BROCCOLI SALAD

This salad is not only beautiful but it is refreshing and nutritious.

Dressing:
2 to 3 tablespoons cider vinegar
3 ounces cream cheese
⅛ teaspoon garlic or onion salt
2 to 3 tablespoons granulated sugar
Dash of ground black pepper
1 tablespoon prepared mustard
2 large eggs, well beaten
2 to 3 tablespoons vegetable oil

Salad:
12 slices of bacon, crumbled
6 to 7 cups chopped broccoli
⅓ cup raisins
3 tablespoons chopped red onion

Place all ingredients for dressing in blender, food processor, or mixer. Blend thoroughly and set aside. Fry bacon in saucepan and dry on paper towels; then crumble into small pieces. Place broccoli, chopped or broken into buds, raisins, onion, and bacon in large salad bowl. Pour dressing over salad and let it stand for at least 1 hour, covered with plastic wrap. Toss before serving.
YIELD: 6 SERVINGS

Variation:

Cauliflower may be substituted for broccoli.

CUCUMBERS AND ONIONS IN DILL SOUR CREAM

Weiner Schnitzel would not be the same without this side dish.

1 large cucumber
1 medium-size onion
1 tablespoon salt
1 tablespoon cider or white wine vinegar
1½ teaspoons granulated sugar
½ cup sour cream
¼ teaspoon dried dill weed
Paprika

Clean and peel cucumber. Slice cucumber and onion as thin as possible.
Place slices in bowl and sprinkle with salt. Let stand at least 1 hour.
Rinse slices in cold water and drain thoroughly. Add vinegar and sugar to
cucumbers and onions and press with hands until sugar is dissolved. Add
sour cream and dill, mixing well. Sprinkle with paprika before serving.
YIELD: 4 TO 6 SERVINGS

SAUERKRAUT SALAD

*Delicious with pork or ham dinners, it is also a wonderful salad for summer picnics
(especially if you have hot dogs or cold cuts). This salad is the perfect way to use up
extra sauerkraut. It can be substituted for cabbage or pepper slaw (see page 45).*

4 cups chopped sauerkraut, fresh or canned, drained
½ cup chopped onion
1 cup chopped celery
1 tablespoon chopped pimiento
¼ cup chopped green bell pepper
½ cup cider vinegar
¼ cup vegetable oil
1½ cups granulated sugar (less if desired)
Lettuce leaves, washed and patted dry

Mix all ingredients but the lettuce and let stand in refrigerator for at least one
hour. Serve on lettuce leaves.
YIELD: ABOUT 6 CUPS OR 6 SERVINGS

MUSHROOM SALAD

This is a great winter salad, especially when you realize that Pennsylvania is the largest producer of mushrooms in the United States.

Dressing:
⅓ **cup olive or walnut oil**
1 **tablespoon fresh lemon juice**
3 **tablespoons Herb Vinegar, 1 each of thyme, rosemary, and chive (page 261)**
¼ **cup chopped fresh parsley**
2 **teaspoons granulated sugar**
½ **teaspoon chopped fresh basil**
⅛ **teaspoon crushed garlic**
¼ **teaspoon salt**
½ **teaspoon coarsely ground black pepper**
¼ **cup red table wine**

Salad:
10 **to 12 ounces fresh mushrooms, cleaned and sliced**
Fresh cutting lettuce or Boston lettuce (about 3 cups)

Combine all ingredients for dressing until thoroughly blended. If you are preparing salad ahead of time, slice mushrooms into dressing to prevent discoloration. Wash and tear lettuce. Drain and pat dry with clean cloth. Arrange lettuce on individual plates or in large bowl. Add mushrooms and dressing and serve chilled.
YIELD: 4 SERVINGS

Variation:

Add wedges of tomatoes or hard-boiled eggs to salad.

 PERFECTION SALAD

We all love molded salads, and this recipe is no exception!

3 tablespoons gelatin (I use Knox)
½ cup cold water
½ cup white wine vinegar
2 cups boiling water
1 teaspoon salt
1 cup finely shredded cabbage
2 tablespoons fresh lemon juice
1 teaspoon grated lemon rind
½ cup granulated sugar
2 cups finely diced celery
½ cup finely diced red or green bell peppers
1 teaspoon celery seed
1 tablespoon sesame seeds
Lettuce
Chopped pecans for garnish

In large mixing bowl soak gelatin in cold water for 5 minutes. Add vinegar, boiling water, salt, cabbage, lemon juice and rind, sugar, celery, peppers, celery seed, and sesame seeds. Stir until sugar dissolves. Pour mixture into 1½-quart mold or 9 x 13-inch baking pan and chill until set. Place on crisp, cleaned lettuce and garnish with chopped nuts. Serve mayonnaise on side.
Yield: 6 to 8 servings

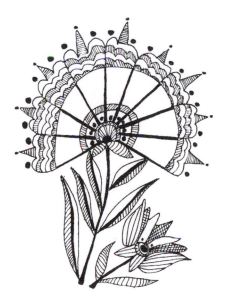

🦅 DANDELION SALAD 🦅
WITH HOT BACON DRESSING

Even though we specify dandelions, any greens are great with this hot dressing. Since we have microwave ovens, we can make a full recipe of the dressing and refrigerate or can it until we need it.

6 cups loosely packed dandelion greens, washed and cleaned
4 hardboiled eggs, peeled and sliced

Dressing:
½ pound bacon
2 tablespoons cornstarch
1½ teaspoons salt
3 tablespoons granulated sugar
2 large or medium-size eggs, lightly beaten
⅓ cup cider vinegar
2 cups milk

Tear dandelion greens into pieces as you would for any salad. Fry bacon in saucepan or deep skillet until crisp. Remove and drain on paper towels, then crumble into small pieces. Combine cornstarch, salt, and sugar. Blend in beaten eggs, then vinegar. Heat milk in pan with leftover bacon fat over medium heat and add egg mixture slowly, stirring with whisk until thickened. Remove from stove and add crumbled bacon, cool slightly, and pour over greens. Top with hardboiled eggs and serve any extra dressing on side.
YIELD: 6 SERVINGS

 CABBAGE SLAW

When I was a child, one of my jobs was squeezing the slaw, sugar, and vinegar until I could see the liquid in the bottom of the bowl. Only after I made slaw for myself did I realize the difference it makes to squeeze it. The raw cabbage taste disappears because the flavors are so thoroughly blended. Try it; I know it works!

1½ pound head of cabbage
1 cup granulated sugar
½ cup cider vinegar
½ teaspoon ground white pepper
½ teaspoon salt
½ teaspoon celery seed
1 tablespoon chopped fresh parsley
1 carrot, grated (optional)

Core cabbage and shred on grate into slaw. Place in large bowl and add sugar, vinegar, pepper, salt, and celery seed. Press together with your hands until completely blended and liquid starts to form in bottom of bowl. Fold in parsley and carrot (for added color and flavor). Cover and chill in refrigerator for at least one hour.
YIELD: ABOUT 5 CUPS

Variation:

Creamed Cole Slaw:
Add 1 cup mayonnaise or ½ cup mayonnaise and ½ cup sour cream when mixing in parsley.

Pepper Slaw:
Add 1 medium-size green bell pepper, chopped, and 1 medium-size red bell pepper, chopped.

CHARLIE'S POTATO SALAD

Ever since our son, Charles, developed this recipe, everyone asks for it. Our guests from Germany say it tastes the way they remember it from "Grandma" while others remember it tasting the same but with the addition of chopped sweet pickles. Try it this way and then add sweet or dill pickles or maybe a bit of chopped fresh tarragon, whichever way you prefer.

3 pounds firm, all-purpose potatoes
1 tablespoon salt
3 cups water
1½ cups mayonnaise
¾ cup sour cream
2½ tablespoons cider vinegar
⅓ cup granulated sugar
1 teaspoon ground white pepper
2 teaspoons dry mustard
1 tablespoon celery seed
2 teaspoons Worcestershire sauce
2 teaspoons fresh lemon juice
2½ tablespoons chopped fresh parsley
2 teaspoons chopped fresh chives
⅓ cup minced onion
⅓ cup minced celery

Peel and cook potatoes in salt and 3 cups of water over medium heat in large saucepan until medium soft. Drain, slice, and let cool. Mix mayonnaise and sour cream together in large mixing bowl, then add all rest of ingredients. Stir in sliced potatoes. If possible, let salad stand for at least 3 hours or overnight before serving. It will keep, refrigerated, for nearly a week if stored in an airtight container.

YIELD: ABOUT 7 OR 8 CUPS OR 4 TO 6 SERVINGS

Variation:

Sunchoke Salad:
Substitute 3 pounds of Jerusalem artichokes (sunchokes) for potatoes in potato salad, cooking as you would potatoes. It will have extra crunch and holds its shape well.

 GERMAN HOT POTATO SALAD

This is a meal by itself if you add sliced smoked sausage.

6 slices bacon
2 tablespoons cornstarch
¼ cup water
1 cup chopped onion
¾ cup diced celery
2 teaspoons salt
1 teaspoon granulated sugar
⅛ teaspoon freshly ground black pepper
½ cup cider vinegar
6 cups firm potatoes (red skins are great), cooked, peeled, diced, and still hot
6 large pimiento-stuffed green olives or 12 small green olives, sliced

Fry bacon in large, heavy skillet until crisp. Remove bacon, drain on paper towels, then crumble and reserve bacon fat. Dissolve cornstarch in water. Saute onion and celery in bacon fat over medium heat about 5 minutes until onions are translucent. Add salt, sugar, pepper, and dissolved cornstarch to skillet. Next, add vinegar and bring to boil over medium heat for 3 minutes. Add hot potatoes and crumbled bacon, stirring gently. Serve hot, garnished with sliced stuffed olives.
Yield: 6 to 8 servings

Variation:

For added flavor, cook potatoes in chicken stock instead of water.

Note:
It takes 8 medium-size potatoes cooked in salted water for
about 30 minutes to make 6 cups of diced potatoes. They
may be cooked in the skins and peeled while still hot.

🪶 WALDORF SALAD 🪶

All the ingredients for this salad are available during the fall, winter, and spring. The old-fashioned way of making this salad always topped it with Cooked Dressing (see page 158). It seems a bit too sweet for those not accustomed to it, so I prefer to use regular mayonnaise.

2 cups cored and diced apples
1 cup chopped celery
1 cup raisins
½ cup broken nuts
½ cup mayonnaise
Fresh lettuce or watercress
Nut halves or maraschino cherries for garnish

Combine apples, celery, raisins, nuts, and mayonnaise gently in large bowl. Chill in refrigerator until ready to serve. Serve on crisp greens. Garnish with nut halves or cherries.
YIELD: 6 SERVINGS

🪶 CHICKEN SALAD 🪶

In the summer, the chicken is cut in chunks, nuts and sometimes grapes or white raisins are added, and the resulting salad is scooped onto fresh cutting lettuce. For sandwiches, the chicken is ground and spread between slices of buttered homemade bread.

2 cups diced, cooked chicken
1 cup chopped celery
4 hardboiled eggs, peeled and chopped
¼ cup chopped pecans (optional)
¼ cup red or white seedless grapes, halved or quartered (optional)
¼ cup white raisins (optional)
1 cup Cooked Dressing (page 158)

Combine all ingredients; stir until thoroughly blended. Chill and serve on lettuce. If making sandwich spread, omit grapes.
YIELD: 4 CUPS

CHAPTER THREE

Cheeses, Doughs, and Batters

MACARONI AND CHEESE

I have made this ever since I was in 4-H club. My family never gets tired of it but my grandchildren like it with Velveeta instead of the sharp cheese. Try it either way.

8 cups water
2 cups (8 ounces) macaroni
Pinch of saffron threads
½ teaspoon salt
1 tablespoon butter or vegetable oil
½ cup grated sharp cheese
1½ cups grated white American cheese
⅓ teaspoon salt or salt substitute
½ teaspoon coarsely ground white pepper
2 cups milk
Several dashes of paprika for garnish
Sliced olives for garnish (optional)

Preheat oven to 375°F.

Bring water to boil in 6-quart pot. Add macaroni, saffron, salt, butter, and boil uncovered until tender, approximately 12 minutes. Drain and place in large mixing bowl. Stir in cheeses, salt, pepper, and milk. When thoroughly blended, pour into buttered 2-quart baking dish and bake for approximately 35 minutes or until golden brown. Remove from oven and top with paprika and sliced olives.

YIELD: 6 SERVINGS

🦢 WELSH RAREBIT 🦢

This is one of the first dishes I mastered in home economics class and my favorite light supper dish. It must be smooth and creamy, so use a wire whisk as well as a wooden spoon when stirring it. The toppings or accompaniments vary according to season.

1 tablespoon butter or margarine
1 tablespoon Worcestershire sauce
¼ teaspoon ground white pepper
⅛ teaspoon red (cayenne) pepper
¼ teaspoon curry powder
½ teaspoon dry mustard
½ teaspoon paprika
1 tablespoon cornstarch
½ cup ale or beer (water may be substituted)
2 cups (about 8 ounces) shredded Cheddar cheese
6 to 8 slices toast
Accompaniments (see below: optional)

Melt butter in heavy, 2- to 3-quart saucepan over medium-low heat (a double boiler may be used to insure it won't stick). Blend in Worcestershire. Gradually stir in all dry seasonings but cornstarch until blended. Dissolve cornstarch in ale and slowly add to mixture. Stir until mixture is warm, but not hot. Add cheese by handful, making sure it is fully melted before adding more. Continue until all cheese is stirred in and melted until hot but not boiling. Serve over toast with desired accompaniments.

YIELD: 4 TO 6 SERVINGS

Accompaniments:
Chopped or thinly sliced roast beef, ground or thinly sliced baked ham or turkey, crisp bacon, or thinly sliced tomatoes, onions, or peppers.

CHEESE SOUFFLE

For those who prefer a meatless meal, this is as attractive and impressive as its flavor.

3 tablespoons butter or margarine
3 tablespoons flour
½ teaspoon salt
½ teaspoon ground white pepper
2 tablespoons dried chopped chives
1 teaspoon prepared mustard
1 teaspoon Worcestershire sauce
Dash of Tabasco sauce
1 cup milk
1 cup grated Cheddar cheese
6 large eggs, separated
¼ teaspoon cream of tartar
1 tablespoon butter
1 tablespoon grated Parmesan cheese or flour

Preheat oven to 350°F.

In large saucepan over medium heat, melt 3 tablespoons of butter, slowly stirring in flour until smooth. Add salt, pepper, chives, mustard, Worcestershire, and Tabasco. Heat milk in microwave or small saucepan. Slowly add warm milk to butter and flour mixture, stirring until thickened. Remove from heat and stir in Cheddar cheese. Beat egg yolks until fluffy and lemon colored. Stir slowly into cheese sauce. Beat egg whites with cream of tartar in large mixing bowl until stiff but not dry. Coat bottom and sides of souffle dish with 1 tablespoon of butter and dust with cheese or flour. Gently fold cheese mixture into egg whites and pour into prepared souffle dish. Bake for approximately 40 minutes or until lightly browned. It should pull away from sides but will shake slightly in center. Serve immediately.
YIELD: 4 TO 6 SERVINGS

🐦 EGG CHEESE 🐦

All kinds of cheese are very important to the Pennsylvania Dutch. It is probably due to the frugality of the dairy farmers. If the milk price is low, they make more cheese. This cheese is made with fresh ingredients and often served as a snack, appetizer, or as a dessert with fresh fruit. The molds that were used for generations to make this cheese are very valuable and sought after, though reproductions of the old molds are now being made. The old heart molds are the most valued (they have little feet on the bottom and the design is pierced from the inside out so the whey can drain, still leaving the design intact when unmolded) but a natural basket–handles removed–works the same way and looks great when unmolded.

I consider it a special treat when I can have a load of hearty bread, golden table molasses, and an egg cheese. It will always be one of my favorites.

2 quarts milk
6 large eggs
2 cups buttermilk
1 teaspoon salt
2 teaspoons granulated sugar

Warm milk in large, heavy 3-quart saucepan or kettle. Beat eggs until fluffy and add buttermilk, salt, and sugar. Slowly add to warm milk, stirring constantly. Reduce heat to low and cover. Simmer for several minutes, stirring occasionally. Remove lid and gently stir with slotted spoon. Watch for curds and whey to separate (liquid will start to clear). Place molds in pan large enough to hold all liquid. Immediately spoon curds into molds with slotted spoon. Allow to drain—if using baskets, place a ring under basket to allow liquid to drain properly. More gently you treat curds, lighter cheese will be. A heavy cheese either has been cooked too long or was bounced carelessly when removed from liquid. When cooled, unmold and serve as desired.
Yield: 3 molds (1¼ pounds)

Variation:

Add 3 tablespoons chopped fresh chives, chopped green onions, or parsley as curds begin to form. Grate nutmeg on top and serve with fresh fruit on side.

EGG NOODLES

The Pennsylvania Dutch often serve noodles as potatoes, especially if sweet potatoes are on the menu. Variations on the basic egg noodle have been added in the past few years, giving color and variety to one of our best loved starches.

2½ cups all-purpose flour
½ teaspoon salt
3 large eggs
¼ cup cold water

Put 2 cups of flour and salt in deep bowl or on pastry board. Make well in middle of flour and add eggs and water. Mix with your hands or in food processor until well blended and smooth. Form into ball and wrap with wax paper or cover until dough feels tender, at least 30 minutes. If using food processor, mix until dough forms ball, adding extra flour if necessary. When ready to roll out, cut dough into three parts if rolling by hand, six parts if using pasta machine. Dust little flour over and under dough to prevent sticking. (It will take more flour if using pasta machine.) Roll paper thin and flour both sides again. Starting at one end of dough, roll up into neat, tight roll, jelly-roll fashion. With very sharp chef's knife, cut roll into thin slices, about ¼ inch wide. As slices fall onto board, toss them lightly with your hand so they do not stick together. Unroll noodles and let them dry on paper towels. If using pasta machine, roll and cut dough to desired thickness. Be sure to add plenty of flour as they fall from machine to prevent them from sticking together. Uncooked noodles may be stored in an airtight container and refrigerated up to 3 days. To cook, drop noodles into 8 cups of water (add tablespoon of vegetable oil or butter to prevent them from sticking together) brought to rolling boil in large pot and continue to boil another 5 minutes or until they reach desired level of doneness. Pour into colander to drain. Serve in heated bowl with Browned Butter (see page 151) or your favorite sauce. To cool and store, or use for cold salads, run cold water over noodles in colander, making sure they are not sticking together. When completely drained and cool, store in an airtight container and refrigerate until ready to use. These will keep for 3 to 4 days.

YIELD: 1 POUND OF NOODLES (ENOUGH FOR 6 TO 8 SERVINGS)

Variations:

Use ¼ cup chopped, drained, cooked spinach or tomato paste instead of water.

🐦 POT PIE SQUARES 🐦

*This is similar to a noodle dough, but the Pennsylvania Dutch roll it out very thin, about
⅛ inch thick, and cut it into 2- to 3-inch squares. It dries nicely if placed on a clean
sheet or linen towels. When properly dried, it will keep in an airtight container for at
least 4 weeks, unrefrigerated. To freeze, place layers between sheets of wax paper and
wrap in double plastic bags. Squares will keep in the freezer for at least 2 months.*

2½ cups all-purpose flour
2 large eggs
⅓ cup water
1 tablespoon butter or vegetable shortening, melted
½ teaspoon salt

Mound flour on pastry board or marble slab and make well in center. Beat
eggs into this well. Add water, butter, and salt. Gradually work flour into
other ingredients with your hand or fork until well blended. Gather into ball
and knead dough until very tender, smooth, and elastic. Generously flour
board and roll dough out very thin, no more than ⅛ inch thick. Thinner it
is rolled, more delicate it will be when cooked. If using pasta machine, roll
out strips of dough. Cut rolled-out dough into 2 to 3-inch squares. Follow
instructions for cooking Pot Pie on page 139.

YIELD: 1½ POUNDS OR 6 SERVINGS

🐦 SPATZLE 🐦

*Often served instead of potatoes, spatzle is great as a garnish when sauteed in
butter and bread crumbs or pan-fried in butter until golden brown. My friend
Sue Hoffman, owner of the Kitchen Shoppe, in Carlisle, Pennsylvania, uses this
recipe in her cooking school classes and it is light, airy, and delicious.*

1½ cups all-purpose flour
¾ teaspoon salt
⅛ teaspoon ground nutmeg
2 large eggs, lightly beaten
½ cup milk
8 cups water

Combine flour, salt, and nutmeg in mixing bowl. Stir in beaten eggs and add
milk gradually. Beat until smooth. Force dough through holes of colander or
use spatzle maker. Bring water to rapid boil in large pot (add 1 tablespoon oil
or shortening to prevent spatzle from sticking together), and drop in dough.
Boil until they rise to surface, about 2 to 3 minutes. Continue to cook over
low heat for 12 minutes. Remove with slotted spoon and drain. Serve as
desired.

YIELD: 3 CUPS

DUMPLINGS

The secret of having beautiful light dumplings is to never lift the lid while they are cooking. Dumplings are often served with sauerkraut as well as poultry or meat.

1½ cups all-purpose flour
1 tablespoon baking powder
1 teaspoon salt
2 tablespoons (¼ stick) butter
1 large egg
½ cup milk
Chopped fresh parsley (optional)

Sift flour, baking powder, and salt together. Cream butter and egg together in large mixing bowl, then add flour mixture and milk to it alternately, blending thoroughly after each addition. Drop by tablespoons into pot of boiling water or liquid in which sauerkraut or meat is cooking. When all are dropped into pot, cover with lid and boil over medium heat for 12 minutes. DO NOT LIFT THE LID during cooking. Remove with slotted spoon and serve hot. Garnish with chopped parsley.

YIELD: 12 TO 15 DUMPLINGS OR 6 SERVINGS

KNEPP

Schnitz und Knepp (recipe on page 136) is one of the best known and publicized dishes of the region, yet few people make it frequently. I suppose it is the combination of salty ham and sweet apples that make it unique. If the ham broth is mild, this dish can be extremely pleasant, but knepp can be used in many other recipes.

2 cups all-purpose flour
1 tablespoon baking powder
¼ teaspoon salt
2 tablespoons (¼ stick) butter or vegetable shortening, at room
   temperature
1½ cups milk

Sift flour, baking powder, and salt together in large mixing bowl. Cut in butter with pastry blender or your fingers. Add milk and stir until dough is smooth. Drop by tablespoons into large pot of boiling water or liquid in which ham is cooking. Cover pot with lid and simmer over medium heat for 12 minutes. DO NOT LIFT THE LID during cooking. Remove with slotted spoon, drain, cover, and keep hot until serving.

YIELD: 6 SERVINGS OR 10 DUMPLINGS

❧ WAFFLES ❧

The earliest waffle irons were brought along with the first settlers. They had beautiful designs, many with tulips, long handles and many different shapes. It is hard to believe the strength needed to hold the iron over the hot coals, but a few had stands to hold the iron.

2 large eggs, separated if desired
2 cups all-purpose flour
½ teaspoon salt
3½ teaspoons baking powder
4 tablespoons (½ stick) butter or vegetable shortening, melted (bacon
    fat may be partially substituted)
2 cups milk

Heat waffle iron while you are preparing batter. (Iron is ready when drop of water dances around on it and quickly evaporates.) If you want fluffy, light waffles, separate eggs and beat whites until stiff in small bowl. In large bowl, beat egg yolks or whole eggs until light in color. Sift flour, salt, and baking powder together. Add melted shortening and mix till just blended.

Alternately add flour mixture and milk to beaten eggs, stirring until blended, about 30 seconds. Do not overbeat. If eggs were separated, now fold in stiffly beaten egg whites. Pour about ¾ cup batter onto heated waffle iron and bake until golden brown, about 5 minutes.

YIELD: 6 TO 8 WAFFLES

Variation:

Nut Waffles:
Add 1 cup chopped, toasted nuts to batter. Wholewheat or Buckwheat:
Use ½ cup all-purpose flour and ½ cup whole wheat or buckwheat flour.

CORNMEAL WAFFLES

These have a beautiful color and a flavor you can't forget.

2 large eggs
1 cup buttermilk
1 cup sour cream
1 teaspoon baking soda
1 cup all-purpose flour
1 cup cornmeal, sifted
2 teaspoons baking powder
½ teaspoon salt
1 teaspoon granulated sugar (optional)
⅓ cup vegetable shortening, softened or melted

Heat waffle iron while mixing batter. In large mixing bowl, beat eggs until light in color. Gradually add remaining ingredients and blend thoroughly. Pour about ¾ cup batter onto hot iron and bake until golden, about 8 minutes. Serve with butter and maple syrup.
YIELD: ABOUT 8 WAFFLES

Variation:

Cheese Waffles:
Fold ⅓ cup grated Cheddar or white American cheese into batter.

BUTTERMILK PANCAKES

We often served Creamed Frizzled Dried Beef (page 125)
and buttermilk pancakes for an easy supper.

2 cups all-purpose flour
¼ cup cornmeal
1 teaspoon baking powder
1 teaspoon salt
2 teaspoons granulated sugar (optional)
1 large egg, lightly beaten
½ cup milk
1 teaspoon baking soda
1 cup buttermilk
2 tablespoons (¼ stick) butter, melted

Sift flour, cornmeal, baking powder, salt, and sugar into large bowl. Stir in beaten egg and milk. Dissolve baking soda in buttermilk and add to flour mixture. Add melted butter and stir until blended. Pour about ¼ cup of batter for each pancake onto hot, seasoned griddle. When golden on bottom and top starts to bubble, turn. If griddle becomes dry, add ½ teaspoon corn oil to hot surface. Serve pancakes immediately.
YIELD: 12 TO 14 PANCAKES

FLANNEL CAKES

The stiffly beaten egg whites make these flannel cakes light and fluffy.

2 cups all-purpose flour
1 tablespoon baking powder
¾ teaspoon salt
2 large eggs, separated
2 cups milk
2 tablespoons (¼ stick) butter, melted

Sift flour, baking powder, and salt together into large bowl. Lightly beat egg yolks into milk and add to flour mixture. Stir in melted butter. Beat egg whites until stiff and fold into batter. Pour about ¼ cup per cake onto hot, oiled griddle and cook until golden brown on both sides.
YIELD: 14 OR MORE CAKES

 BUCKWHEAT CAKES

There was always a yeast starter stored in a crock on the arched cellar steps. It was made with potatoes and was used for breads and griddle cakes. Today it is easier to use packaged yeast. These cakes are lighter than the usual baking powder griddle cakes.

1 package dry granular yeast or 1 yeast cake
1 cup warm water
Pinch of granulated sugar
1 cup milk, scalded
1 teaspoon salt
1 cup all-purpose flour
1 cup buckwheat flour
½ teaspoon baking soda
2 tablespoons table molasses (golden, barrel, or King Syrup) do not
**   use baking molasses**
1 tablespoon butter, melted
1 large egg, lightly beaten

Proof yeast by combining it with water and sugar in small bowl. If it foams, it's active and ready. Cool milk to lukewarm, then mix with salt and both flours in large mixing bowl. When thoroughly blended, gradually stir in yeast mixture. Cover and let stand in warm, draft-free place overnight. When ready to use, preheat griddle and spray with nonstick vegetable spray or brush lightly with vegetable oil. Then, dissolve baking soda in 1 tablespoon of water. Stir it, molasses, butter, and egg into flour mixture. This should create thin batter. If it is too thick, add extra milk. Pour about ¼ cup of batter for each cake onto hot griddle (it's hot enough when drop of water dances around on it until it disappears). Turn when golden or when bubbles break and top begins to look dry, about 5 minutes.

Yield: 4 servings or about 12 medium to large cakes

CREPES OR THIN PANCAKES

The country folks serve thin pancakes in many ways. They fill them with thinly sliced meats, roll, and stack them on a heated platter, topping them with beef or chicken gravy. For dessert (see Variation), they're often filled with ice cream, folded tightly and fried in butter, brown sugar, and orange juice. When served hot with meat, they are known as Pfatzlings in Pennsylvania Dutch. When used as desserts, they're called Fancy Pancakes.

1 cup all-purpose flour
3 large eggs
½ teaspoon salt
½ cup beer or water
¾ cup milk
¼ cup water
2 tablespoons (¼ stick) butter, melted
1 tablespoon vegetable oil

Combine all ingredients but oil in large mixing bowl and stir until well blended. Cover and refrigerate overnight or at least several hours (this will make crepes more tender). Season your crepe pan by adding oil to it and heating it until it smokes. Remove pan from heat and sprinkle it with salt. Wipe pan with paper towels and it's ready. If you always use this pan for making crepes, you only need to clean it with clean towel and spray pan with nonstick vegetable spray or brush it with few drops of oil whenever you use it.

Return pan to stove and heat it over a medium-high flame. When hot, pour ¼ cup of batter into pan and cook until light, golden brown on top. Flip over and remove when golden. Store between sheets of wax paper until ready to fill.

YIELD: 12 TO 14 CREPES

Variation:

Fancy Pancakes:
Add 2 tablespoons granulated sugar and ½ teaspoon fresh lemon juice or extract to batter. These are delicious with Fried Ice Cream (page 248).

CHAPTER FOUR

Vegetables and Side Dishes

APPLESAUCE

A staple in Pennsylvania Dutch cookery, homemade applesauce is so tasty and satisfying, it is a shame to buy store-bought unless you add some extra flavor to make it your own. For this recipe, I like to use one of the following types of apples: Stayman, Smokehouse, Winesap, Baldwin, York Imperial, Rome, or Jonathan.

8 apples (about 3 pounds), peeled, cored, and quartered
1½ cups water
2 teaspoons fresh lemon juice
½ teaspoon grated orange rind
¼ teaspoon salt
⅛ teaspoon ground nutmeg
¼ cup lightly packed light brown sugar
¼ cup red cinnamon candies (optional)
Ground cinnamon or nutmeg for garnish

Place apples in large, heavy 6-quart saucepan or kettle. Add water and cook over low heat, covered, until soft, about 15 minutes. Stir to prevent them from sticking to bottom of pan. If there is any extra liquid, drain off before pureeing. Put apples through food mill or processor until they are smooth (or chunky, if you wish). Pour them back into saucepan and add all ingredients but cinnamon. If you want your applesauce to have cinnamon flavor and pinkish color, add candies. Bring apples to boil over low heat and let boil for at least 2 minutes. Serve warm, garnished with sprinkle of cinnamon or nutmeg. If making large amount, can applesauce in hot, sterilized jars with new lids after boiling for 5 minutes (see section on canning, pages 249-250).
Yield: About 4 cups

🐉 APPLE DUMPLINGS 🐉

Apple dumplings are sold individually at most of our markets and bakeries. When there were twelve around our table, we made deep-dish dumplings, cutting them into large slices. I much prefer baking them separately, basting them with the syrup. They're almost as good cold as hot.

6 baking apples, such as Stayman, Smokehouse, or Granny Smith, peeled and cored
½ cup cinnamon hearts (hard candies)
2 cups all-purpose flour
2½ teaspoons baking powder
½ teaspoon salt
½ pound (2 sticks) butter or margarine
½ cup milk
2 cups lightly packed light brown sugar
2 cups water
⅛ teaspoon ground cinnamon
⅛ teaspoon ground nutmeg

Preheat oven to 350°F.

Fill cored center of each apple with cinnamon candies. Sift flour, baking powder, and salt together. Cut ⅔ cup of butter into flour mixture until fine and crumbly. Sprinkle milk over mixture until moist, pressing it into ball. Roll out dough about ¼ inch thick on floured board and cut into 6-inch squares. Place an apple on each square and bring dough up around to cover it completely. Moisten top edges with water and fasten securely on top of apple—whole cloves may be used to secure it. Place dumplings 1 inch apart in greased 9 x 13-inch baking dish or pan. Combine brown sugar, water, cinnamon, and nutmeg in large saucepan and bring to boil. Simmer over low heat for 3 minutes, remove from heat and stir in remaining butter. Pour syrup over dumplings and bake for 35 to 40 minutes, basting every 15 minutes. Serve hot with chilled rich milk, cream, or whipped cream.
YIELD: 6 SERVINGS

APPLE FRITTERS

Fritters are eaten as a snack, vegetable, or dessert. I suggest using either Smokehouse, Winesap, Jonathan or Stayman, Rome, or York Imperial.

4 or 5 large apples
1½ cups all-purpose flour
2 large eggs, separated
½ cup water or milk
1 tablespoon butter, melted
1 tablespoon fresh lemon juice or white wine
1 teaspoon baking powder
¼ teaspoon salt
¼ cup granulated sugar
2 cups vegetable oil (or 2 inches deep in the skillet)
Confectioner's or cinnamon sugar for topping

Peel, core, and slice apples into rings about ¼ to ⅓ inch thick. Dredge in ½ cup of flour. Whip egg yolks in large mixing bowl until light in color, then whip in water, butter, and lemon juice. Sift baking powder, salt, sugar, and remaining flour together. Slowly add to egg yolk mixture until thoroughly blended. Beat egg whites until stiff and fold into batter. Dip apple slices in batter, covering them completely. Heat oil in large, heavy skillet or fryer to 375°F and fry until golden brown, about 2 minutes on each side. Drain on paper towels, sprinkle with sugar, and serve hot.

JERUSALEM ARTICHOKES

These artichokes grow wild along fencerows and meadows. Even though they were growing here before the first settlers arrived, they were nearly forgotten over the past 40 years.

1½ pound Jerusalem artichokes (or sunchokes)
1 cup water
½ teaspoon salt
3 slices bacon or 3 tablespoons butter
½ teaspoon celery salt
½ clove garlic, minced, or 1 tablespoon minced onion
½ teaspoon ground black pepper

Scrub chokes and cook them in water and salt, covered, in large, deep saucepan until nearly tender over medium heat, about 15 to 20 minutes. Drain, cool, and peel. Cut into ⅓-inch slices or wedges. Fry bacon in large, heavy skillet until limp, then drain off fat, add chokes, celery salt, minced garlic, and pepper, and continue to fry over medium heat until chokes are golden. The extra fat from bacon will be enough to fry chokes and bacon should be crisp by time dish is ready to be served, about 4 minutes. If you prefer not to have bacon, follow same instructions, only frying chokes in 3 tablespoons butter.

 ESCALLOPED ASPARAGUS

*This is a very delicate dish. Make sure you serve it
immediately from the oven (almost like a soufflé).*

3 cups asparagus, cleaned and cut in pieces
2 large eggs, lightly beaten
½ teaspoon ground white pepper
1½ teaspoons salt
1½ cups milk
2 cups fresh bread crumbs
¼ cup grated Cheddar cheese
Several slices of Cheddar cheese for topping

Preheat oven to 350°F.

Blanch, steam, or microwave asparagus for two minutes until bright green
but not fully cooked. Blend eggs, pepper, salt, and milk thoroughly. Butter or
oil 1½-quart casserole dish and alternate layers of bread crumbs, asparagus,
cheese, and milk mixture until all are used. Top with slices of cheese and
bake for 40 minutes. If cheese starts to darken, lightly cover with foil for last
15 minutes. Serve immediately.

Yield: 6 servings

ASPARAGUS IN CREAM

*This is the old standby. Everyone served it with toast tips or poured it into
patty shells (pie dough baked in muffin cups) for a special occasion.*

1½ pounds asparagus
½ cup water
½ teaspoon salt
Pinch of granulated sugar
1 cup Medium White Sauce (page 152) or heavy cream
2 tablespoons Browned Butter (page 151)
Toast Cups (page 107) or Patty Shells (page 181)

Make sure all tough ends are removed, then cut asparagus into 1-inch pieces
and place in saucepan. Add water, salt, and sugar, and bring to boil. Cover
and blanch for only few minutes. Drain water off, then add white sauce or
cream to asparagus and simmer over low heat until thoroughly heated. Pour
into heated serving dish, warm toast cups, or warm patty shells and top with
browned butter.

Yield: 6 servings

 BAKED BEANS

Everyone loves baked beans but this recipe is exceptionally versatile.

8 slices bacon
½ cup chopped onion
1 teaspoon dry mustard
½ teaspoon ground white pepper
1 teaspoon chopped fresh chives
1 teaspoon dried parsley flakes
½ teaspoon salt
½ cup pure maple syrup
½ cup catsup or barbecue sauce
½ cup red or white wine
4 (15-ounce) cans butter beans, drained, or 1 pound dried lima beans
soaked in water overnight
3 slices bacon or ½ cup fresh bread crumbs for topping

Preheat oven to 350°F.

Fry bacon in large, heavy skillet until crisp. Remove bacon, drain on paper towels, and crumble when cool. Saute onion in bacon fat over medium heat until golden brown, about 3 minutes. Add crumbled bacon, mustard, pepper, chives, parsley, salt, syrup, catsup, wine, and beans. Blend thoroughly. Pour into greased 9 x 12-inch casserole or baking dish and top with bacon or bread crumbs. Bake for 1 hour, uncovered.

YIELD: 6 TO 8 SERVINGS

Variation:

Add 2 cups chopped beef or pork and substitute an equal
amount of beef broth for wine and maple syrup.

BEAN LOAF

*A great substitute for meat loaf, this is perfect for stretching
the budget as well as pleasing to the vegetarian.*

**3 cups dried beans, cooked, or 5 cups canned and drained (use navy,
    great northern, butter or kidney beans, or chick peas)**
2 tablespoons vegetable shortening
½ cup chopped celery
1 medium-size onion, chopped
1 tablespoon chopped fresh parsley
1 tablespoon chopped green or red bell pepper
½ teaspoon chopped fresh marjoram
½ cup chopped tomatoes or catsup
1 teaspoon salt
½ teaspoon ground black pepper
2 large eggs, lightly beaten
1½ cups fresh bread crumbs

Preheat oven to 350°F.

Chop beans in food processor if you prefer smoother loaf. If shells of beans
are not problem for your family, leave beans whole. Heat shortening in skillet
and saute celery, onion, parsley, bell pepper, and marjoram for 5 minutes
over medium heat or until celery and onion are clear. In large mixing bowl
combine beans, tomatoes, celery mixture, salt, pepper, eggs, and bread
crumbs. Mix thoroughly, form into loaf. If loaf seems dry, add a little tomato
or vegetable juice. Place in greased 9 x 5-inch loaf pan or 9 x 13-inch cake
pan and bake for 45 minutes.
YIELD: 6 SERVINGS

Hint:
For extra flavor, add strips of bacon to top of loaf before baking.

 GREEN BEANS

Plain green beans, lightly steamed and crunchy, are still the
most colorful vegetable to complement any dish.

1 pound green beans, washed and trimmed
¼ (if steaming beans) to ½ cup (if boiling beans) water
½ teaspoon salt
1 tablespoon Browned Butter (page 151, optional)
1 tablespoon Mushroom-Herb Sauce (page 154, optional)

Leave beans whole or cut into desired lengths. Place beans and water into covered saucepan or deep skillet. Bring to boil and cook or steam over high heat until beans are bright green and give when squeezed. Drain and sprinkle with salt if desired. Top with Browned Butter or sauce of choice.

YIELD: 4 SERVINGS

Variation:

Cook green beans with 4 white potatoes, whole or quartered, and ham hock in large saucepan until everything is tender. Remove meat from bone, cut off fat and cut mean into chunks. Serve with beans and potatoes in deep serving dish. Top with Hollandaise Sauce (page 153).

PICKLED BEETS

These are usually made with small beets and used as a relish. If using
large beets, cut them into quarters after they are cooked.

2½ pounds fresh beets
½ cup granulated sugar
½ cup cider vinegar
½ cup water
1 teaspoon salt
1 teaspoon coarsely ground black pepper
1½ teaspoons minced mixed herbs (dried salad herbs are fine)

Wash but do not peel beets. Cut tops 1 inch above beets to keep them from bleeding. Place them in large pot and cover with water. Bring to boil and cook over medium heat until tender, approximately 30 minutes. Drain, reserving beet liquid. Peel beets and cut up if necessary. Place all ingredients (except beets) and 1 cup of beet juice back into pot, stir together, and bring to boil. Add beets and boil an additional 2 minutes over medium-high heat. Pack and seal in hot sterilized jars or store in covered container in refrigerator until ready to use.

YIELD: 3 PINTS

🪷 HAPPY BEETS 🪷

One day while making Harvard Beets, our cook mistook the homemade wine
for vinegar and this recipe became a favorite of everyone in the restaurant.
Some folks who wouldn't think of eating beets just ask for the "sauce."

4 cups beet juice from pickled beets
2 tablespoons arrowroot or cornstarch
¼ cup water
½ cup dry red wine or dry fruit wine
¼ cup granulated sugar
4 cups Pickled Beets (page 67)

Place beet juice in large saucepan and bring to boil over high heat. (If you do
not get 4 cups beet juice from pickled beets, add equal parts water and part
wine to make proper amount.) Dissolve arrowroot in water and add to wine
along with sugar. Stir into beet juice and cook until thickened over medium
heat, about 5 minutes. Add beets and continue to simmer for several minutes
until thoroughly heated and flavor goes through beets. Check for seasonings
and add salt or sugar as desired.
YIELD: 4 TO 6 SERVINGS

Variation:

Sunshine Beets:
Add juice and grated rind of 1 orange, ¼ cup maple syrup, ½ teaspoon
ground ginger, and 2 tablespoons (¼ stick) butter to above recipe.
Omit wine if desired and substitute ¼ cup white vinegar. Harvard
Beets: Substitute an equal amount of red wine vinegar for wine.

STUFFED BEETS

The extra work of stuffing the beets will be rewarded when you try this old recipe.

6 large beets, with tops
2 cups water
½ teaspoon salt
2 green onions
2 tablespoons (¼ stick) butter
¾ cup fresh bread crumbs
¼ teaspoon dried dillweed
½ teaspoon salt
⅛ teaspoon ground white pepper
⅓ cup sour cream
1 hardboiled egg, chopped

Preheat oven to 350°F.

Scrub beets and cut tops one inch from beets to prevent bleeding. Place in large saucepan with water and salt. Cook over medium heat, covered, until tender, about 1 hour. While beets are cooking, wash tops thoroughly, save few choice tops for garnish, and chop rest coarsely. Chop or slice onions, tops and all. Melt butter in large heavy skillet and saute tops, onions, bread crumbs, dillweed, salt, and pepper over medium heat approximately 6 minutes. When beets are ready, let cool, then slip off skins. Scoop or cut center out of each beet. Chop centers and add to crumb mixture. Trim bottom of each beet so it will stand upright in 9-inch baking dish and on plate. Add those trimmings to crumb mixture. Fill each beet with mixture and place filled beets in 9-inch buttered baking dish or pan. If you have extra filling, arrange it around beets and bake for 25 minutes. Top with dollop of sour cream and some chopped egg and continue baking for 5 more minutes. Serve on heated plate garnished with beet tops.

YIELD: 6 SERVINGS

Hint:
Any of the homemade vinegars will complement this dish
nicely. Serve the vinegar in a cruet, letting each person
sprinkle a few drops on the beet after cutting it.

 BRUSSELS SPROUTS WITH CHESTNUTS

*I cannot understand why folks shy away from this wonderful vegetable.
Maybe it's because it's a member of the cabbage family. After you try
this combination I think you will be pleasantly surprised.*

2 pounds small Brussels sprouts
2 cups water
½ teaspoon salt
6 tablespoons (¾ stick) butter or margarine
1 tablespoon granulated sugar
**1 cup boiled or canned chestnuts (do not use water chestnuts; pecans
    may be substituted)**
⅓ cup seasoned beef broth
Freshly ground black pepper

Clean and trim sprouts. (If freshly picked, some people like to soak them in
cold salted water for 15 minutes to remove any garden insects that may be
inside.) Place sprouts, water, and salt in large saucepan, cover, and cook until
tender, about 8 minutes. They should not fall apart, but give when squeezed.
Drain. Melt 3 tablespoons of butter in large, heavy skillet and saute sprouts
over medium heat until lightly golden, about 5 minutes. Pour into heated
serving dish, keep warm. Melt remaining butter in same skillet, add sugar
and stir over medium heat until lightly caramelized, about 3 minutes. Add
chestnuts and stir until golden brown, about 4 minutes. Add beef broth,
simmer, still over medium heat, check for seasonings, then pour over sprouts.
Top with pepper and serve immediately.

YIELD: 4 TO 6 SERVINGS

🦅 RED CABBAGE 🦅

*Our ancestors raised red cabbage and considered it an ordinary part of a meal.
I think it is exciting and delicious, especially when served with a fine red wine.*

½ **cup granulated sugar**
1 **tablespoon salt**
½ **cup water**
½ **cup cider vinegar**
8 **cups shredded red cabbage**
1 **tablespoon butter**
½ **cup red wine (grape jelly may be substituted)**

Combine sugar, salt, water, and vinegar in large 6-quart saucepan or kettle.
Bring to boil and add cabbage and butter. Lower heat to simmer and cook,
covered, until tender, at least 30 minutes. Add red wine and check for
seasoning, adding extra salt and pepper if desired. Simmer 10 minutes more
or until ready to serve.
YIELD: 6 SERVINGS

Hint:
Several apples, peeled, cored, and sliced thin may
be added to cabbage while it is boiling.

🦅 BROCCOLI 🦅

*Many folks prefer eating broccoli raw, but if steamed for a very
short time, it takes on a beautiful bright green color.*

1 **pound broccoli**
½ **cup water**
½ **teaspoon salt**
1 **tablespoon butter**
½ **teaspoon dried salad herbs (optional)**
2 **tablespoons Browned Butter (page 151), your favorite sauce, or**
    Herb Vinegar (page 261)

Wash and trim broccoli. Break into flowerets and peel stem. Cut stem into
⅓-inch-thick slices or into strips to cook with flowerets. Put broccoli, stems,
water, salt, butter, and herbs in large saucepan, cover, and bring to boil
over high heat. Reduce heat to medium, cover, and simmer 3 to 5 minutes,
depending on how crunchy you like them. Drain and top with browned
butter, your favorite sauce (walnut-mustard sauce or hollandaise is very nice),
or few splashes of herb vinegar.
YIELD: 4 SERVINGS

BAKED CABBAGE

I have to include this recipe because everyone asks me why they like this cabbage when they do not eat cabbage–could it be the cheese?

1 medium-size head cabbage
½ cup water
2 tablespoons all-purpose flour
½ teaspoon salt
½ teaspoon ground white pepper
1 tablespoon granulated sugar
3 tablespoons butter
1 cup milk
½ cup grated Cheddar or white American cheese

Preheat oven to 350°F.

Cut cabbage into wedges and parboil in water in covered saucepan for about 4 minutes. Drain and place cabbage in buttered or greased 2-quart casserole. Sprinkle with flour, salt, pepper, and sugar. Dot with butter or melt and pour over evenly. Pour milk over cabbage and top with grated cheese. Bake for about 35 minutes or until golden brown on top and bubbling around sides. Time will be affected by depth of baking dish.

YIELD: 4 SERVINGS

🦅 SAUERKRAUT 🦅

Every good "Dutchman" eats pork and sauerkraut on New Year's
Day to bring the family good luck for the coming year.

2 pounds sauerkraut (4 cups), fresh or canned
2 cups beer or water
1 tablespoon light brown sugar
1 tablespoon caraway seeds (optional)

Wash and drain sauerkraut and place it in large, heavy kettle. Cover with
beer or water. If you use water, add several cored and sliced apples to mellow
kraut. Add brown sugar and caraway. Bring to boil and simmer over low
heat for at least 1 hour. Longer it simmers, better it tastes. If you want to
add meat, put this in during last 15 minutes before serving. Brownings from
pork or beef roast give an excellent flavor.

To make your own sauerkraut, finely shred fresh cabbage with coarse grater
or thin slicer of a food processor. A firm medium head of cabbage will fill
3 pint jars of kraut. Pack into sterilized jars. Sprinkle top of each quart with
one teaspoon of salt (if using pints, ½ teaspoon salt per pint) and fill to neck
of jar with boiling water. Seal with new lids and rings and store in cool place.
To prevent liquid from staining shelves mold foil in baking pan to form tray.
Place jars of kraut on foil—it will ferment in jars and seep from lids—to age.
Let kraut age for at least 1 month—longer better—but 3 months is good. Old-
fashioned way was to place it in crock and let it ferment, partially covered
with plate weighted down with washed stone, until it was tender, about
365 days. This method keeps kraut much lighter and is so easy—without
near the odor!
YIELD: 6 SERVINGS

Variation:

Sauerkraut and Knepp:
Add extra liquid to sauerkraut and drop knepp in tablespoonsful
into boiling broth, following recipe on page 55.

🐦 CARROT SOUFFLE 🐦

*Many folks think souffles are new, but my research proves
they've been made for many, many years.*

1 pound carrots, peeled and coarsely chopped
5 tablespoons butter
1 tablespoon minced onion
2 teaspoons dried chervil
½ teaspoon dried tarragon
½ teaspoon chopped fresh mint
1 teaspoon Worcestershire sauce
¼ teaspoon paprika
½ teaspoon salt
¼ teaspoon ground black pepper
3 tablespoons all-purpose flour
1½ cups milk
3 large eggs, separated

Preheat oven to 350°F.
Place carrots in large saucepan and cover with water. Bring to boil, then
simmer over medium heat until carrots are tender, about 10 minutes; drain.
Melt 2 tablespoons of butter in large heavy skillet or saucepan over medium
heat. Add carrots, onion, chervil, tarragon, mint, Worcestershire, paprika, salt,
and pepper, and saute for 4 minutes or until thoroughly heated. Remove from
heat and let cool slightly. In 1½-quart saucepan, melt remaining butter and
gradually stir in flour with whisk over medium heat, stirring until smooth and
bubbly, about 2 minutes. Slowly add milk and cook about 3 minutes or until
thickened. Beat egg yolks. Remove milk mixture from heat and whip in yolks.
Fold it into carrot mixture. Beat egg whites until stiff and fold into warm
mixture. Pour into buttered 1½-quart ring mold, bundt pan, or baking dish.
Place it in pan with 1 inch of water and bake for approximately 45 minutes or
until knife inserted in deepest part of souffle comes out clean. Work point of
knife around outer edge to loosen souffle and invert it onto heated serving dish.
Do not remove mold immediately—let souffle come out gradually.
YIELD: 4 TO 6 SERVINGS

Variation:

Before serving, fill center of baked souffle with cooked snow
peas, garden peas, green beans, or buttered spinach.
Corn Souffle: Substitute 4 cups corn kernels for carrots and omit
mint. For fine, light souffle, puree corn in food processor or blender.

Broccoli Souffle: Substitute 1½ pounds broccoli buds for
carrots and omit mint. If baking in ring mold or bundt pan, fill
baked souffle with any sauteed or steamed vegetables.

CARROTS

*Nutritious and colorful, carrots are loved by children. Here
are some of my favorite recipes for tempting them.*

1 pound carrots, peeled and cut into 1-inch pieces
1 cup water
½ teaspoon salt
2 tablespoons Browned Butter (page 151)

Place carrots into large saucepan, add water and salt, cover, and cook over
medium heat until tender but not mushy, about 12 minutes. Drain and serve
in heated serving dish. Top with browned butter.
YIELD: 4 TO 6 SERVINGS

Variations:

Fried Carrots:
After draining cooked carrots, roll them in ½ cup flour, coating thoroughly.
Melt 2 tablespoons butter or vegetable oil in large, heavy skillet over
medium heat. Add carrots and 1 teaspoon granulated sugar and fry
until golden brown around edges, approximately 6 minutes. Serve
immediately. This recipe is especially good with whole baby carrots.

CAULIFLOWER

*You can also make this recipe using the whole head of the
cauliflower; it's more showy looking for company.*

1 head cauliflower, about 10 inches across the top
1 cup water
½ teaspoon salt
1 teaspoon chopped fresh chervil (optional)
½ teaspoon ground white pepper
1½ cups Medium White Sauce (page 152)
½ cup grated Cheddar or white American cheese
Paprika or chopped fresh chervil for garnish

Trim and wash cauliflower, breaking it into flowerets if you prefer. Place
in large saucepan with water, salt, chervil, and pepper. Cook over medium
heat until tender, about 10 minutes if separated into flowerets, 20 minutes
if whole. Drain cauliflower and top with butter pats if you like it plain and
serve immediately. If you plan to sauce it, heat white sauce while cauliflower
is cooking, adding grated cheese and stirring until completely blended. Pour
sauce over drained cauliflower and sprinkle with paprika or chervil. Serve
immediately or place under preheated broiler until top is golden brown.
YIELD: 4 SERVINGS

 NUTTY SWEET-AND SOUR CAULIFLOWER

*With the abundance of walnuts in Pennsylvania Dutch country, is
it any wonder they are used in sauces and as garnishes?*

1 large head cauliflower
1 cup water
1 teaspoon salt
2 tablespoons (¼ stick) butter
1 large egg, lightly beaten
2 tablespoons granulated sugar
¼ teaspoon ground white pepper
3 tablespoons light brown sugar
2 tablespoons Dijon mustard
1 tablespoon cornstarch
⅓ cup cider vinegar (herb or wine vinegar may be substituted)
½ cup milk or evaporated milk
½ cup broken or coarsely chopped walnuts, toasted
Walnut halves for garnish

Trim and wash cauliflower. Place it in large saucepan with water and
½ teaspoon of salt. Cover and cook over medium heat until tender but
crisp, approximately 20 minutes. Meanwhile, melt butter in small skillet
or saucepan and whisk in egg, sugar, pepper, salt, brown sugar, mustard,
and remaining salt. Cook over low heat until slightly thickened, about
3 minutes. Dissolve cornstarch in vinegar and add to egg mixture, stirring till
well blended. Add milk and stir until thickened and smooth, about 6 minutes.
Add walnuts. Drain cauliflower and place in heated serving dish. Spoon
sauce over cauliflower and garnish with walnut halves.
YIELD: 4 SERVINGS

CELERY BAKED WITH ALMONDS

Bleached celery hearts are always presented chilled and usually in an antique glass celery dish. The green stems around the outside of the stalk were used to their best advantage in this recipe.

8 to 10 stems of green celery or 2 whole stalks of celery with leaves, washed, trimmed and cut into 1-inch pieces
1 cup chicken broth
1 teaspoon chopped fresh parsley
½ cup grated carrots (optional)
½ teaspoon salt
½ teaspoon ground black pepper
3 tablespoons butter
3 tablespoons all-purpose flour
1 cup milk
⅓ cup toasted slivered or sliced almonds
⅓ cup fresh bread crumbs
⅓ teaspoon celery seed and ⅓ cup toasted slivered almonds for garnish

Preheat oven to 400°F.

Place celery in large saucepan with broth, parsley, carrots, salt and pepper. Bring to boil and simmer over medium heat until tender but still crisp, about 10 minutes. Strain, reserving liquid for sauce. Melt butter in deep skillet or saucepan and stir in flour over medium-low heat until smooth and bubbly. Gradually add celery liquid and milk. Cook over medium heat, stirring constantly until sauce is thick and creamy, about 6 minutes. Add almonds and sauce to celery and pour into buttered 2-quart baking dish. Top with bread crumbs, celery seed, and almonds and bake for 10 minutes or until golden brown, or place under preheated broiler until lightly browned.
YIELD: 6 SERVINGS

Variation:

Use ½ cup grated Cheddar cheese instead of almonds.

CELERY WITH SESAME-HONEY PEANUT BUTTER

This takes very little time to make and lasts forever in the refrigerator (if you can keep from eating it!).

¼ cup sesame seeds
3 tablespoons honey
1 cup creamy peanut butter (crunchy if desired)
Celery stems, cleaned and cut in 3-inch lengths

Preheat toaster oven to 350°F.

Toast sesame seeds in small skillet over medium heat or toaster oven for 5 minutes, stirring constantly until golden brown. Blend honey into peanut butter and add 3 tablespoons of sesame seeds. Mix well and spread on celery stems. Top with remaining sesame seeds.
YIELD: 1½ CUPS

Variation:

Place spread in small bowl and serve with fresh carrot sticks, cauliflower or broccoli florets, or sliced turnips. Fill leaves of fresh cabbage with peanut butter mixture, roll them, and serve as finger food.

 CORN, LIMAS, AND RED PEPPER STIR-FRY

*When everyone is enjoying the outdoors, make this recipe in your wok or electric
skillet or use your heavy iron skillet on the grill and prepare it outdoors–that
way you can keep the heat out of the kitchen and be part of the family fun.*

6 slices bacon
6 ears corn or 4 cups corn kernels
2 medium-size red bell peppers, sliced or diced
2 cups Fordhook or baby lima beans
¾ teaspoon salt
½ teaspoon coarsely ground black pepper

Fry bacon until crisp in large skillet. Remove and drain on paper towels.
Cut corn kernels from cob and add to hot bacon fat along with peppers, lima
beans, salt, and pepper; stir-fry over medium-high heat until vegetables are
tender but crunchy, about 8 minutes. Top with crumbled bacon and serve
immediately.
YIELD: 6 TO 8 SERVINGS

CORN FRITTERS

*Excellent as a vegetable dish, fritters are a perfect finger food to serve
from an electric skillet during a buffet (or at poolside).*

3 cups corn kernels, fresh or frozen
1 teaspoon salt
½ teaspoon granulated sugar (optional)
¼ teaspoon coarsely ground black pepper
½ teaspoon crushed dried basil (optional)
2 large eggs, lightly beaten
2 tablespoons butter or vegetable oil

Blend all ingredients together, coarsely, in food processor or blender, unless
you are using frozen corn; in that case, add all other ingredients first or frozen
corn will harden and burn out blender's motor. Heat butter or oil to medium-
high in large heavy skillet and drop batter in by tablespoonsful. Turn over
when golden brown. Remove from skillet when other side has browned.
Serve with maple syrup, molasses, or powdered sugar. (I like my corn fritters
plain.)
YIELD: 25 TO 30 FRITTERS

🦚 DRIED CORN 🦚

When fresh sweet corn is dried it retains all its natural sugar. When reconstituted, it almost tastes as though there was a bit of caramel syrup added. You can purchase dried corn by mail: Write John F. Cope Co., Inc., Rheems, Lancaster County, PA 17570

8 ounces dried sweet corn, almost 2 cups
3½ cups milk
2 tablespoons (¼ stick) butter or margarine
¼ teaspoon salt (optional)

Grind corn in food processor or mill until fine. Soak corn in 2-quart buttered casserole overnight, refrigerated, in milk. Pour into 2-quart saucepan, add butter and salt, and simmer over low heat for at least 40 minutes, stirring frequently to prevent sticking. Take off heat, stir once, and let stand for 15 minutes. Return to low heat and cook 15 minutes more. Serve immediately.

YIELD: 6 SERVINGS

Variation:

Baked Corn:
Add 4 eggs, lightly beaten, and 1 teaspoon salt to corn and bake in preheated 350°F oven for 45 minutes.

🦚 EGGPLANT CASSEROLE 🦚

2 eggplants, peeled
1 medium-size green bell pepper
1 medium-size onion
½ cup water
1½ teaspoons salt
1½ cups grated Cheddar cheese
1 cup broken saltine crackers
½ teaspoon coarsely ground black pepper
4 tablespoons (½ stick) butter, melted

Preheat oven to 350°F.
Slice, dice, or chop eggplants, pepper, and onion, and place them in 3-quart saucepan with water and salt. Cover and cook over medium heat until eggplant is clear, about 5 minutes. Drain well. Generously butter 2-quart baking dish or pan and layer vegetables, cheese, and crackers. Sprinkle with pepper and dribble melted butter over top. Bake for 30 minutes until golden brown.

YIELD: 6 TO 8 SERVINGS

🦎 FRIED EGGPLANT 🦎

The secret to good eggplant is the weighting down process. It has a lot of liquid which is best removed before preparation by slicing the eggplant, sprinkling it lightly with salt, covering the slices with a dish, and weighting it down with a heavy can, stone, or jar. This presses out all of the liquid in less than 1 hour. Many folks used eggplant as a substitute for oysters.

2 eggplants, about 1 pound, peeled
Salt
2 cups fresh bread crumbs or half cracker and half bread crumbs
½ teaspoon dry mustard
½ teaspoon ground white pepper
3 large eggs, lightly beaten
1 cup vegetable oil

Slice peeled eggplants ¼ to ⅓ inch thick. Place in large bowl or casserole, sprinkling each layer lightly with salt. Cover slices with dish and weight it down with heavy object. Let stand for at least 1 hour. Drain liquid. Mix crumbs, mustard, and pepper together on plate or sheet of wax paper. Dip eggplant slices into beaten egg, then dredge completely in crumbs. Fry in oil, heated to 375°F in a large, skillet or deep fat fryer until golden brown, about 4 minutes.

YIELD: 4 TO 6 SERVINGS

Variation:

Slice 3 firm tomatoes ½ inch thick and fry or broil same way.
When serving, alternate tomato and eggplant slices around serving
dish. Two large zucchini may be substituted for eggplant.

Note:
You may broil eggplant instead of frying it, placing slices in
preheated broiler until golden brown, about 3 minutes per side.

 BATTER-DIPPED CUCUMBERS

When cucumbers are plentiful, this will be one of your favorite ways to enjoy them.

4 to 6 medium-size cucumbers
1 recipe of Beer Batter (page 160)
Vegetable oil for frying

Do not peel cucumbers unless they are waxed. Cut into ¼-inch slices and dip in batter. Heat 3 inches of oil in fryer to 380°F; fry batter-dipped slices until golden brown. Drain on paper towels. Serve hot with catsup on side.
YIELD: 4 SERVINGS

 DANDELION, LIMAS AND POTATOES

An excellent way to enjoy the first fresh dandelions.

6 slices bacon
1 cup baby limas, fresh or frozen
2 cups diced potatoes
½ cup water
4 cups fresh baby dandelion leaves
½ teaspoon salt
½ teaspoon ground black pepper

Fry bacon until crisp. Remove from pan and drain on paper towels. Reserve 2 tablespoons of bacon fat. Cook limas and potatoes over medium-high heat with water in saucepan, covered, until tender, approximately 12 minutes. Drain. While vegetables are cooking, wash dandelion leaves thoroughly and trim stems and roots. Heat bacon fat over medium heat and saute leaves until wilted; then add potatoes, lima beans, salt, and pepper. Stir and cover, simmering over medium heat for about 3 minutes. Do not overcook or dandelion leaves will become bitter. Top with crumbled bacon or stir in before serving. Serve from skillet or heated serving dish.
YIELD: 4 SERVINGS

HOMINY CROQUETTES

*Hominy, the center of a grain of corn, was an important part of the early settlers'
diets. Today we have the advantage of the availability of flaked hominy, known
as grits, or canned hominy. Hominy picks up the flavor of anything it is cooked
with, much like noodles, potatoes, or rice. Usually served with pork or ham dishes,
these croquettes, when sweetened, are served with poached fruit as a dessert.*

1¼ cups instant grits
1½ cups water
1¾ cups canned hominy (small or chopped), drained
3 large eggs, separated
1 tablespoon butter, melted
1 teaspoon granulated sugar
¼ teaspoon salt
2 cups milk

Preheat oven to 350°F.

Cook instant grits in water over medium heat in covered saucepan for about
4 minutes. If using whole canned hominy, chop in food processor. Lightly
beat egg yolks with fork. Whip whites until they form peaks. Mix grits,
hominy, butter, sugar, salt, and beaten egg yolks together until well blended.
Gradually add milk and mix until smooth. Fold in beaten egg whites. Pour
into buttered 2 to 2½-quart casserole dish. Bake for 1 hour or until golden
brown.
YIELD: 6 SERVINGS

Variation:

Add 1 cup of grated Cheddar cheese to mixture before baking.

For Dessert:
Add 2 to 3 tablespoons granulated sugar and 1 teaspoon
vanilla extract to mixture before folding in egg whites.

🪶 HOMINY CAKES 🪶

These can be baked in the oven, but most people find it easier to fry them. Hominy is a great substitute for potatoes or rice and may be served for breakfast, lunch, or dinner.

1¼ cups cooked hominy, drained
½ cup milk
1 large egg
1 tablespoon butter, melted
½ teaspoon salt
1 teaspoon granulated sugar
Flour for dredging
2 tablespoons (¼ stick) butter or vegetable oil

Preheat oven to 375°F.
Place hominy, milk, egg, melted butter, salt and sugar in food processor or mixer and puree. Form into cakes about 3 inches round and dredge in flour. Melt butter in skillet and fry until golden brown on each side. Cover pan with lid to keep from splattering during frying. If baking in an oven, generously grease baking dish, put dab of butter on top of each cake, and bake them for 20 minutes.
YIELD: 6 CAKES APPROXIMATELY 3 INCHES IN DIAMETER

🪶 KOHLRABI 🪶

Kohlrabi, like turnips, are delicious peeled, sliced, and eaten raw with a sprinkle of salt. It is such an interesting vegetable, reasonably priced and nutritious.

1½ pounds kohlrabi, peeled and cut into ½-inch slices
1 cup chicken broth or water
½ teaspoon salt (less if broth is salty)
½ teaspoon ground black pepper
2 tablespoons Browned Butter (page 151)

Place kohlrabi, broth, salt, and pepper in large saucepan. Cook, covered, over medium heat until tender, about 25 minutes. Drain and top with browned butter.
YIELD: 4 SERVINGS

Variation:

½ pound turnips and ½ pound rutabaga, peeled and sliced,
may be added to above recipe for 6 to 8 servings.

LANCASTER COUNTY LIMA BEANS

My Dad's family always served their vegetables in cream. Limas do need more cooking than some of the green vegetables, and when they are simmered in cream, they are unbelievable. We still make them with cream for special occasions.

4 cups (about 2 pounds) fresh or frozen lima beans (I prefer the pole limas or Fordhook limas)
½ cup water
½ teaspoon salt
½ teaspoon granulated sugar
1 tablespoon butter
Pinch of ground white pepper
1 cup half and half
1 tablespoon Browned Butter (page 151)

Put beans in large saucepan with water, salt, sugar, butter, and pepper. Cover and bring to boil. Simmer over medium heat for 10 minutes. Add cream and heat to nearly boiling. Turn off heat and let stand covered until ready to serve (the cream thickens as it stands). Pour into heated serving dish and top with browned butter.

YIELD: 4 TO 6 SERVINGS

Variation:

Baby Limas with Herbs:
Omit cream and add ½ teaspoon each of ground thyme, dried chervil, and dried parsley to lima beans while cooking. A pinch of baking soda added while cooking will make them more tender. Top with Browned Butter if desired.

Limas with Roquefort:
Use 1 cup Thin White Sauce (page 152) instead of cream and add ⅓ cup crumbled Roquefort just before serving or top with cheese instead of browned butter.

 LIMAS IN TOMATO SAUCE

A great winter dish. Everyone dried their own beans and canned their own tomatoes. Today it is much easier to buy the canned ones.

6 slices bacon
2½ cups prepared tomato sauce
2 or 3 tablespoons light brown sugar (depending on your taste)
½ teaspoon salt
½ teaspoon celery salt
½ teaspoon ground black pepper
2½ cups canned butter beans, drained
Seasoned croutons

Fry bacon in large, heavy skillet until crisp. Remove bacon and drain on paper towels. Discard all but 2 tablespoons of bacon fat. Put fat in large saucepan, over medium heat, stir in tomato sauce, brown sugar, salt, celery salt, and pepper. When thoroughly heated, add beans and simmer over medium heat for 30 minutes or until they absorb some of liquid. Crumble bacon and stir about ¾ of it into beans. Serve beans in saucers topped with croutons and remaining bacon.

YIELD: 4 TO 6 SERVINGS

 GLAZED ONIONS

Glazed onions were always served for special occasions. I can't understand why we didn't use them all the time–maybe because it takes time to peel them. I think any onions are wonderful and exciting when prepared this way, even if you quarter the large ones.

1 pint pearl onions (about ½ pound), cleaned
½ cup water
½ teaspoon salt
2 tablespoons (¼ stick) butter
1 tablespoon granulated sugar
Dash of ground white pepper

Parboil cleaned onions in water and salt in covered saucepan over high heat for 3 minutes. Remove from heat and let stand for another 2 minutes. Drain and pat dry onions between paper towels. Melt butter in heavy skillet and add sugar and onions. Cook slowly over medium heat, stirring constantly with wooden spoon until all sides are golden and shiny, about 5 minutes. Serve as vegetable side dish or as garnish around entree. Sprinkle with pepper before serving.

YIELD: 4 SERVINGS

🦚 ONION RINGS 🦚

Fried (pan fried with butter) onions were the normal way to serve onions as a side dish. I like to fry them in deep fat in single rings, but many people prefer to partially fill the basket and fry them altogether. Either way, they're great with this light batter.

6 large onions, cut into ¼-inch slices (Bermuda or red onions are best because they are mild and sweet)
Vegetable oil for frying
1 recipe Beer Batter (page 160)

Preheat 3 inches of oil to 375°F.
Separate onion slices into rings. Dip rings in beer batter and drop them into oil. Fry until golden brown, about 4 minutes. Drain on paper towels. Place on heated platter and serve immediately.
YIELD: 4 TO 6 SERVINGS

🦚 BAKED ONIONS 🦚

Grandma always said, "When you feel a cold coming on, eat lots of onions." Most of the time we ate them raw, but I loved baked onions because they are so sweet after baking.

6 to 8 medium-size onions, peeled and cut in half
Salt and ground black pepper or herbed salt
3 tablespoons butter, margarine, or vegetable oil

Preheat oven to 350°F.
Place onion halves in buttered muffin cups. Sprinkle with seasonings and add pat of butter (or brush with oil) to each half. Bake for 45 minutes or until golden on top. Serve hot.
YIELD: 4 TO 6 SERVINGS

Variation:

Baked Stuffed Onions:
Follow above recipe but remove centers of each half and chop them up. Fry 3 slices bacon in skillet until golden and crisp. Remove bacon and drain on paper towels. Saute chopped onion in bacon fat over medium heat until golden brown. Remove from heat and add ½ cup fresh bread crumbs, 1 egg, lightly beaten, ½ teaspoon salt, ⅓ teaspoon coarsely ground black pepper, ½ teaspoon chopped fresh chives, ¼ teaspoon celery salt, and crumbled bacon. Mix thoroughly and spoon into onion halves. Dot with butter or oil. Bake in greased 9-inch square or 9 x 13-inch baking dish as directed above.

 GARDEN PEAS WITH MINT

Peas are always colorful, and the mint makes them taste extra fresh.

4 lettuce leaves
2 cups peas, fresh or frozen
½ teaspoon salt
½ teaspoon granulated sugar
1 tablespoon butter
2 or 3 sprigs fresh mint or 1 teaspoon dried
⅓ cup water
2 tablespoons Browned Butter (optional; page 151)

Line 1½-quart saucepan or vegetable steamer with lettuce leaves. Add peas, salt, sugar, butter, and mint. Pour water underneath lettuce, cover pan, and bring to boil, then turn down to medium heat. Steam peas for 3 minutes or until tender. Drain peas, discard lettuce, and serve peas in heated serving dish. Top with Browned Butter.

YIELD: 4 SERVINGS

Variations:

Saute or steam 2 cups small pearl onions or chopped green onions in
1 tablespoon butter until tender. Add to peas before serving.
Scrub 6 tiny new potatoes and leave their skins on and cook
in 1 cup lightly salted water over medium heat until tender,
approximately 20 minutes. As it will take longer to cook potatoes,
start them before you steam peas. Add peas before serving.

In Patty Shells:
Use Basic Pie Dough recipe (page 181) to make shells or use Toast
Cups (page 107). Fill with peas. If you prefer, add ½ cup heavy cream
to peas and heat thoroughly before topping with Browned Butter.

SUGAR PEAS

The original sugar peas grown in the Pennsylvania Dutch country were of two varieties. One was the flat, thin ones, much like the snow peas available everywhere but sweeter and smaller. The other was the sickle pod sugar peas which were rounder and plumper, since developed into the sugar snap peas. The pods of both are a delicate surprise; newcomers to the area often thought the peas were to be shelled and threw the best part away.

4 cups sugar peas
½ teaspoon salt
1 tablespoon butter
½ cup water
2 tablespoons Browned Butter (page 151)

Wash peas, then remove stem end and pull string back to blossom end. Trim any browned or dry tips. Place peas, salt, butter, and water in 2-quart saucepan. Cover and bring to boil. Reduce heat to medium and cook for about 2 minutes. Do not overcook. Serve in heated serving dish and top with Browned Butter.
YIELD: 4 SERVINGS

UNBELIEVABLE PEAS IN SOUR CREAM

The name says it all!

1 large cucumber or zucchini, peeled
Pinch of chopped fresh chervil
Pinch of chopped fresh tarragon
Pinch of chopped fresh dill
Pinch of chopped fresh mint
1 pound fresh or frozen garden peas
1 tablespoon butter
½ teaspoon salt
¼ cup water
½ cup sour cream
½ cup Cook Dressing (page 158), mayonnaise, or salad dressing
1 tablespoon fresh lemon juice

Slice cucumber into ¼-inch slices. Place them in large saucepan and add herbs, peas, butter, salt, and water. Cover and bring to boil. Reduce heat to low and simmer for 6 minutes, less if frozen peas are used. Blend sour cream, mayonnaise, and lemon juice, and pour over peas. Heat thoroughly, stirring to prevent sticking. Serve immediately.
YIELD: 6 SERVINGS

🎕 BAKED POTATOES 🎕

*So many young cooks find it hard to believe that few cookbooks tell how to bake
a potato. Since I am a potato freak, I'll give you several ways to enjoy them. It
saves time and insures uniform baking if you choose fresh baking potatoes,
not wrinkled ones or ones with sprouts, and preferably the same size.*

1 potato per person
Butter, salt, pepper, sour cream, chopped chives, and all your favorite
   extras

Preheat oven to 400°F.

Scrub potatoes thoroughly and prick with fork several times to prevent skin
from exploding during baking. If you like skin soft, rub with vegetable oil or
salad dressing. Place on oven rack or in shallow baking pan and bake for
1 hour or until potato feels soft when squeezed gently with pot holder. Cut slit
on top of each potato and squeeze each end, popping it enough to let in butter
or sour cream, etc. Serve immediately.

For microwave baking, place potatoes on paper towel in circle, leaving at
least 1 inch between each. Prick each potato with fork. Each medium-size
potato takes about 4 minutes on high (meaning, if you are baking 2 potatoes
they should be in microwave for 8 minutes). Halfway through, turn potatoes
over. When cooked, cover with clean towel and let stand at least 10 minutes
or until ready to serve.

Variation:

Baked Sweet Potatoes or Yams:
Follow same recipe as baked potatoes, but reduce baking time to 45 minutes.

Baked Potatoes Stuffed with Sausage:
When potatoes are nearly baked, cut them in half and scoop out middles.
Crumble ½ pound fresh or smoke sausage in large, heavy skillet and fry
over medium heat for 6 minutes. Drain off most of fat. Mash scooped-out
potatoes with fork and add them to sausage in pan. Add chopped chives
and ground black pepper if desired and simmer over medium heat until
thoroughly cooked, about 10 minutes. Spoon filling back into potato skins
and continue baking until golden brown, approximately 15 minutes.

SCRAPED NEW POTATOES

Don't bother trying to scrape new potatoes for a large dinner party if you haven't tried it before. It takes about 1 hour to scrape enough for 6 people. Of course, it is well worth the effort, but I would suggest preparing them the day before and storing them in cold water until needed. When you buy new potatoes, scrape one with your nail. If the skin does not come off easily, they are not freshly dug and will be hard to scrape.

8 small new potatoes, scrubbed clean
2 cups water
½ teaspoon salt
2 tablespoons Browned Butter (page 151) or browned bread crumbs

Place potatoes in large bowl of water (dipping potato in water as you scrape off skin speeds up scraping time). Scrape toward you with paring knife, holding potato firmly in one hand and guiding knife with other. Do not pare, but scrape gently, with blade at 90° angle to potato, until all skin is removed. Place scraped potatoes in another bowl filled with cold water to prevent them from turning brown. When ready to cook, put potatoes in large saucepan with 2 cups water and salt and cook over medium heat with lid cracked until tender, about 20 minutes. Edges should crack; if they don't, just prick potato with fork several times. Drain and place in heated serving dish. Top with browned butter.

YIELD: 4 SERVINGS

PAPRIKA BROWNED POTATOES

These are so easy to make and so good to eat.

6 medium-size potatoes, peeled
½ cup all-purpose flour
1 tablespoon paprika
1 teaspoon salt
½ teaspoon ground white pepper
2 to 3 tablespoons corn oil

Cut potatoes into wedges or thick slices. Combine flour, paprika, salt, and pepper in paper bag. Shake cut potatoes in flour mixture until thoroughly covered. Heat oil in skillet and fry over medium heat until potatoes brown and are soft in middle, approximately 20 minutes.

YIELD: 4 TO 6 SERVINGS

❧ POTATO CAKES ❧

These are often served with chipped beef or Creamed Frizzled Dried Beef as a light lunch or supper dish. I like them with everything.

3 cups seasoned, cooked mashed potatoes
2 large eggs, lightly beaten
¼ teaspoon coarsely ground black pepper
⅓ cup all-purpose flour, 2 tablespoons if the potatoes are stiff
2 teaspoons chopped fresh chives
2 tablespoons (¼ stick) butter or vegetable oil

Mix everything but butter together until blended thoroughly. Form into 3-inch-diameter cakes about 1 inch thick. Heat butter or oil over medium-high heat until bubbly hot, then add potato cakes. Reduce heat to medium and fry until golden brown on each side. Serve immediately or place in low oven until ready to serve.

YIELD: 6 TO 8 CAKES

❧ RAW FRIED POTATOES ❧

It took me years to realize why some raw fries were so much better than others. The secret is to add water while frying. The best ones I ever ate were made by George Yoder of Shoemakersville. He prepares them on his huge outdoor grill. First he fries the onions, slides them to the side, then fries the potatoes, covered with a lid. Every time he turns them he adds a little water. Unbelievable!

1½ pounds white potatoes
6 slices bacon or 3 tablespoons vegetable shortening
½ teaspoon salt (optional)
½ teaspoon coarsely ground black pepper
1 medium-size onion, thinly sliced (optional)
1 tablespoon chopped fresh chives
⅓ cup water

Scrub potatoes, peel if desired, and slice very thin in food processor. Fry bacon in large heavy skillet until crisp. Remove and drain on paper towels. If you do not use bacon, melt 3 tablespoons shortening or oil in skillet; otherwise, reserve 3 tablespoons of bacon fat and heat in skillet over medium flame. Add sliced potatoes, salt, pepper, onion, and chives, cover and fry, turning potatoes often to prevent burning. Each time you turn potatoes, sprinkle little of the water in pan before you cover it with lid. Fry until potatoes brown on each side and are soft in middle, approximately 25 minutes. Crumble bacon on top before serving.

YIELD: 4 TO 6 SERVINGS

POTATO CHIPS

2 pounds Irish Cobbler or good baking potatoes
1 tablespoon cider vinegar
2 cups peanut oil
Salt (optional)

Heat oil in deep skillet or deep fat fryer to 360°F.

Wash and peel potatoes. Slice as thin as possible, thickness of penny, place them in deep bowl, add vinegar, and cover with cold water. Dry chips on clean towels handful at time to prevent them from discoloring, and drop them into hot fat one at time. As they turn golden, remove them with slotted spoon and drain on paper towels. Sprinkle lightly with salt if desired. After chips cool, store them in airtight container. Chips fried in peanut oil will keep longer than those fried in lard or shortening.
YIELD: 1½ POUNDS

POTATO FILLING

The Dutch of Berks County make this dish more beautifully than anyone else I've met. It is soupy when mixed and bakes high and golden brown, but they make swirls in the batter with a spoon before baking that gives it that "extra touch."

3 tablespoons butter or vegetable oil
¾ cup chopped celery with leaves
½ cup chopped onion
Pinch of saffron thread
¼ cup chopped fresh parsley
½ teaspoon salt
½ teaspoon ground black pepper
2 cups cooked mashed potatoes
2 cups white bread cubes
1 cup milk

Preheat oven to 350°F.

Heat butter or oil in skillet and saute celery, onion, saffron, parsley, salt, and pepper over medium heat until celery is tender, approximately 6 minutes. Mix with mashed potatoes, bread cubes, and milk until well blended. Pour into buttered 2-quart souffle dish and bake for 40 to 45 minutes or until golden brown.
YIELD: 6 SERVINGS

ESCALLOPED SALSIFY

The best substitute for oysters, salsify was brought in from the garden before the first frost. Stored in the root cellar of the coolest part of the cellar in a tub and layered with dirt, they stayed firm and fresh for most of the winter. It sill works today, but for many folks without cellars it is easier to buy salsify at the local grocery or farmers' market. Most folks know this vegetable as "oyster plant" and use it in casseroles, stews, or fritters. Mother Groff often fries the slices like oysters, but this is her favorite way to use salsify.

1 pound salsify
1 cup water
½ teaspoon salt
1 cup fresh bread crumbs
1 cup small oyster crackers (broken Saltines may be substituted)
½ teaspoon salt
½ teaspoon coarsely ground white pepper
4 tablespoons (½ stick) butter or part margarine, melted, less if
    desired
1 cup light cream or milk

Preheat oven to 375°F.

Scrub salsify and cook in water and salt in large saucepan until tender over medium-high heat, about 15 minutes. Drain and peel. Cut in ½-inch-thick slices. Use bit of butter to grease 1½-quart baking dish. Layer crumbs, salsify, crackers, butter, and cream. Sprinkle with half salt and pepper and layer rest, ending with butter poured over remaining crumbs. Bake for 35 minutes.
YIELD: 4 SERVINGS

Variation:

Scalloped Salmon:
Substitute 2 cups flaked, cooked salmon for salsify, add ½ teaspoon dried dill weed, ½ teaspoon celery salt, and substitute lemon pepper for white pepper.

🝫 PARSNIPS 🝫

Parsnips have a rather sweet flavor and are usually fried or added to beef stew. This recipe will give you several choices. Try them all.

1 pound parsnips
1 cup beef broth or water
¼ cup wine
2 tablespoons vegetable shortening or oil
Salt and ground black pepper to taste (depending on strength of broth)
½ cup heavy cream or Medium White Sauce (page 152)

Scrub parsnips, prick them several times with fork, and place them in large saucepan with broth and wine. Bring to boil over medium heat and boil until tender, about 40 minutes. Remove from heat and cool until able to hold in hands. Peel and either slice, cut in half, or leave whole. Heat shortening in large, heavy skillet and saute parsnips over medium heat until golden brown, about 5 minutes. Check for seasonings and add salt and pepper if desired. Add cream and heat through.

YIELD: 4 SERVINGS

Variation:

Glazed:
Cook as recipe above but omit cream. Mix together 2 tablespoons white wine and ¼ cup light brown sugar or maple syrup and pour over parsnips. For extra flavor, add 1 tablespoon Dijon mustard to glaze.

 STUFFED ACORN SQUASH

Acorn squash are so attractive and, when stuffed, they become individual one-dish meals. Our early settlers roasted them over an open fire and we can enjoy the same flavors by using our outdoor grills.

3 pounds acorn squash (2 or 3, depending on the size), washed, halved crosswise, and seeded
1 cup water
½ teaspoon salt

Stuffing:
1½ cups long-grain rice
3 cups water
½ teaspoon salt
3 tablespoons butter
1 small onion, chopped (about ½ cup)
2 stems celery, chopped
2 cups chopped, cooked ham
½ cup chopped fresh parsley or 3 tablespoons dried
½ teaspoon dried marjoram
½ teaspoon dried mint, crushed
¼ teaspoon dried rosemary, crushed
½ teaspoon Krazy or seasoned salt
½ teaspoon lemon pepper
2 tablespoons (¼ stick) butter or vegetable shortening, melted
½ recipe Tomato Sauce (page 153) but add ½ teaspoon each chopped fresh basil and chopped fresh oregano to the recipe
1 tablespoon chopped fresh basil for garnish

Preheat oven to 350°F.

Boil squash in large, heavy saucepan in water and salt, covered, over high heat for about 10 minutes. Drain upside down until ready to fill. To make stuffing, cook rice in water and salt over high heat until almost tender, about 20 minutes. Drain. Melt butter in large skillet and saute onion and celery over medium heat until clear, about 6 minutes then add ham, herbs, salt, and pepper. Stir in rice and mix thoroughly. Brush each squash half with melted butter and fill by placing tablespoon of tomato sauce in bottom of each half and then filling with stuffing, topping with at least 2 tablespoons of sauce. Bake for 20 minutes, turn off heat and let stand in oven until ready to serve. Garnish with chopped basil. If you have extra stuffing and sauce, mix it together and bake it in buttered baking dish to serve on side or freeze for later use.
Yield: 4 servings

(continued on next page)

(continued)

Variations:

Maple Baked Squash:
Prepare squash as above, omitting stuffing. Brush with melted butter and ½ cup pure maple syrup. Sprinkle with dash each of grated nutmeg and ground cinnamon. Bake for 30 minutes or until tender and golden brown.

 BAKED SQUASH AND CRANBERRIES

This casserole will brighten any winter day. Fill two small baking dishes, bake and serve one, freeze the other.

2 pounds butternut squash, peeled, seeded, and cubed
½ teaspoon salt
2 cups water
2 large eggs, lightly beaten
5⅓ tablespoons (⅔ stick) butter, melted
⅓ cup lightly packed light brown sugar
1 teaspoon salt, less if desired
½ teaspoon coarsely ground black pepper
1½ cups raw cranberries, washed and picked over for stems
Freshly grated nutmeg

Preheat oven to 350°F.

Cook squash, covered, in salt and water in large saucepan over high heat until soft, about 15 minutes. Drain well; let stand in colander for at least 30 minutes or press down with your hand to force out most of liquid. Puree pulp in food processor or put through food mill; it should yield about 4 cups. Add eggs, butter, sugar, salt, and pepper. Blend thoroughly. Fold cranberries into mixture. Pour into buttered 2-quart baking dish or two small ones. Top with grated nutmeg and bake until golden and does not shake in middle when jiggled, about 45 minutes for one casserole, 30 minutes for two.
Yield: 8 servings

 CREAMED SPINACH

If people would eat spinach that is lightly steamed, they would never say they hate it again. I hate to wash sandy spinach, so I put it in a net bag and agitate it in the washing machine (no soap, of course) in cold water and in a minute it is as clean as a whistle.

1 pound spinach, with stems if they are young leaves
1 teaspoon salt
½ cup heavy cream or Medium White Sauce (page 152)
2 tablespoons Browned Butter (page 151)

Wash spinach thoroughly, trim stems (I like to chop them into pieces) and shake. Water that is left on leaves will be just enough to steam it perfectly. Place leaves in saucepan, add salt, and cover. When it starts to steam and leaves turn bright green, turn off heat. Add cream and heat thoroughly over medium heat until slightly thickened. Serve hot with browned butter dribbled over it. Many folks prefer omitting cream and use just browned butter— choice is yours.
YIELD: 4 SERVINGS

Hint:
Grated cheese or chopped hard-boiled egg makes an excellent garnish.

 FRIED SPINACH

Many people of Pennsylvania Dutch country served vinegar–often an herb vinegar–with their spinach. It gives a special added flavor.

2 pounds spinach, including stems if leaves are young
6 slices bacon or 3 tablespoons butter or vegetable shortening
½ clove garlic, minced (optional)
½ teaspoon salt
1 teaspoon coarsely ground black pepper

Wash spinach thoroughly and dry thoroughly. Chop stems into 1-inch pieces and tear leaves as you would for salad. Fry bacon until crisp in large skillet; remove bacon and drain on paper towels. If you don't use bacon, heat butter or oil in skillet; otherwise add garlic to fat and saute over medium heat until golden. Then add spinach, salt, and pepper and fry over medium-high heat for about 2 minutes. Do not overcook. Remove spinach from pan with slotted spoon, place in heated serving dish, and crumble bacon on top.
YIELD: 4 TO 6 SERVINGS

Variation:

Use 1 teaspoon lemon pepper instead of garlic and ground black pepper.

FRIED SWEET POTATOES

There's a difference between Jersey White sweet potatoes and yams. Jersey Whites are small, dry, and firm compared to the big orange sweet potatoes and yams. Yams and sweets have more liquid and are sweeter than the whites.

1½ pounds sweet potatoes
½ teaspoon salt
2 cups water
3 tablespoons butter or vegetable oil
Salt and ground black pepper (optional)

Scrub potatoes and put them in large saucepan with salt and water. Cook over medium heat, covered, until tender, about 30 minutes. Drain, cool, and peel. Cut in half, lengthwise, or into thick slices to fry. Heat butter or oil in large, heavy skillet and fry over medium heat until golden brown on all sides, about 10 minutes. Sprinkle with salt and pepper if desired. (My family always sprinkled sugar on Whites during frying.) Potatoes may be frozen for future use before they are fried.

YIELD: 4 TO 6 SERVINGS

Variations:

Maple-Glazed Sweet Potatoes:
Add ⅓ cup pure maple syrup to butter while frying. Sweet
Potatoes and Apples: Fry 4 apples, cored, peeled if desired,
and sliced into rings or wedges with potatoes.

 TOMATOES STUFFED WITH SPINACH

A perfect color combination for the holidays, this dish can be prepared ahead of time and slipped in the oven as the guests arrive. Serve it as a vegetable or use cherry tomatoes and serve them as an appetizer.

1½ pounds tomatoes
1 pound fresh spinach or 10 ounces frozen
¼ cup water
4 ounces cream cheese, at room temperature
1 large egg
¾ cup fresh bread crumbs
½ cup shredded Cheddar cheese
¼ cup grated Parmesan cheese
¼ cup milk
½ teaspoon salt
½ teaspoon ground nutmeg
Dash of ground white pepper

Preheat oven to 350°F.

Wash tomatoes, cut off top of each, and carefully scoop out center and seeds. Chop about ½ cup of pulp. If using fresh spinach, remove stems and wash leaves thoroughly. Place them in large saucepan, add water, and steam over high heat until limp, about ½ minute. Drain and chop fine. If using frozen spinach, allow to defrost and then chop. In large mixing bowl, beat cream cheese and egg together until fluffy. Gradually add crumbs, cheese, milk, salt, nutmeg, pepper, chopped tomato pulp, and chopped spinach, blending thoroughly. Fill each tomato shell with mixture and place in greased baking dish. Bake for 35 to 40 minutes or until toothpick comes out clean when inserted in middle of tomato. If baking cherry tomatoes, reduce baking time to 15 minutes. If you want to freeze these, do so before baking; they will keep for at least 6 weeks, if tightly covered. Defrost them for 10 minutes before baking.

Yield: 6 servings or 25 to 30 stuffed cherry tomatoes

 PLAIN BAKED TOMATOES

These are a great addition to any meal.

1½ pounds tomatoes
¾ cup all-purpose flour
5⅓ tablespoons (⅔ stick) butter or margarine, melted
1 tablespoon light brown sugar
½ teaspoon dry mustard
½ teaspoon salt
½ teaspoon ground black pepper

Preheat oven to 375°F.

Peel tomatoes by dipping them in boiling water for ½ minute or until skins slip off easily. Core and cut in half crosswise. Dredge each half completely in flour then dip in melted butter; place in buttered baking dish. Mix brown sugar, mustard, salt, and pepper together and sprinkle over tomato halves. Bake for 25 to 30 minutes or until golden brown. If broiling, place halves on rack of broiler pan and broil for 5 to 7 minutes until golden brown.
YIELD: 4 TO 6 SERVINGS

Variation:

Baked with Wine:
Bake with 1 cup white wine added to baking dish.

Hint:
For extra flavor, sprinkle tomato halves with chopped fresh herbs and herb blossoms, such as chives, chervil, oregano, parsley, or mint before baking.

SCALLOPED TOMATOES WITH CORN

Perfect for picnics and dramatic when served in a beautiful casserole dish or basket.

1½ pound tomatoes
6 slices bacon or 3 tablespoons butter or margarine
2 cups corn kernels, fresh or frozen
½ cup chopped onion
½ teaspoon salt
½ teaspoon ground black pepper
1 tablespoon chopped fresh parsley
1 teaspoon chopped fresh sweet basil
1 teaspoon chopped fresh chervil
1 teaspoon granulated sugar (optional)
1 cup fresh bread or cracker crumbs

Preheat oven to 350°F.

Core and slice tomatoes about ⅓ inch thick. Fry bacon or melt butter in a large skillet. When bacon is crisp, remove and drain on paper towels. Add corn, onion, salt, pepper, parsley, basil, chervil, and sugar (if desired) to skillet and saute for several minutes. Butter 2-quart baking dish or casserole and alternate layers of tomatoes, corn mixture, and bread crumbs, ending with about ⅓ cup crumbs for topping. Bake for 45 minutes, covered. Top with crumbled bacon and bake until bubbly and golden brown, about 10 minutes more.

Yield: 6 servings

Variations:

Core and scoop out whole tomatoes. Saute bread crumbs with corn mixture. Stuff tomatoes with corn mixture and place them in buttered baking dish or in buttered muffin cups and any extra corn mixture in casserole. Bake for 35 to 40 minutes.

With cheese:
Add 1 cup grated cheese of your choice when layering casserole.

 FRIED TOMATOES

The tomatoes must be firm to fry. Some fry green tomatoes with onions–super good!

2 pounds firm tomatoes
1 cup all-purpose flour
2 tablespoons light brown sugar
½ teaspoon ground white pepper
½ teaspoon salt
1 teaspoon chopped fresh chervil
¼ cup vegetable oil
Chopped fresh chervil or parsley for garnish

Core tomatoes and trim ends. Cut into ⅓-inch-thick slices. Combine flour, brown sugar, pepper, salt, and chervil on plate or sheet of wax paper. Dredge slices completely and fry one layer at time in heated oil over medium heat in large, heavy skillet until golden brown and crispy, about 3 minutes on each side. Place slices in buttered baking dish and keep warm until all are fried and ready to serve. Garnish with chopped fresh chervil or parsley.
YIELD: 4 TO 6 SERVINGS

Variations:

Use green tomatoes and 1 medium-size onion, sliced. Saute onions without dredging in flour, adding them along side tomatoes while frying.

FILLED ZUCCHINI BLOSSOMS

The best way to keep from getting too many zucchini is to break off the blossoms. They're good batter dipped and fried, but this recipe is so dramatic it will be remembered forever.

1 dozen zucchini blossoms (must be fresh, picked the morning they fully open)
½ recipe Cheese Souffle (page 51)

Preheat oven to 350°F.

Rinse blossoms and remove any green stems. Spray or butter muffin cups. Pour souffle batter ½ inch deep in each cup. Place blossom in each cup and fill to little below top with batter, leaving room for souffle to expand while baking without running over. If blossoms are very long, fold blossom tips into middle, over top of souffle batter. Bake for 18 minutes, or until lightly browned. Serve immediately.
YIELD: 12 (MUFFIN-CUP SIZE) FILLED BLOSSOMS, 6 SERVINGS

❧ STUFFED ZUCCHINI ❧

What do you do with all your large zucchini? For one, you can stuff them with any of your favorite meats or stuffings. They make a one-dish meal that's attractive and filling.

1 large zucchini or several small ones, totaling 1 pound
1 teaspoon vegetable oil
½ pound lean ground beef
½ cup chopped onion
1 cup Tomato Sauce (page 153) or 1½ cups chopped tomatoes, canned or fresh
1 tablespoon chopped fresh parsley
½ teaspoon salt
½ teaspoon ground black pepper
½ teaspoon celery seed
½ teaspoon chopped fresh basil
Dash of Tabasco sauce
1 teaspoon fresh lemon juice or Herb Vinegar (page 261)

Preheat oven to 350°F.

Clean and cut zucchini in half lengthwise. Scoop out center of each half, leaving at least ½-inch thick shell, then discard seeds and chop up good pulp. Heat oil in large, heavy skillet over medium-high heat, crumble beef, and brown it with onion; then add chopped zucchini, tomato sauce, parsley, salt, pepper, celery seed, and basil. Reduce heat to medium and stir until thoroughly heated. Spoon into zucchini shells. Whisk Tabasco and lemon juice together and sprinkle over top. Place in 9 x 13-inch baking pan and bake for 30 minutes. Cut baked zucchini into 3- to 4-inch pieces for serving.
YIELD: 4 SERVINGS

CHAPTER FIVE

Poultry and Wild Game

 ## CHICKEN AND ASPARAGUS

This is perfect for spring entertaining. Wild asparagus grows on lots of country roadbanks and fence rows. The tender tiny tips make this an elegant dish that tastes as good as it looks.

2 cups chunked cooked chicken
2 cups fresh asparagus, cut in 1½-inch pieces
¼ cup water
4 tablespoons (½ stick) butter or margarine
¼ cup all-purpose flour
½ teaspoon salt
¼ teaspoon ground white pepper
½ teaspoon paprika
1 cup light cream or milk
1 cup chicken broth or milk
Toast Cups (recipe follows)
Paprika or fresh parsley sprigs for garnish

Preheat oven to 400°F.
If you are starting with fresh chicken, cook, covered, over medium heat, until tender, about 45 minutes, in 6 cups water seasoned with ½ teaspoon each salt and ground black pepper. When cool, remove skin and debone. Cut into chunks and set aside. Place asparagus and ¼ cup water in saucepan, cover and cook until just tender—no more than 5 minutes. Do not overcook! Drain. Make roux in heavy saucepan by melting butter over medium heat, slowly adding flour, salt, pepper, and paprika. Stir until smooth and golden-colored. Gradually whisk in cream and broth, stirring until smooth and thickened. Reduce heat to low and add chicken. When it is warmed through, add asparagus and heat thoroughly. Serve in warm Toast Cups or over toast points. Garnish each cup with dash of paprika or sprig of parsley. To make Toast Cups, remove crusts from slices of bread. Butter each slice on one side. Generously butter or oil muffin cups and mold bread, buttered side down to form cups. Bake 10 to 12 minutes or until lightly browned. (These may be made ahead of time and stored in airtight container.)
YIELD: FILLS 6 TO 8 TOAST CUPS

OLD-FASHIONED CHICKEN PIE

A country favorite, we can't have a complete cookbook without one chicken pie!

1 roaster chicken, 4 to 5 pounds
2 cups water
⅛ teaspoon paprika
2 stems celery, with leaves
¼ cup chopped onion
¼ cup teaspoon ground black pepper
½ teaspoon chopped fresh parsley
½ teaspoon salt

Place chicken in large pot with above ingredients and cook, covered, over medium heat for about 45 minutes, or until tender. Strain broth, skim off fat, reserve, and debone chicken.

4 medium-size potatoes, peeled and sliced
2 large carrots, peeled and sliced
1 large onion, chopped
4 stems celery with leaves, diced
3 cups reserved chicken broth
3 tablespoons cornstarch
1 teaspoon salt
½ teaspoon ground black pepper
1 tablespoon chopped fresh parsley
1 recipe Baking Powder Crust (page 182)

Preheat oven to 350°F.

Cook potatoes, carrots, onion, and celery in ⅔ cup chicken stock, covered, over medium-high heat until nearly tender approximately 15 minutes. Drain and use broth from vegetables and add enough stock to make 3 cups. Stir cornstarch into broth until it dissolves. Bring to boil over medium heat, check for seasonings, and add salt and pepper if desired. Add parsley and cook until thickened. Combine diced chicken, vegetables, and gravy, and pour into buttered 9 x 13-inch baking dish. Top with baking powder crust, making sure to slit crust to allow steam to escape. Bake for 45 minutes or until golden brown.

YIELD: 6 SERVINGS

Variation:

Use any type of meat or wild game instead of chicken.

CHICKEN CROQUETTES

The white sauce is the secret to this moist delicious croquette.

2 cups diced cooked chicken
⅓ cup finely chopped celery
1 teaspoon dried celery leaves
¼ teaspoon celery salt
1 teaspoon fresh lemon juice
1 teaspoon chopped fresh parsley
¾ cup Thick White Sauce (page 152)
½ teaspoon salt
1¼ cups fresh bread crumbs
1¼ cups fresh cracker crumbs
2 large eggs, lightly beaten
Vegetable oil for frying
2-3 cups Chicken Gravy (page 111 using the gravy recipe for Chicken
   Fricassee)
Fresh parsley sprigs for garnish

Preheat oven to 300°F.

Combine chicken, celery, celery leaves, celery salt, lemon juice, parsley, white sauce, and salt thoroughly in large mixing bowl. Refrigerate until easy to form croquettes, about 30 minutes. Use about ½ cup each of mixture to form into cones or rectangular croquettes. Mix crumbs together, then roll croquettes in crumbs, dip them in beaten eggs, and roll them in crumbs again. Chill for at least 30 minutes until firm. Deep fry in 3 inches of vegetable oil in large, heavy skillet or fryer at 375°F until golden brown, about 5 minutes. Keep on plate in preheated oven until ready to serve. Serve with gravy on side and garnish with fresh parsley.
YIELD: 8 TO 10 CROQUETTES

Variation:

Any type of meat may be substituted for chicken. Turkey is excellent, too.

Hint:
These make great appetizers when made small and served with
dipping sauce, such as sour cream, dill, or mustard sauce.

CRISPY FRIED CHICKEN

Everyone loves fried chicken and this recipe is perfect for picnics.

1 cup fresh cracker crumbs
½ cup all-purpose flour
1 teaspoon Krazy salt (a course salt with herbs added)
½ teaspoon dried chervil
½ teaspoon dried parsley
½ teaspoon ground white pepper
½ teaspoon celery seed
2 pounds chicken parts
1 large egg, lightly beaten
1 tablespoon milk or heavy cream
⅓ cup vegetable oil

Combine all dry ingredients, including herbs. Roll or shake chicken parts in crumb mixture. Let stand 15 minutes. Combine beaten egg and milk. Dip chicken parts in egg mixture and roll in crumbs again. Heat oil in deep skillet and fry over medium heat, turning occasionally, until golden brown, approximately 15 minutes.

YIELD: 4 TO 6 SERVINGS

 CHICKEN STOLTZFUS

*I couldn't write a book without including my trademark dish. You
may make the pastry the day before if time is limited.*

1 roaster chicken, 4 to 5 pounds, giblets removed
6 cups water
2 teaspoons salt
½ teaspoon ground black pepper
Pinch of saffron threads
12 tablespoons (1½ sticks) butter or margarine
¾ cup all-purpose flour
1 cup heavy cream, or half milk and half evaporated milk or all milk
¼ cup finely chopped fresh parsley
½ recipe Pastry Squares (page 181)
Fresh parsley sprigs for garnish

Put chicken, water, salt, pepper, and saffron in 6-quart kettle and bring to
boil. Reduce heat to medium, partially cover with lid and simmer for 1 hour.
Remove chicken, cool, debone, and remove skin. Cut chicken into bite-size
pieces. Strain stock through double thickness of cheesecloth and reduce it
over high heat until it makes 4 cups. Melt butter in heavy saucepan, whisk
in flour, and stir over medium heat until golden and bubbling. Slowly whisk
in stock and cream, stirring constantly until smooth, creamy, and thickened,
about 10 minutes. Add chicken and parsley and heat thoroughly. Arrange
pastry squares on heated platter and pour chicken on top. (Make sure to
leave edges of pastry squares showing.) Garnish with parsley sprigs. Serve
immediately or pastry will become soggy.
Yield: 6 to 8 servings

Variation:

Chicken Fricassee:
Follow above recipe, but while reducing broth, add ½ cup each of
chopped celery and onion. Use an equal amount of chicken broth
instead of cream. Most chicken fricassee is prepared with stewing hen
but I prefer to use roaster; it is more tender, takes half time to cook,
and has better flavor. Serve over biscuits instead of pastry squares.

🐦 PAPRIKA CHICKEN 🐦

Paprika and saffron are spices that have been used and valued highly by Pennsylvania Dutch cooks. Their antique spice boxes are family treasures that give us an insight into their early cooking techniques.

4 pounds chicken parts
1 teaspoon salt
1 teaspoon ground black pepper
6 tablespoons (¾ stick) butter or margarine
1 cup chopped onion
1½ teaspoons paprika
1 tablespoon all-purpose flour
2 cups chicken broth
1 cup sour cream
1½ tablespoons chopped fresh dill
Fresh dill sprigs for garnish

Sprinkle chicken parts evenly with salt and pepper and let stand, covered, for a few minutes. Melt butter in large, heavy saucepan and saute onion over medium heat until clear, about 3 minutes. Stir in paprika. Add seasoned chicken parts, sprinkle with flour and simmer over medium-low heat until clear, about 3 minutes. Stir in paprika. Add seasoned chicken parts, sprinkle with flour and simmer over medium-low heat for 30 minutes, turning pieces as they get golden brown on all sides. Stir in broth, cover, and simmer for 15 minutes more. Remove chicken to heated serving dish and keep covered. Stir sour cream and dill into chicken broth and heat thoroughly over medium heat. Pour over chicken and garnish with dill sprigs (or parsley).
Yield: 6 servings

🦃 ROAST TURKEY 🦃

One of the most versatile meats turkey is so easy to prepare.
Turkey is a great substitute in veal recipes, too.

1 15-pound turkey
Salt and ground black pepper, to taste
½ teaspoon salt
½ teaspoon ground black pepper
2 cups water
8 cups stuffing (A moist bread stuffing is the most popular but if you
want to save one hour of baking time, omit the stuffing or cook it
in its own dish.)

Preheat oven to 375°F.

Remove giblets and neck from inside cavity. Rinse bird thoroughly, pat dry, and lightly salt and pepper inside. Put giblets and neck in small saucepan with water to cover, add salt and pepper. Bring to boil and simmer, covered, over low heat until soft, about 45 minutes. Remove, trim fat and gristle, and debone neck meat; set aside in small bowl. Spoon stuffing lightly into cavity, taking care not to press it together. This prevents heavy stuffing and seepage while baking. Truss bird with skewers and baking cord, folding wings under its back. Generously salt and pepper outside of turkey, rubbing skin with vegetable oil to brown skin evenly if desired. Add water to roasting pan, place turkey breast down, tent with aluminum foil and bake for 4 hours. Remove foil, drain broth into bowl, turn turkey breast side up, and continue to bake until golden brown and legs are easily moved, about 45 minutes. After removing turkey, deglaze pan with ½ cup water to get all pan juices and brownings. Skim fat from reserved broth and add to brownings. Add 2 tablespoons cornstarch dissolved in ¼ cup water for every 2 cups broth. Cook over medium heat until thickened, about 3 minutes. Add chopped giblets to gravy and serve on side with turkey.
YIELD: 15 SERVINGS

🪶 TURKEY HASH 🪶

*What do you do with leftover turkey—that old, familiar refrain? For one thing,
never reheat more than once or it will lose all flavor. Use what you need for serving,
then freeze or refrigerate the rest. This is an excellent brunch or breakfast dish.*

4 tablespoons (½ stick) butter or margarine
½ cup chopped onion
½ cup chopped bell peppers, preferably ½ red and ½ green
1 cup sliced mushrooms
3 tablespoons all-purpose flour
1½ cups turkey or chicken broth
4 cups coarsely chopped turkey
2 tablespoons chopped fresh parsley
1 teaspoon Worcestershire sauce
⅛ teaspoon red (cayenne) pepper
⅛ teaspoon curry powder
½ teaspoon salt
¼ teaspoon ground white pepper
½ cup heavy cream or evaporated milk
Fresh parsley sprigs or pimiento slices for garnish

Melt butter in large, heavy skillet over medium heat and saute onion, peppers,
and mushrooms for 5 minutes. Sprinkle with flour and stir, then gradually
pour in broth, stirring until thickened, about 5 minutes. Add turkey and
seasonings. Blend thoroughly, then add cream. Heat well but do not bring to
boil. Garnish with parsley. Serve in skillet.
YIELD: 6 SERVINGS

 MAPLE-GINGER DUCK WITH WILD RICE

The use of maple syrup and ginger is interesting and traditional.

1 large duck, about 6 pounds
Salt and ground black pepper, to taste
1 cup pure maple syrup
1 tablespoon ground ginger
3 cups chicken broth
1½ cups wild rice
1 tablespoon butter or margarine
½ cup chopped onion
½ cup chopped celery with leaves

Preheat oven to 400°F.

Sprinkle inside and outside of duck with salt and pepper. Place duck, breast side down, on wire rack in roaster pan and pour in ½ inch of water—this is to prevent duck from drying out. Roast in oven for 30 minutes, then turn on its back and roast 30 minutes more. Reduce heat to 350°F. Mix syrup and ginger together and spread over duck. Continue to roast until duck is tender and leg joints are easy to move, approximately 45 to 60 minutes more. After you glaze duck, bring chicken broth to boil in large kettle. Add rice, butter, onion, and celery. Lower heat to simmer and cook until rice is tender. Place rice on heated platter with carved duck or place duck whole and carve tableside.

YIELD: 6 SERVINGS

ROAST DUCK WITH APPLE GLAZE AND APPLE STUFFING

The worst think about duck is getting the feathers off. When we were children, cousin Dick and I raised ducks and chickens for extra spending (or saving) money. We had to dress them ourselves (that made us real money), which wasn't too pleasant but taught us the economics of business. To get the pin feathers off the ducks, we dipped them in scalding water with paraffin melted into it. This caused all the feathers to stick together, making it much easier to pull them out, and the birds always looked terrific when they went to our customers.

1 large duck, about 6 pounds
Salt and ground black pepper
Apple Stuffing (page 161)
1 cup orange juice
¼ cup grated orange rind
1 cup applesauce
1 tablespoon cornstarch
Pinch of ground thyme
Pinch of dried or fresh hyssop (optional)
½ cup sherry or sweet red or white wine
½ cup lightly packed light brown sugar
1 teaspoon grated lemon rind
1 tablespoon fresh lemon juice
½ cup water
⅓ cup brandy (optional)

Preheat oven to 400°F.

Remove giblets from duck and sprinkle it inside and out with salt and pepper. Stuff loosely with apple stuffing, baking rest of stuffing in buttered baking dish for last 30 minutes of duck's cooking, and place it, breast side down, on rack in roasting pan. Prick skin several times on each side to allow fat to drain. Add ½ inch of water. Roast duck in oven for 45 minutes. Then turn it breast side up, reduce heat to 375°F and roast another 45 minutes. Combine orange juice and rind, applesauce, cornstarch, thyme, hyssop, sherry, brown sugar, and lemon rind and juice in large saucepan and cook over high heat until thickened, about 5 minutes. Pour 1 cup of sauce over duck and continue to roast until tender, about 45 minutes to 1 hour more. Duck is ready to serve when legs move easily. After removing duck to heated serving platter, skim off all fat in roasting pan. Add ½ cup water and loosen all brownings from bottom over low heat, stirring constantly with wooden spoon until all brown particles are dissolved. Add this to remaining sauce along with brandy and ignite at table for that extra touch.

Yield: 6 servings

🦅 HONEY-HERBED DUCK 🦅

*Duck was not considered a delicacy years ago, but with the addition of fresh
herbs it took on a different and interesting flavor. This was especially true
of wild duck. If using wild ducks for this recipe, use two. I prefer fresh
herbs, but if you use dried herbs, cut the amounts listed in half.*

1 duck, 5 to 6 pounds
⅓ cup honey
1 teaspoon chopped fresh rosemary
1½ teaspoons chopped fresh hyssop
1 teaspoon chopped mint
1 teaspoon chopped fresh chervil
1 teaspoon chopped fresh dill
½ teaspoon chopped fresh thyme
½ teaspoon ground fresh marjoram
¼ cup orange liqueur or orange juice
½ teaspoon coarsely ground black pepper
½ teaspoon salt

Preheat oven to 400°F.

Halve duck and score skin with sharp knife several times on each side.
Brush skin with honey (if you heat it, it will spread more easily). Mix all
herbs, substituting mild herbs if you cannot get ones mentioned above, with
half of orange liqueur in small bowl and brush it over duck. Sprinkle with
pepper and salt. Let stand for 1 hour or more to absorb all herb flavors.
Place on wire rack in roasting pan and roast in oven for 1 hour, basting
with remaining orange liqueur mixture until tender. It should be browned
and crispy on outside and tender on inside. Serve with your favorite rice or
stuffing.

YIELD: 4 TO 6 SERVINGS

🪶 ROAST GOOSE 🪶

Goose is considered very fatty and hard to prepare. That's just not true–it's as easy to prepare as turkey. For those who love the dark meat of fowl, goose is hard to beat. I like to count on 1 pound per person when serving whole roasted fowl because of the bones.

1 large goose, 6 to 8 pounds
¼ cup Herb Vinegar (page 261)
1 teaspoon salt
1 teaspoon ground black pepper
Stuffing of your choice: I recommend Apple or Dried Fruit Stuffing
  (see Index)
3¼ cups water
2 tablespoons cornstarch
¼ cup water

Preheat oven to 350°F.

Remove giblets and neck from dressed goose and rinse them thoroughly. Pat dry with paper towels. Sprinkle goose with vinegar, salt, and pepper inside and outside. Pat it with your hands to insure seasonings stick to skin. Stuff cavity loosely, secure it with skewers, tie legs together with cords, and fold wings under back. Pour 2 cups of water in bottom of roasting pan fitted with wire baking rack. Place giblets, not including liver, alongside goose. Tent it with foil and roast in oven for 4 hours for a 6-pound goose to 5 hours for an 8-pound goose. When legs move easily, remove foil, turn breast side up, and brown it, about 20 minutes. This cooking method will keep meat moist. Transfer goose to heated platter. Deglaze pan with 1 cup of water and simmer over low heat until brownings are easily scraped from pan. Pour into bowl and cool until fat comes to top, about 15 minutes. Remove fat. To make gravy, pour broth into 1-quart saucepan, dissolve cornstarch in ¼ cup water, and add to broth. Bring to boil over medium heat and cook until thickened, approximately 5 minutes. Check for seasonings, adding salt and pepper if desired.

YIELD: 6 TO 8 SERVINGS

ROAST SQUAB OR QUAIL

*Count on at least one bird per person. They are so delicate in flavor and look
so nice when served whole, it is a pity to debone them in the kitchen.*

4 to 6 birds, about 3 to 4 pounds, total
Salt and ground black pepper
1 ½ cups stuffing of your choice—I recommend Salsify or Chestnut
  Stuffing (pages 163, 164), or filling the cavity with fried oysters
  (see page 146)
1 cup water

Preheat oven to 400°F.

Remove giblets and neck from dressed birds and rinse thoroughly. Sprinkle
lightly with salt and pepper inside and out. Stuff birds lightly, baking any
extra stuffing in oven for last 15 minutes. Truss birds with cord or skewers,
folding wings under backs. Add water to roasting pan, place birds breast side
down, and tent with aluminum foil. Bake for 40 minutes. Meanwhile, cook
giblets and necks in remaining water with salt over medium heat until tender,
about 30 minutes. When soft, trim fat, debone meat, and cut into small pieces
to add to gravy. Remove foil from roasting pan, drain broth into bowl and
turn birds breast side up to brown. Add extra stuffing to pan and continue
roasting for another 15 minutes. Remove birds and stuffing from pan
onto heated serving platter. Deglaze pan with ½ cup water to make gravy.
Thicken with cornstarch dissolved in ¼ cup water over medium heat and add
giblets. Taste for seasoning, adding salt and pepper if needed. Serve in gravy
boat.
YIELD: 4 TO 6 SERVINGS

Variations:

Braised Squab:
Split birds in half, sprinkle lightly with seasoned salt and ground black
pepper. Melt 3 tablespoons butter or vegetable oil in heavy skillet
and saute them breast side down over medium-high heat until golden
brown, about 12 minutes. Turn, add ½ cup dry wine and ¼ cup pure
maple syrup. Cover and simmer over medium heat until birds are
tender, about 20 minutes. Baste sauce over birds while cooking.
Place on heated platter and spoon over sauce or serve it on side.

Grilled Squab, Quail or Partridge:
Marinate in ½ cup white wine vinegar or ½ cup walnut or vegetable oil
with your favorite herbs for one hour before placing on grill. Do not
overcook; if grill is very hot, needs approximately 7 minutes on each side.

ROAST GUINEA HEN

Considered the best "watch dog" because they make so much noise when strangers arrive, guineas are delicious, tender, and unique in flavor. They have a rather spicy taste, much like that of pheasant. The meat is very dark, especially the legs, and moist if roasted properly. Many farmers raise the fowl for the feathers, which they sell to fishermen for flying. The eggs are sought after for pickling because they are so small and the beautiful brown speckles make them attractive for egg decorators.

**2 guineas, 2½ to 3 pounds each
Salt and ground black pepper
1 tablespoon vegetable oil
Stuffing of your choice (recommend Raisin-Pecan on page 165)
3 cups water
½ teaspoon salt
½ cup currant or grape jelly
½ cup dry white wine or water
2 teaspoons cornstarch (optional)**

Preheat oven to 350°F.

Remove giblets and neck from dressed birds and rinse birds thoroughly. Pat dry inside and out with paper towels. Sprinkle lightly inside with salt and pepper. Rub outside with oil and sprinkle lightly with salt and pepper. Stuff lightly, baking extra stuffing in buttered baking dish for last 15 minutes of birds' cooking. Truss birds with skewers or cord. Add 2 cups of water to bottom of roasting pan. Place birds, breast down, in pan and tent with aluminum foil. Bake for 2 hours. Meanwhile, cook giblets and necks in salt and remaining water over medium heat until tender, about 45 minutes, if you want to add them to gravy. When soft, trim fat and gristle from good meat and chop into ½-inch pieces. After 2 hours of baking, remove aluminum foil and brush birds with jelly. Bake another 15 to 20 minutes or until jelly bubbles. Remove birds from pan when legs or wings move easily, and deglaze pan with ½ cup white wine or water. Continue to stir with wooden spoon until all brownings are loosened from pan. If you prefer gravy, dissolve 2 teaspoons cornstarch in ⅓ cup water and add to brownings. Heat over medium heat until thickened, approximately 4 minutes or until smooth.

YIELD: 4 TO 6 SERVINGS

Variation:

Roast Pheasant with Bourbon:
Follow recipe above, substituting 2 pheasants of equal weight, and stuff with any of your favorite stuffing. Baste with ½ cup bourbon instead of jelly.

 RABBIT

Rabbit tastes very much like chicken, so I recommend substituting it in any of the chicken recipes. Our family always loved rabbit pot pie and fried (really crisp) rabbit. If the hare is fully grown, wild, and large, it is best to marinate the meat in wine and herbs overnight before roasting or frying.

SQUIRREL

Squirrels are small, but the meat is so mild and delicious, you will need several for a meal for four. Much like rabbit, they are wonderful in stews or pot pie. Follow the same recipes as for chicken, pork, or veal.

VENISON

Venison is very popular in this area for hunters' families. Deer feed on many things, but most of the time they graze on corn or acorns. The taste is very similar to that of beef, but if the season has been dry, or the deer is old, the meat has a tendency to have a "wild" taste. Here's a recipe that will overcome that gamey flavor; the secret is in the marinade and the removal of fat before preparation.

2 tablespoons cider vinegar
2 tablespoons soy sauce
1 pound venison, fat removed

Mix vinegar and soy sauce together in shallow baking dish. Dip both sides of meat in it and let it marinade overnight in refrigerator, covered. Then follow any beef recipe. If pan frying, steaks will need more time than 3 minutes to cook. If steaks are 1 inch thick, fry over high heat for 3 minutes on each side.

 VENISON CHOPS

Count on at least 2 chops per person.

1 recipe Venison Marinade (see preceding recipe)
4 venison chops (about 1 pound), cut ¾ inch thick and trimmed of fat
⅓ cup all-purpose flour
Salt and ground black pepper
3 tablespoons vegetable oil or butter
1 small onion, chopped
⅓ cup chopped green or red bell pepper
½ cup sliced water chestnuts or sliced broccoli stems
1 large tomato, diced, seeded, and juice drained
1 stem celery, chopped
½ cup grated Cheddar cheese
½ cup sour cream
¼ cup brandy
1 tablespoon chopped fresh parsley

Marinate chops in marinade overnight. Pat dry, dredge in flour and sprinkle with salt and pepper. Set aside. Melt oil or butter in large skillet and saute onion, pepper, chestnuts, tomato, and celery for several minutes over medium-high heat until clear and thoroughly heated. Remove everything from pan and add chops, sauteing them to golden brown on each side over medium-high heat, no more than 4 minutes per side. When browned, add vegetables and reheat completely, covered. Remove and place on heated platter. Melt cheese in small saucepan over low heat, add sour cream, brandy, and parsley and heat through but do not boil. Pour over chops before serving or serve on side.
YIELD: 4 SERVINGS

CHAPTER SIX

Meats

 **BRISKET OF BEEF WITH BEANS**

This dish has terrific flavor but little eye appeal. Serve it with
a bright salad or colorful relishes on the side.

2 to 2½ pounds beef brisket
2 slices bacon or 1 tablespoon vegetable oil
¾ teaspoon salt
½ teaspoon ground black pepper
2 cups water
4 cups dried navy, butter, or lima beans, cooked and drained, or
1 pound of dried beans soaked overnight in 8 cups of water and
drained
¼ cup pure maple syrup or table molasses (golden, barrel, or King
Syrup), do not use baking molasses
⅓ cup lightly packed brown sugar
½ teaspoon dry mustard
Fresh parsley or watercress sprigs for garnish

Brown fat side of beef in Dutch oven or heavy pot over medium-high heat.
Add bacon or oil and brown other side. Add salt, pepper, water, and beans.
Reduce heat to medium and cook, covered, for 2 hours or until beef and
beans are tender, stirring occasionally to prevent sticking. Remove beef and
keep warm. Add maple syrup, brown sugar, and mustard to beans. Mix
thoroughly and simmer over medium heat another 10 minutes. Slice brisket
thin and serve with beans garnished with fresh parsley or watercress.
YIELD: 6 SERVINGS.

🦚 CORNED BEEF 🦚

There is a certain pride in saying "I made this" when everyone enjoys a meal. Corned beef takes a while to cure, but after it is made, it can be frozen. It will keep in the freezer for months if properly sealed, so make a good amount at one time or you can cut this recipe in half.

5 cups salt
¼ cup saltpetre (this is available in drug stores, but should be ordered in advance)
10 pounds beef, brisket, round, or rump
20 cups water
1 teaspoon ground white pepper
½ cup pickling spices
1 teaspoon paprika
½ teaspoon ground nutmeg
3 bay leaves
3 cloves garlic
1 teaspoon whole black peppercorns, cracked
1½ cups lightly packed light brown sugar

Combine 1 cup of salt and 1 tablespoon of saltpetre and rub it into beef, covering it generously on all sides. It should take about half mixture; reserve what's left over. Let stand in cold place or refrigerator, covered for one day. The next day cover beef with rest of salt mixture and let stand overnight again. Wipe salt mixture from meat the next day. Make brine of the water, 4 cups salt, 3 tablespoons saltpetre, and remaining ingredients in large pot. Bring to boil and simmer over medium heat for 5 minutes. Let cool. Place meat in crock or container big enough to hold it along with brine. Use stainless steel or plastic; brine will react with aluminum. Pour brine over meat, weight down meat with a plate to keep it submerged. Refrigerate and leave in brine for 3 to 4 weeks, turning every other day. If brine seems to lose its strength, add more salt or make a new brine. Wash several times in cold water to remove the extra salt before cooking or freezing. Cut meat, remembering that it is strongly flavored, into size desired. Three pounds of meat will serve at least six people. Freeze remainder by double wrapping it in heavy aluminum foil or plastic freezer bags.
YIELD: ABOUT 9 POUNDS BEEF.

Variation:

Pickled Beef Tongue or Heart:
Use the recipe above, but with the same amount of either fresh tongue or heart, leaving it in the brine for two weeks. Wash off the salt, peel the skin from the heart, and cook the same as for tongue on page 141. They freeze well and keep for months.

 GLAZED CORNED BEEF

*Although boiled corned beef is most common, glazing it looks
better, tastes better, and is worth the extra baking time.*

3 pounds corned beef (see preceding recipe)
Whole cloves
½ cup pure maple syrup
¼ cup dry white wine

Preheat oven to 350°F.

Place beef in large, heavy saucepan or Dutch oven, cover it with water, bring
to boil and simmer it over medium-low heat for about three hours, covered, or
until it's tender. Remove, stud with whole cloves and place in greased baking
dish. Combine maple syrup and wine and pour it over meat. Bake for
20 minutes or until the glaze is lightly browned. Baste meat with syrup
several times during baking. Serve thinly sliced.
YIELD: 6 SERVINGS.

Variation:

Boiled Corned Beef:
Cook as above, omitting the glaze.

 CREAMED FRIZZLED DRIED BEEF

*One of my favorites, this is as good for light suppers as well as for breakfast. We always
brown the flour as we brown the dried beef, giving the dish a rich, nutty flavor.*

3 tablespoons butter or margarine
6 ounces thinly sliced dried beef, shredded
¼ cup all-purpose flour
1 teaspoon chopped fresh chives
½ teaspoon chopped fresh parsley
⅛ teaspoon ground white pepper
3 cups milk

Melt butter in heavy skillet. Add shredded dried beef and cook over medium-
high heat until golden brown, approximately 3 minutes. Add flour and
seasonings and stir until well blended and flour turns a light brown. Lower
to medium heat, then slowly add milk, stirring constantly until thickened and
creamy, approximately 6 minutes. Add more milk if desired. Serve in Toast
Cups (page 107), or with toast tips, pancakes, or potato cakes.

BEEF PIE WITH POTATO CRUST

Old-fashioned, tasty, and great for those busy days, this pie also freezes well.

3 tablespoons butter or vegetable shortening
½ head cabbage, sliced
1 medium-size onion, sliced
1 pound thinly sliced roast beef or corned beef
2 cups seasoned mashed potatoes
½ cup beef broth

For crust:
1 cup mashed potatoes
1 large egg, lightly beaten
2 tablespoons (¼ stick) butter, melted
1 cup all-purpose flour
About ¼ cup milk
1 large egg
1 tablespoon water

Preheat oven to 350°F.

Melt butter in large, heavy skillet over medium heat and saute cabbage and onion until clear, about 6 minutes. Butter 1½ -quart baking dish or pan and layer half of beef, mashed potatoes, and cabbage mixture. Pour broth over everything. Repeat again and top with potato crust. To make the crust, place the mashed potatoes, 1 egg, butter and flour in large ball. Gradually add milk until right consistency to roll out. It should not be too dry. Place dough between 2 sheets of wax paper and roll about ⅓ inch thick. Place on top of beef pie, and slit a design in center. Mix beaten egg and water and brush over crust. Bake for 35 minutes or until golden brown on top.
YIELD: 6 SERVINGS.

Hint:
This potato crust is super for any meat or vegetable pie.

 RIB ROAST

Many folks ask why our prime rib is so moist, rare in the middle, and consistently excellent. We buy top quality standing ribs, we roast in a slow oven with a small amount of water in the bottom of the roasting pan, and we season the meat under the fat. It is hard to get all of these advantages if you are roasting anything less than a 6-pound roast. The roast should be thick enough to insure getting it rare in the middle.

6 pounds standing prime rib roast of beef
1 teaspoon salt (less if desired)
½ teaspoon coarsely ground black pepper
2½ cups water
2 tablespoons cornstarch (optional)
¼ cup water (optional)

Preheat oven to 275°F.

With a very sharp knife trim fat close to the meat – making smooth, clean cuts, not sawing– if you didn't have the butcher cut it, making sure fat is still connected at bottom; do not cut it off completely. Fold fat back and sprinkle meat generously with salt and pepper. Replace fat and place in roasting pan. Add 1½ cups of water and tent it with foil. Bake for 4 hours. Place meat thermometer in meat, making sure it does not touch a bone. The thermometer will show baking temperatures so you can roast it from rare, medium, to well done. Remove foil after roasting for 3 hours. When done, place roast on heated platter, skim fat from pan and deglaze it with 1 cup of water for a broth or gravy. If you prefer gravy, dissolve cornstarch in ¼ cup water and add it to broth. Cook over medium heat until thickened, approximately 5 minutes. The broth is excellent for stews and soups. Remove fat from roast for easy carving.
YIELD: 6 TO 8 SERVINGS.

Variations:

Rolled Rib Roast:
Have butcher trim and roll roast, tying it every 2 inches, to form a neat, tight roll. Moisten outside with a bit of water so salt and pepper will stick. Bake as instructed above, using meat thermometer to insure the rare, medium or well done temperature you want, approximately 3½ hours. This is wonderful for slicing cold.

Barbecued Short Ribs:
After cutting out the eye, cut each rib apart, trim some of the fat and brush with your favorite barbecue sauce. Place on a grill or in a preheated 425°F oven in a shallow pan, baking until crisp, approximately 40 minutes.

🐉 SAUERBRATEN 🐉

Our heritage really shows through in this recipe. It is interesting to see how this dish has remained nearly the same since it came over from Europe in the early 1700s.

1 cup dry red wine
¾ cup red wine vinegar
1½ cups water
1 medium-size onion, sliced thin
1 teaspoon salt
1 teaspoon whole black peppercorns, broken
½ teaspoon whole cloves
2 bay leaves
¼ teaspoon ground ginger
4 pounds beef, top round, rump or chuck
3 tablespoons vegetable shortening
½ cup chopped onions
½ cup grated carrots
½ cup chopped celery
3 tablespoons all-purpose flour
⅔ cup water

Combine wine, vinegar, water, onion, salt, peppercorns, cloves, bay leaves, and ginger in 2-quart saucepan and bring to boil. Place beef in casserole dish or pot large enough to hold it and the marinade—make sure it is not made of aluminum, as there will be a chemical reaction. Pour hot liquid over beef, cover partially with lid, and refrigerate for 3 days, turning meat twice each day. When ready to cook beef, remove it from marinade and pat dry. Strain marinade through double thickness of cheesecloth, discarding onions and spices. Melt shortening in Dutch oven and brown beef over medium-high heat on all sides. Remove from pan. Add vegetables and saute over medium heat until onions and celery are clear, about 6 minutes. Add flour; reduce heat to low, stir until mixture is golden brown and thick, about 10 minutes. Gradually add reserved marinade and water and bring to boil over medium heat. Then add meat, cover and simmer over low heat for 1 to 1½ hours or until meat is tender. Remove meat and slice thin, serving marinade gravy in gravy boat. Serve with boiled potatoes, potato dumplings, or Potato Cakes (page 94).
YIELD: 6 TO 8 SERVINGS.

BEEF POT ROAST

*Everyone's favorite one-dish meal on a cold day; this recipe
may be a bit different in presentation and flavor.*

6 slices bacon
4 to 5 pounds beef roast (top round or brisket is best)
1 tablespoon chopped fresh parsley
½ tablespoon coarsely ground black pepper
1 teaspoon salt
¼ teaspoon ground nutmeg
1 teaspoon ground thyme
6 medium-size onions, whole or halved
8 large carrots, cut in 3-inch pieces
8 to 10 medium-size potatoes, peeled and quartered
½ cup sherry or white wine
½ cup brandy
1 cup water

In Dutch oven or large kettle, fry the bacon until crisp. Drain on paper
towels and crumble. Over medium-high heat, brown roast on all sides in
bacon fat, adding parsley, pepper, salt, nutmeg, and thyme as you turn beef
first time. When brown, remove meat and brown vegetables, then remove
half the vegetables to microwave dish or skillet. Place roast back in pot with
remaining vegetables, making sure meat makes direct contact with bottom
of pot. Add sherry or wine, brandy and water, reduce heat to low, cover and
simmer for at least 2½ hours, turning meat and vegetables occasionally to
prevent sticking. Pour gravy into bowl, skim off fat, then return to pot. Add
other half of vegetables and simmer over low heat for 30 minutes or until the
beef is very tender and all vegetables are tender. Add ½ cup water during
cooking if pot roast seems to be drying out or is sticking to bottom of pot.
Gravy should be thick when served. Carve roast and place on heated platter.
Arrange vegetables around sides of roast and top with crumbled bacon.
YIELD: 6 TO 8 SERVINGS.

Variations:

Pork Pot Roast:
Use pork roast, 4 peeled turnips, 4 potatoes, add 1 teaspoon dry
mustard in addition to herbs, and follow above recipe.

Beef Pot Roast with Parsnips:
Use half potatoes and half peeled parsnips.

🦅 SWISS STEAK 🦅

Many folks will always prefer their beef well done, but it should be tender and very flavorful. We always canned round steak in quart jars for that moment when we needed a meal in a hurry. It's not hard to do, tastes great, and I think it's easier than to make it the usual way. For those of you who still buy a quarter of a side of beef, why not can a few jars of beef for a special occasion?

2 to 2½ pounds round steak, cut 1 inch thick
½ teaspoon ground white pepper
1 teaspoon salt
¼ cup all-purpose flour
1 tablespoon butter
1 tablespoon vegetable oil
2½ cups water or 1¼ cups water and 1¼ cups red wine
2 tablespoons cornstarch

Lightly pepper and salt one side of steak. Generously dredge in flour, then pound with meat mallet or back of butcher knife. Turn it over and salt and pepper and pound it again. Heat butter and vegetable oil in deep pan or skillet. When very hot, add steak and brown on both sides. Pour off fat, cover steak with water, cover pan, and simmer over low heat for 1½ hours or until tender. Remove onto a heated platter and thicken pan gravy with cornstarch dissolved in ¼ cup water. Serve gravy in boat. Some folks like to leave the steak whole; others cut it into thin slices before serving.
YIELD: 4 TO 6 SERVINGS.

🦅 PAN-FRIED STEAK 🦅

My dad, Clarence Herr, was known as the steak king to anyone who purchased beef at our butcher shop on the farm. He would cut a small steak from each quarter of beef and fry it for the customer, right in the butcher shop. He used a Coleman burner and an old tin pan. With his usual twinkle, he would warn "Never" cook a steak more than 2 to 3 minutes. He scored the fat around the outside of the steak, had the pan as hot as it could get, sprinkled the pan with a bit of salt, waiting until it popped up and down like popcorn, then placed the steak proudly in the pan. As the smoke rolled to the ceiling, he would gently press the fat into the pan, pepper the steak generously, turn it and brown the other side, and look at his watch. "Two minutes—you'll see—now try it." He always won the customer to his side (even those that swore they would never eat anything pink!).

Steaks should be cut at least ¾ inch thick or they'll be hard to keep rare. If you're frying 2-inch-thick steaks, make sure you have a lid tilted over the top of the pan to keep the splattering to a minimum.

STUFFED FLANK STEAK

For steak lovers, this economical meal is sure to please.

2 pounds flank steak, about 1½ inches thick with pocket cut in
3 tablespoons butter
3 tablespoons chopped onion
½ cup chopped celery with leaves
½ cup grated carrots
½ cup grated raw white or sweet potatoes
1 tablespoon chopped fresh parsley
1 teaspoon salt
½ teaspoon ground black pepper

If your steak does not have a pocket, cut a long slit alongside the steak, cutting ⅔ the way through to other side. In Dutch oven or deep saute pan, melt butter and saute the vegetables for approximately 5 minutes over medium heat, then salt and pepper them. Stuff this vegetable mixture into pocket of steak and close it with skewers. There should be enough butter left in pan to brown the steak; if not, add 1 tablespoon vegetable oil and brown steak on both sides over medium high heat. Remove, place a baking rack in pan, and lay stuffed steak on it. Add enough water to cover rack but not steak. Cover, reduce heat to medium low and simmer for 1½ to 2 hours until meat is very tender. If you have a pressure cooker, follow the directions and you'll save a lot of time. Add extra vegetables (if desired) to pan for the last 40 minutes of cooking. If you want to serve gravy with steak, check broth in pan for seasoning and add extra beef broth if needed. Thicken as for any gravy, adding 2 tablespoons cornstarch dissolved in ¼ cup water to each cup of beef broth. Cook over medium heat until thickened.
YIELD: 6 SERVINGS.

❧ CITY CHICKEN DRUMSTICKS ❧

When young, tender chickens were only available in the springtime, the creative housewife found many ways to substitute. City chicken was sold in the farmers' markets and butcher shops year-round. It tasted like chicken and at that time veal and pork were cheaper than young chickens. That's hard to imagine now that chicken is so available and reasonably priced.

1 pound lean ground beef
1 pound lean ground pork
½ pound ground veal
3 large eggs
1 cup coarsely crushed cracker crumbs
1½ teaspoons salt
½ teaspoon ground white pepper
1 teaspoon chopped fresh parsley
2 tablespoons milk
1 cup fresh bread crumbs
6 to 8 wooden skewers
3 to 4 tablespoons vegetable oil

Preheat oven to 350°F (if baking rather than frying).

In large mixing bowl, combine ground beef, pork, and veal with 2 of the eggs, cracker crumbs, salt, pepper, and parsley. Using about ½ cup of mixture for each serving, form it into shape of a drumstick. Combine remaining egg with milk in deep soup bowl and pour bread crumbs into deep bowl as well. Roll each drumstick in egg wash and then into bread crumbs. Insert a skewer into base of each drumstick. Heat oil in large skillet over medium heat. Fry until golden brown on all sides, cover with a lid, reduce heat to low, and simmer for at least 30 minutes. If skillet becomes dry on bottom, add two tablespoons of oil or water to prevent burning. If you prefer to bake drumsticks, place in a greased 9 x 13-inch baking dish and bake in oven for 35 minutes. If they are not as brown as you would like, increase the heat to 400°F and bake an additional 10 minutes. Serve as you would fried chicken.

YIELD: 6 SERVINGS.

MEAT LOAF WITH SWEET POTATOES

Everyone tries to do something different with this all-time favorite. Hot or cold, this recipe is delicious!

2 pounds ground meat; preferably equal parts of beef, pork, and veal (or turkey)
1 medium-size onion, chopped
½ cup chopped celery
1 tablespoon chopped fresh parsley
2 large eggs, lightly beaten
¾ cup dry bread crumbs
1 teaspoon salt
½ teaspoon ground white pepper
1½ cups cooked, mashed sweet potatoes
¼ cup finely chopped green bell pepper or green onion
¼ cup pure maple or light corn syrup (I use Karo)

Preheat oven to 350°F.

Mix ground meats, onion, celery, parsley, eggs, crumbs, salt, and pepper in large bowl. Place between two large sheets of wax paper and roll in a rectangle about 14 x 10-inches. Remove the top paper and spread meat with mashed potatoes. Sprinkle with chopped pepper or onion or both. Roll mixture jelly-roll fashion, seal outside edge, and place in shallow greased baking pan, seam side down. Bake for 45 minutes. Drain off excess fat and drizzle syrup on top of loaf. Bake 25 minutes more or until juices are clear and loaf is golden brown.
YIELD: 4 TO 6 SERVINGS

Variation:

Stuffed Peppers:
Clean, core, and seed 6 large green bell peppers, trimming the bottoms enough to make them stand straight in a greased 9-inch square baking dish. Fill the peppers with one recipe of meat loaf. Add ½ cup water to bottom of dish, tent with aluminum foil, bake for 45 minutes. Remove foil and continue baking for another 10 minutes or until lightly browned on top.

LAMB ROAST WITH CRUSTY MINT

Lamb should be basted in creme de menthe, preferably white, to prevent an unusual taste, especially if you do not use an abundance of garlic.

6 to 8 pounds leg, or roast, of lamb
½ cup white crème de menthe (or sherry)
1 clove garlic, minced
1 teaspoon Krazy salt or steak salt (a coarse salt with herbs added)
1 teaspoon coarsely ground black pepper
1 cup water
⅓ cup lemon curd jelly or marmalade
⅓ cup mint jelly
1 teaspoon chopped fresh or dried mint
½ teaspoon chopped fresh or dried marjoram
1 cup fresh bread crumbs
Fresh mint or parsley sprigs for garnish

Preheat oven to 325°F.

Moisten roast with creme de menthe, then sprinkle with minced garlic and salt and pepper on all sides. Place on rack in roasting pan, add water to bottom of roaster and tent it with aluminum foil. Roast in oven for 25 minutes per pound or until meat thermometer registers 145°F (medium rare). Baste with remaining creme de menthe during first hour of roasting. About 30 minutes before roast should be done, combine lemon and mint jellies, mint, marjoram, and bread crumbs. Spread mixture over roast, patting firmly with blade of cold knife. Roast until golden brown. Garnish with fresh mint.
YIELD: 6 TO 8 SERVINGS

Variation:

Lamb Chops with Crusty Mint:
Use all above ingredients in ½ measurements and spread over 2 pounds of chops. Place them in a buttered baking dish and bake in preheated 350°F oven for one hour; then turn and bake until golden brown and crusty, approximately 20 minutes.

🦎 LAMB PAPRIKA 🦎

I love this for all the extra flavor, plus, it's so easy to prepare.

1 pound lamb, cubed
3 tablespoons all-purpose flour
5 or 6 slices bacon, cut in small pieces
½ cup chopped onion
2 cups diced potatoes (about 4 medium-size)
1 tablespoon paprika
½ teaspoon caraway seeds
¼ teaspoon crushed fresh rosemary
½ teaspoon salt
¼ teaspoon ground white pepper
1 cup diced and drained tomatoes (fresh or canned)
½ cup beef broth
½ cup red wine

Preheat oven to 350°F.

Dredge meat cubes in flour. In heavy, deep skillet, saute bacon and onion over medium high heat until golden brown. Add potatoes and floured meat and brown lightly. Sprinkle with paprika, caraway, rosemary, salt, and pepper. Add tomatoes, broth, and wine, and simmer over medium heat, covered, for 10 minutes. If you prefer, finish cooking in skillet over medium heat for 30 minutes or place in 2-quart baking dish and bake for 30 minutes. If placed in oven, it will be drier when served.
YIELD: 6 SERVINGS.

🦎 BAKED HOME-CURED HAM 🦎

Everyone asks why their hams become so salty and dry when they bake them. The answer for keeping a ham moist, mild, and tender is to roast it in water at a low temperature. If the ham is very salty, pour off the water after 2 hours of baking and add fresh water. This gives you the wonderful smoky flavor without all the salt.

12 to 14-pound smoked, home-cured ham
2 cups water

Preheat oven to 300°F.
Soak ham overnight in cold water. When ready to roast, remove rind and place bone side down in roaster pan. Add water, tent with aluminum foil, and bake for 2½ hours. Remove and debone. If broth seems salty, pour it off and add 2 cups fresh water. Put deboned ham in water and continue baking for one more hour.

❈ SCHNITZ UND KNEPP ❈

Here is a fine example of combining sweet and salty foods to make a delicious meal.

3 pound smoked ham butt or end
½ pound sliced dried apples (the schnitz)
6 cups water
2 tablespoons light brown sugar
¼ teaspoon ground cloves
¼ teaspoon ground cinnamon
1 recipe Knepp (page 55)

Place ham, apples, water, brown sugar, and spices in 6-quart Dutch oven or heavy kettle. Cover and bring to a boil. Simmer over medium heat for about 1½ hours or until ham is tender. (If you are using precooked ham, it will only take 30 to 45 minutes.) Remove ham from broth and let cool enough to debone, remove fat, and cut in bite-size pieces. Prepare knepp dough. Return the cut meat to broth and bring to full boil over medium high heat. Continue with this heat until all dumplings are added. There must be enough liquid to boil the dumplings, so add extra water if necessary. Drop dough by tablespoonfuls into boiling broth. Cover with lid and simmer over low heat for 12 minutes. DO NOT PEEK OR LIFT THE LID! Remove knepp with slotted spoon and set aside while pouring ham and apples into heated bowl or deep platter. Arrange knepp around the sides and serve at once.
YIELD: 6 SERVINGS.

 FRIED HAM SLICES

The best way to have several memorable meals from one home-cured ham is to cut three or four slices, 1 inch thick, from the center of the ham for frying. This leaves the butt end (best for a meal of ham, green beans, and potatoes) for cooking and the other end for roasting. This is the most common practice–the whole ham is roasted only for special occasions.

**2 slices of center-cut ham (home-cured is the best), about 1 pound
   each**
1 tablespoon butter or vegetable oil
1 teaspoon dry mustard (optional)
2 teaspoons light brown sugar (optional)

For gravy, if desired:

1 tablespoon cornstarch
1 cup milk or water
1 teaspoon chopped fresh parsley

Trim rind from ham slices. Melt butter in large heavy skillet. Sprinkle slices with mustard and brown sugar if desired. Place them in skillet and fry over medium heat until golden brown on each side, about 15 minutes a side. Remove slices to heated platter and slice them thin. For gravy, dissolve cornstarch in milk and add to skillet. Reduce heat to low, stir in parsley and bring to boil. Make sure browning is loosened from pan and stir until thickened, about 5 minutes. Serve with biscuits or whole browned potatoes.
YIELD: 4 TO 5 SERVINGS.

❧ SOUTHERN-STYLE HAM ❧

My mother's cookbook, written by her during her teenage years, gives us one way of retaining the wonderful flavor of home-cured ham without the strong, salty flavor.

1 pound of center cut, home-cured ham, cut about 1 inch thick
1 teaspoon dry mustard
⅓ cup lightly packed light brown sugar
2 tablespoons (¼ stick) butter
1 cup milk

Preheat oven to 325°F.

Rub mustard on top of ham. Place in 9 x 11-inch baking dish and sprinkle with brown sugar. Dot with butter. Pour milk in dish and bake for 1 hour. It will develop a browned crust on top which sometimes looks curdled. That's fine, as the milk helps take away the salty taste. Remove the ham to heated platter. Cut into thin slices.
Yield: 4 to 6 servings

❧ HAM, GREEN BEANS AND POTATOES ❧

Everyone loves this one-dish meal. During the busy summer harvest days, we counted on this dinner at least once a week.

4 pound butt end of ham
4 cups water
6 to 8 medium-size potatoes, peeled
2 pounds green beans, fresh or frozen
1 teaspoon coarsely ground black pepper

Trim rind from ham. Place ham in Dutch oven or large kettle, add water and cook, covered, over medium heat until tender, about 3 hours. Remove ham and debone. Cut potatoes in half and add, along with the beans and pepper, to the ham broth. Simmer over medium heat until vegetables are soft, about 30 minutes. Add ham and heat thoroughly.
Yield: 6 servings

Variation:
Add 2 cups corn kernels, fresh or frozen. This may replace the potatoes or be added in addition to them.

 POT PIE

*Give me a good, rich broth and some fine meat and I'll assure you a great meal. Pot
pie in the Pennsylvania Dutch country is not a baked pie but a slippery dough
noodle dish with lots of flavor. Every kind of meat works well in this recipe.*

**4 to 6-pound roast with bones (ham, pork, chicken, squirrel, rabbit, or
beef)**
½ cup coarsely chopped celery with leaves
2 medium-size potatoes, peeled and thinly sliced
6 cups reserved broth
Pot Pie Squares (page 54)
Fresh parsley sprigs for garnish

Cover meat with water, season, and cook, covered, over medium heat until
tender, about 2 hours. Remove and debone, discarding any fat or skin. Cut
meat into bite-size chunks and set aside. Add celery, potatoes, and parsley
to 6 cups of broth and simmer over medium heat. Meanwhile, roll out pot
pie dough ⅛ inch thick and cut it into 2-inch squares. Drop them into the
simmering broth only one layer at a time, cooking about 3 minutes before
pushing the cooked dough under the broth before dropping in the next layer.
If several layers are put in at the same time, they will become thick and
doughy. After all dough is in broth, add meat chunks and simmer for
15 minutes more. Garnish with parsley before serving.

YIELD: 6 TO 8 SERVINGS

PORK LOIN ROAST
STUFFED WITH DRIED FRUIT

This is a very elegant dish and will make any meal seem special.

4 pounds pork loin, without the bone
1 recipe of Dried Fruit Stuffing (page 165)
1 cup water
1½ teaspoons salt
1 teaspoon ground black pepper
1 teaspoon dry mustard
1 tablespoon light brown sugar
½ cup sherry

Preheat oven to 375°F.

Cut loin lengthwise, about ⅔ the way through, and fill with stuffing. Tie with cord and skewers to keep filling inside. Place water in roasting pan. Season loin with salt, pepper, mustard, and brown sugar and place in pan. Tent with aluminum foil and bake for 2 hours basting every 30 minutes with sherry. Remove foil and reduce heat to 350°F, baking another 15 minutes (or turn off oven and let it stand uncovered for 30 minutes until ready to serve). If using meat thermometer, let roast reach an internal temperature of 185-190°F. If you have extra filling, bake in buttered baking dish for last 15 minutes and arrange around roast before serving.
YIELD: 6 TO 8 SERVINGS

Variation:

Pork Chops with Wine:
Use 4 pounds pork chops and season the same as above. Omit water, fry chops in large, heavy skillet over medium heat in 2 tablespoons (¼ stick) butter or oil and baste with sherry or an equal amount of red or white wine as they are browning, about 35 minutes. Serve stuffing as a side dish.

 COOKED BEEF TONGUE

Smoked tongue was considered a delicacy when I was growing up. I can remember all the older folks picking out the sliced, smoked tongue from the platters of cold cuts. I like tongue hot as well as cold and I love it when it is smoked. If you have a smoker or grill, cook the tongue and smoke it for extra flavor. The cooked tongue tastes like a tender beef roast with a very fine texture, so go ahead and try it; you'll find your family will enjoy it.

1½ pounds beef tongue, cleaned
1 green bell pepper, cut in quarters
4 stems celery with leaves, cut in 2-inch pieces
1 tablespoon chopped fresh parsley
½ teaspoon chopped fresh thyme
2 teaspoons salt
1 teaspoon coarsely ground black pepper

Place tongue in 6-quart stockpot, add rest of ingredients, and cover with water. Bring to a boil over high heat, cover with a lid, and reduce heat to medium. Cook until tongue is tender, approximately 3 hours. Let tongue cool in broth. Peel off skin of tongue when you remove it from broth. If you prefer tongue served hot, strain broth through a double thickness of cheesecloth, slice tongue, and heat it thoroughly in broth. To serve cold, refrigerate and slice thin, serving with a horseradish sauce or mustard. To smoke tongue, follow directions for smoker, smoking over wet hickory chips for no more than four hours. Refrigerate smoked tongue, tightly covered, until ready to serve. Freeze tongue that is left over. It will keep in freezer for at least six weeks.

YIELD: 6 SERVINGS

 WIENER SCHNITZEL

Turkey may be substituted for the veal, but Wiener schnitzel and red cabbage are a meal that most of us cannot live without for any length of time.

2 pounds veal cutlets, cut ½ inch thick
½ cup all-purpose flour
1½ teaspoons salt
½ teaspoon freshly ground black pepper
2 large eggs, lightly beaten
1 tablespoon evaporated or whole milk
2 cup dry bread crumbs
½ cup saltine cracker crumbs, rolled fine
¼ cup vegetable oil
Lemon slices and fresh parsley sprigs for garnish

Score edges of cutlets with sharp knife to prevent curling. Pound cutlets between 2 sheets of wax paper until ¼ inch thick and set aside. Combine flour, salt, and pepper on plate or sheet of wax paper. Mix eggs and milk in shallow dish and combine bread and cracker crumbs on plate or sheet of wax paper. Then, take each cutlet and first generously dredge it in flour mixture, then dip it in egg mixture, and finally dredge it in crumbs until thoroughly coated. Heat oil in large, heavy skillet over medium heat and fry cutlets until golden brown on each side, approximately 3 minutes per side. DO NOT OVERCOOK! Serve on a heated platter and garnish with lemon slices and sprigs of parsley.

Yɪᴇʟᴅ: 4 sᴇʀᴠɪɴɢs

 SCRAPPLE

Scrapple is finely ground pork cooked with cornmeal and seasoning, then poured into loaf pans, and cooled and refrigerated for several days. Cut into slices, it should be fried on a grill or in a skillet and served crispy on the outside. We always served scrapple for supper, spreading it with apple butter, molasses, or syrup. Everyone else seems to like it best for breakfast, so you decide when to enjoy it.

16 cups water
3 cups finely ground pork or the chopped meat from pork rib rack, heart, or feet (3 cups pork sausage meat is also fine)
2 teaspoons salt
2 teaspoons coarsely ground black pepper
½ teaspoon dried basil (optional)
Pinch of dried rosemary (optional)
3½ cups cornmeal
2 tablespoons vegetable oil

In large 6-quart stockpot, combine water, pork, salt, pepper, and herbs. Bring to a boil, skim, cover and simmer over medium heat for 3 hours or until meat falls off bones. Remove meat and strain broth through a double thickness of cheesecloth. Debone and remove all fat, gristle, and skin. Chop or grind meat in food processor or grinder. Skim fat from broth, making sure you have 12 cups of broth. If not, add enough water to make 12 cups. Place broth and meat in large, heavy saucepan and bring to a boil. Slowly add cornmeal, continually stirring with a whisk to prevent lumping. Simmer over low heat for 1 hour, stirring frequently with a wooden spoon. Mixture should be thick like mush. Remove from heat and pour into three greased 8 ½ x 4½-inch loaf pans. Cool and refrigerate, covered with wax paper, until ready to use. It does not freeze well, but will keep for weeks in refrigerator. To serve, slice ⅓ inch thick and fry on grill or in skillet greased with vegetable oil over medium heat until golden and crisp, about 3 minutes on each side.
Yield: Three 8 ½ x 4½-inch loaf pans

SAUSAGE AND SQUASH STIR-FRY

Appealing to the eye and the palate, it is also easy and quick to prepare.

1 pound smoked pork sausage
2 yellow (summer) squash, each about 10 inches long
1 zucchini, about ⅓ pound
1 tablespoon butter
1 teaspoon steak salt
1 teaspoon dried chervil
½ teaspoon celery seed
½ teaspoon ground white pepper

Slice sausage about ⅓ inch thick. Slice squash and zucchini same size or into thin strips. Melt butter in large, heavy skillet or wok and stir-fry sausage over high heat for 5 minutes. Add all remaining ingredients and continue to stir-fry until vegetables are nearly tender and sausage is golden, about 8 minutes. Serve immediately.

YIELD: 4 SERVINGS

PAN-FRIED LIVER AND ONIONS

If you are used to eating liver that has been dredged in flour and fried to death til it's tough, try this recipe. You won't believe liver could be so tender!

3 tablespoons butter
1 cup sliced onions
1½ pounds fresh calf's liver, sliced 1 inch thick, skinned
¾ teaspoon salt
¼ teaspoon ground white pepper

Melt butter in large, heavy skillet and saute onions over medium heat until they are clear and golden around edges, about 3 minutes. Remove onions onto a heated platter and increase heat to high. Add slices of liver, pressing with a fork to seal in all juices. Fry until browned, about 2 minutes, sprinkle with salt and pepper and turn. Fry on other side for 2 minutes, add onions, and heat through, covering pan with the lid until heated. Serve immediately. If the liver is left a bit pink it will be tenderer.

YIELD: 4 SERVINGS

CHAPTER SEVEN

Seafood

🖎 DEVILED CLAMS 🖎

These are delicious either baked or pan-fried.

12 large clams or 2 cups frozen or canned chopped clams with broth
4 large eggs, lightly beaten
½ cup chopped onion
⅔ cup chopped celery
½ cup chopped green bell pepper
2 tablespoons chopped fresh parsley
1 teaspoon chopped fresh chervil
½ teaspoon salt
½ teaspoon ground white pepper
4 cups fresh bread crumbs

Preheat oven to 375°F.

Scrub clams and open with shucking knife, or place in baking pan. Bake in oven at 300°F until shells open enough to remove clam, reserve broth. Do not bake clams! Remove clams from shells and chop up or use frozen or canned ones. Oil inside of scrubbed clam shells. Mix remaining ingredients together until well blended then divide among shells. Place them in shallow baking pan and bake until golden brown, approximately 25 minutes. If pan frying, place filled clam shells upside down in large, heated and buttered saucepan, and fry, covered, over medium heat until golden brown, approximately 8 minutes.
Yield: 12 deviled clams (1 usually serve 2 per person)

BOX PANNED OYSTERS

These are for the true oyster lover.

3 dozen large shucked oysters with the liquor
3 tablespoons butter
¼ teaspoon ground white pepper
Dash of paprika
Old Bay (seafood) seasoning (optional)
Chopped fresh parsley for garnish

Check oysters for shells. If large, heavy saute pan, lightly brown butter over medium-high heat and add oysters. Fry only till edges curl, about 1 minute. Add reserved liquor and seasonings. Heat thoroughly over medium heat and serve immediately in heated bowls with toast tips or crackers. Garnish with parsley.

YIELD: 4 TO 6 SERVINGS

FRIED OYSTERS

Excellent!

3 dozen large shucked oysters (reserve ½ cup oyster liquor)
3 cups assorted cracker crumbs
¼ teaspoon Old Bay (seafood) seasoning
¼ teaspoon Hungarian paprika
½ teaspoon dried dillweed
¼ teaspoon ground white pepper
¼ teaspoon red (cayenne) pepper
1 large egg, well beaten
⅓ cup vegetable oil or butter

Check oysters for shells. Combine crumbs and seasonings in medium-size bowl. Combine beaten egg and oyster liquor in small bowl. Roll each oyster in crumbs, let stand 30 minutes, then dip in egg liquid. Roll again in crumbs and fry both sides over medium heat in large, heavy skillet until golden brown.

YIELD: 4 TO 6 SERVINGS (MY DAD AND GRANDFATHER ALWAYS ATE AT LEAST
      8 OYSTERS EACH, SO YOU BE THE JUDGE.)

 OYSTER PIE

A traditional, favorite one-dish meal served with salad or relishes. The Shirks prepared this for one of the most memorable dinners we've enjoyed. It is their old family recipe and it deserves special applause.

3 medium-size potatoes, peeled and sliced ¼-inch thick
1 stem celery, chopped
1 cup water
1 teaspoon salt
Pastry for a double crust 10-inch pie (page 181)
1½ cups shucked oysters including the liquor, about 2½ dozen
4 large eggs, lightly beaten
½ teaspoon ground white pepper
1 tablespoon all-purpose flour
3 tablespoons butter, melted
1 tablespoon chopped fresh parsley

Preheat oven to 350°F.

Place sliced potatoes, celery, water, and ½ teaspoon of salt in medium-size saucepan. Boil until vegetables are tender, about 10 minutes, over medium heat. Reserve liquid. Roll out bottom crust of pie, fit into 9-inch pie pan, and puff in oven for about 3 minutes to prevent soggy bottom crust. Check oysters for shell particles. Blend oyster liquor with beaten eggs, remaining salt, pepper, and flour. Layer half potatoes, celery, and oysters onto bottom crust. Pour in half egg mixture. Add rest of potatoes, celery, and oysters, and pour remaining egg mixture plus melted butter and parsley over top. If there is not enough liquid to cover vegetables and oysters, use potato liquid to cover. Moisten edges of bottom crust with liquid. Cover it with top crust, piercing it in several places first. Flute edges, place pie pan on aluminum foil or baking sheet and bake for 45 minutes or until juices start to bubble through edges or vents. Serve hot.

YIELD: ONE 9-INCH PIE FOR 4 SERVINGS

🦅 SALMON CROQUETTES 🦅

My mother, Bertha, and Abe's mother, Elizabeth, both made these quite often. If they were used as an appetizer, they were made smaller. As the main course, they were shaped like large cones and served with a thin white sauce. I like serving them with a wine-caper sauce.

1 pound fresh salmon, filleted and poached (canned salmon may be substituted)
2 tablespoons finely chopped onion
1 tablespoon minced fresh dill or ½ tablespoon dried
1 teaspoon minced fresh basil or ½ teaspoon dried
1 teaspoon seasoned salt
¼ cup evaporated milk or whole milk
3 large eggs, lightly beaten
2 tablespoons (¼ stick) butter, melted
1½ cups fresh bread crumbs
3 tablespoons vegetable oil
½ cup dry white wine
1 tablespoon capers
Fresh dill sprigs or lemon slices for garnish

Remove any skin or small bones from salmon. Flake fish with fork in large mixing bowl. Combine it with onion, dill, basil, salt, milk, beaten eggs, butter, and 1 cup of bread crumbs. Cover with plastic wrap and refrigerate for 30 minutes. Form into balls, cones, or patties and roll in remaining bread crumbs. Heat oil in large, heavy skillet over medium-high heat and fry croquettes until golden brown on all sides, about 10 minutes altogether. Remove them from skillet, then add wine and capers and deglaze pan. Pour sauce over top of croquettes before serving. Garnish with sprigs of dill or lemon slices.

YIELD: ABOUT 12 TWO-INCH BALLS, 4 SERVINGS

🦐 SHAD AND ROE BAKED AND FRIED 🦐

*Shad is a strong-flavored fish, the roe very mild and delicious, especially when
fried with bacon. The old-fashioned way of baking shad was to use the whole
fish and bake at 350°F for 3 to 4 hours. They say the bones, at least the small
ones, would then be soft enough to eat. I have not found that to be true, so I
have the fish filleted. It saves time in the oven and they are just as tasty.*

Shad:
6 to 8 slices bacon
3 pounds shad fillets
1 teaspoon salt
½ teaspoon ground white pepper
Thin slices of lemon or lime

Roe:
3 pairs shad roe
¼ cup all-purpose flour
½ teaspoon salt
½ teaspoon ground white pepper
6 slices bacon
Lemon wedges

Preheat oven to 400°F.

Place 2 or 3 slices of bacon in bottom of buttered baking pan, add fillets,
sprinkle them with salt and pepper, and top with slices of lemon and
remaining bacon. Bake for 30 minutes. The fillets should be golden brown
on top but flake when you pierce them with fork. Separate pairs of roe by
cutting fiber that holds them together. Shake roe in paper bag with flour, salt,
and pepper until coated. Wrap roe halves in bacon and place them in large
skillet. Slowly heat skillet until bacon has warmed enough to fry roe; cover
skillet partially while you do this, as roe has tendency to splatter. Fry until
golden over medium-high heat, about 8 minutes for each side. Serve with
lemon wedges or special vinegar, such as Celery Vinegar on page 261.
YIELD: 6 SERVINGS

Variation:

Shad Stuffed with Spinach:
Spread spinach stuffing used to stuff tomatoes (recipe on page 102) between
fillets. Bake one hour or until golden on top and flaky on bottom.

🦋 TROUT CAMERON ESTATE STYLE 🦋

Simon Cameron, native of Lancaster County and first Secretary of War for Abraham Lincoln, used the fresh springs of Donegal to nurture the trout he brought to the area. The Cameron Estate was his summer residence and is now a beautiful country inn with the streams stocked with lots of trout. This recipe honors him for his great contribution to our area.

1 trout or 2 fillets, about 14 ounces
Flour for dredging
1 large egg, slightly beaten
1 teaspoon water or milk
Pecan Breading (page 166)
2 tablespoons butter (¼ stick) or vegetable oil
Dash of ground white pepper
⅓ cup dry white wine
1 tablespoon fresh lemon juice
1 teaspoon capers
Lemon slices and watercress for garnish

You may want to use trout that are boned and beheaded, but if you are catching your own, give my way a try. Don't remove fins or head until fish is cooked. At that point, fork inserted under backbone will be all that's needed to neatly fillet fish in matter of seconds. Dredge trout in flour, then dip in egg wash made from beaten egg and water. Dredge trout in Pecan Breading. Heat butter or oil over medium-high heat in large saute pan or skillet and place trout skin side up. Season lightly with pepper and salt if desired. Saute until edges start to curl, then flip over and cook until fish flakes when fork is inserted at thickest part. Gently remove fish onto heated platter. Add wine, lemon juice, and capers to pan brownings. Deglaze pan and pour sauce over fish or serve on side. Garnish with lemon slices and watercress.
YIELD: 1 SERVING

Variation:

Use this recipe for any mild, fresh fish. Two tablespoons chopped scallions may be added when deglazing pan.

CHAPTER EIGHT

Sauces, Dressings, and Stuffings

🌸 GRAVY 🌸

Gravy may be made from any broth or a combination of broth, brownings from the roast, and milk. Cornstarch may be substituted for flour as a thickener.

2 cups broth
½ cup water
3½ tablespoons all-purpose flour or cornstarch
**Season to taste with salt, ground black or white pepper, chopped
    fresh parsley, or paprika**

If you want to make gravy from roast, pour all drippings into bowl. Skim and discard fat. Heat pan over medium heat and deglaze with water. Scrape and stir with wooden spoon until all brownings are loosened. Reduce heat to low and whisk in flour, stirring until all lumps are dissolved. Slowly add broth and whisk until velvety smooth, about 5 minutes. Season to taste. Serve piping hot.
YIELD: 2½ CUPS

🌸 BROWNED BUTTER 🌸

I like to make a large amount at one time because it will keep, covered, in the refrigerator for at least two weeks. All I have to do is spoon it onto any hot vegetable and the butter melts into the vegetables. And mashed potatoes are heavenly when topped with browned butter.

¼ pound (1 stick) butter or margarine

Melt butter in 1-quart saucepan over medium heat. After it has melted, stir constantly until butter begins to turn nutty, golden brown, approximately 4 minutes. Remove from heat immediately, before it burns. It will have what some call spicy taste. This is caused by browning of milk particles in butter. Spoon small amount over hot vegetables before serving. Cover remaining butter and refrigerate until ready to use. Dark particles will settle to bottom, so when spooning cold butter, make sure you touch bottom of pan for all good parts.
YIELD: ½ CUP

 CLARIFIED BUTTER

*Clarified butter will keep for at least a week if stored,
covered, in a cool place or in the refrigerator.*

¼ pound (1 stick) butter

Place butter in deep saucepan and cook over medium heat until it foams.
Remove it from heat and skim foam from top. Clear yellow liquid is the
clarified butter. Carefully pour it off from solids and milky liquid at bottom of
pan.

YIELD: ½ CUP

 WHITE SAUCE

Thin:
1 tablespoon butter or vegetable shortening
1 tablespoon all-purpose flour
1 cup milk
¼ teaspoon salt
Dash of freshly ground black or white pepper

Medium:
2 tablespoons (¼ stick) butter or vegetable shortening
2 tablespoons all-purpose flour
1 cup milk
¼ teaspoon salt
Dash of freshly ground black or white pepper

Thick:
3 tablespoons butter or vegetable shortening
3 tablespoons all-purpose flour
1 cup milk
¼ teaspoon salt
Dash of freshly ground black or white pepper

In 1-quart saucepan, melt better over medium heat. Gradually add flour,
stirring with whisk until it becomes smooth paste, approximately 2 minutes.
Gradually add milk, stirring constantly until thickened. Add salt and pepper
and reduce heat to very low. Stir for at least one minute before adding to
prepared dish.

YIELD: 1 CUP

 HOLLANDAISE SAUCE

When serving hollandaise sauce, it must be kept warm, not hot, as the sauce will break (curdle). If that happens, add another egg yolk and beat sauce vigorously.

2 large egg yolks
1 tablespoon white wine
½ cup Clarified Butter (page 152)
2 drops Tabasco sauce
2 tablespoons fresh lemon juice
⅛ teaspoon salt
⅛ teaspoon ground white pepper

In top of double boiler, beat egg yolks and wine together thoroughly as water below heats up. Do not allow water to boil. If you are not using double boiler, beat yolks and wine in bowl set in pan of near-boiling water. Be careful not to cook yolks, just heat them, always beating with wire whisk. When egg yolks are warm, slowly add clarified butter, mixing all time, until smooth and thickened, approximately 1½ to 2 minutes. Gradually whisk in Tabasco, lemon juice, salt, and pepper. As soon as it is thick and creamy, remove from heat. Keep warm, but not hot, until ready to serve.
YIELD: ¾ CUP

TOMATO SAUCE

The Dutch like their tomato sauce sweet, and either chunky or smooth, and often serve it with mashed potatoes.

3 tablespoons butter or margarine
½ cup chopped onion
⅓ cup all-purpose flour
½ teaspoon salt
½ teaspoon ground black pepper
1 to 2 tablespoons light brown sugar
1 tablespoon chopped fresh parsley or 1 teaspoon dried
3 cups diced or pureed (depending on preference), peeled tomatoes, fresh or canned (with juice)
Croutons, toasted crackers, or hardboiled egg slices for garnish

Melt butter in large saucepan over medium heat. Saute onion until golden, then add flour. Stir until smooth and add salt, pepper, brown sugar, parsley and tomatoes. Cook over medium-low heat until thick, about 12 minutes. When ready to serve, garnish with croutons, toasted crackers or hardboiled egg slices.
YIELD: 4 CUPS

 MUSHROOM-HERB SAUCE

This sauce is perfect over beans, peas, or nearly everything.

¼ cup chopped onion
2 tablespoons (¼ stick) butter
1¼ pounds mushrooms, sliced
1 large egg yolk, beaten with fork
1 teaspoon ground white pepper
½ teaspoon salt
1 teaspoon dried parsley flakes
½ teaspoon dried tarragon
¼ teaspoon dried dillweed
1 cup half and half (milk may be substituted)
½ cup dry white wine

In saucepan or skillet, saute onions in butter over medium-high heat until clear, then add sliced mushrooms. After evaporating almost all mushrooms' liquid, stir in beaten yolk, pepper, salt, and herbs. Reduce heat to medium. Slowly add cream, stirring with wooden spoon until slightly thickened. Gradually add wine and heat thoroughly. Serve over vegetables or in sauce boat on side.
YIELD: 2 CUPS

WINE SAUCE

This is delicious served over puddings and cakes.

10 tablespoons butter, (1¼ sticks) at room temperature
3 cups confectioner's sugar
¼ teaspoon salt
¾ cup boiling water
⅔ cup white wine or sherry
1 teaspoon ground nutmeg
¼ teaspoon ground cinnamon

Place butter, sugar, and salt in large mixing bowl and beat vigorously until light and fluffy. Slowly add boiling water to mixture, beating rapidly until very creamy. Gradually add wine, nutmeg, and cinnamon, beating thoroughly. It should look milky white, if beaten properly. Set bowl over very hot water, either in saucepan or bottom of double boiler is fine, and keep hot until ready to serve, do not boil.
YIELD: ABOUT 4 CUPS

🌿 STRAWBERRY-RHUBARB SAUCE 🌿

This is a great sauce to serve with fresh strawberries or puddings. Fill baked meringues with a combination of fresh fruit and sauce to make an elegant dessert.

1 pound fresh rhubarb
⅓ cup granulated sugar
1¼ cups frozen strawberries or 1½ cups sliced fresh strawberries
2 tablespoons fresh lemon juice
⅓ teaspoon ground nutmeg
3 drops red food coloring
3 tablespoons arrowroot or cornstarch
6 tablespoons water

Wash and cut off leaves (they are poisonous) and stem ends of rhubarb. Cut into ½-inch pieces. Place the diced rhubarb, sugar, and strawberries in food processor or blender. Chop fine and pour into 1½-quart saucepan. Add lemon juice, nutmeg, food coloring, arrowroot, and water, stirring until completely dissolved. Bring to boil and cook over medium heat, stirring until thickened, about 10 minutes. Cool and refrigerate, covered, until ready to serve.

YIELD: 2½ CUPS

🌿 FRESH FRUIT GLAZE 🌿

This is a perfect glaze for all fresh, uncooked fruits. While cornstarch has a tendency to gel and turn cloudy, arrowroot remains clear. The most economical way to buy arrowroot is to order it from your grocery store buyer in large ½-pound boxes. The major companies package it in large boxes for commercial restaurant use and will sell it to the grocery buyers by special order. It keeps at least a year if stored with the lid sealed.

1 tablespoon arrowroot
½ cup water
⅓ cup granulated sugar
1 teaspoon fresh lemon juice (optional)
Dash of ground nutmeg (optional)
Drop of food coloring (optional)

Blend all ingredients together, except food coloring, in 1-quart saucepan and bring to boil over medium-high heat. Reduce heat to low and simmer until thickened, approximately 3 minutes. Add food coloring, if desired, stir until blended, and cool before adding to fruit.

YIELD: ABOUT 1 CUP

🪶 HARD SAUCE 🪶

Especially good on plum pudding or warm gingerbread, many folks serve it on top of any warm pudding. It can be poured into a fancy mold, kept hard in a cool place, and then dipped in warm water for a few seconds to loosen before unmolding into a pretty glass dish for serving.

¼ **pound (1 stick) butter, at room temperature**
2 **cups confectioner's sugar**
¼ **teaspoon salt**
1 **teaspoon vanilla extract**
Dash of ground nutmeg
⅓ **cup brandy or rum or 2 to 3 tablespoons rum flavoring**

Place butter, sugar, and salt in large mixing bowl and beat until light. Slowly add in vanilla, nutmeg, and brandy. Beat until fluffy. Pour into 3-cup mold or dish. It can be refrigerated, covered, for at least 3 weeks. Spoon over any warm pudding or cake.

YIELD: ABOUT 2 CUPS

🪶 CHOCOLATE SYRUP 🪶

Make a full recipe of this because it keeps, refrigerated, for a long time.

1 **cup unsweetened cocoa**
4 **cups (2 pounds) granulated sugar**
1 **teaspoon salt**
6 **cups water**
2 **tablespoons arrowroot, dissolved in** ¼ **cup water**
1 **tablespoon vanilla extract**

Sift cocoa, sugar, and salt together in large mixing bowl. Put in 5-quart kettle and gradually whisk in water over medium heat. Bring to boil, stirring constantly. As it comes to boil, mix in arrowroot and cook for 5 minutes, until thickened. Remove from heat and stir in vanilla. Store in airtight jars and refrigerate.

YIELD: AT LEAST 1½ QUARTS

 # LEMON-LIME SAUCE

*A little goes a long way. Adding rum makes this a delightful
sauce for gingerbread or plum pudding.*

1½ cps granulated sugar
¼ pound (1 stick) butter
¼ teaspoon salt
1 large egg, lightly beaten
1 lemon, juiced and rind grated
1 lime, juiced and rind grated
¾ teaspoon ground nutmeg
¼ cup boiling water

Cream sugar, butter, and salt together in large mixing bowl until fluffy.
Gradually add in beaten egg, juice and grated rind of lemon and lime, nutmeg,
and water, beating thoroughly. Heat in top of double boiler over simmering
water, stirring frequently, until sauce is clear and thickened, about
20 minutes. Serve warm.
YIELD: 2 CUPS

Variation:

For lemon-rum sauce, omit lime juice and rind. Add
½ cup light rum just before serving.

COOKED DRESSING

This is an old-fashioned dressing that was always used in salads. The only problem in serving this dressing is that it becomes watery if it stands too long (more than two hours). It is important to stir the salad or pour off the excess liquid and toss before serving. It is the original dressing used for chicken, turkey, or ham salad.

3 tablespoons granulated sugar
1 tablespoon butter, melted
1 teaspoon all-purpose flour
1 teaspoon dry mustard
¼ teaspoon ground turmeric
½ teaspoon salt
1 large egg, lightly beaten
1 cup milk, scalded
½ cup cider vinegar

Combine sugar, melted butter, flour, mustard, turmeric, and salt in small saucepan. Whisk in beaten egg and gradually add hot milk. Place on stove over medium heat. When hot, briskly beat in vinegar, stirring until thickened. Remove from heat and cool. If using for potato or macaroni salad, add to salad while warm so flavor permeates entire salad. If using with apples, add minutes before serving.
YIELD: ABOUT 2 CUPS

FRUIT DRESSING

This is a perfect touch for molded salads.

½ cup granulated sugar
1½ tablespoons arrowroot or cornstarch
1 cup pineapple juice
2 large eggs, slightly beaten
¼ teaspoon ground nutmeg
1 cup heavy cream

In small saucepan, combine sugar and arrowroot with pineapple juice until thoroughly blended. Gradually mix in beaten eggs and nutmeg. Bring to boil over medium heat and stir until thickened, about 5 minutes. Remove from heat, cool, and refrigerate until ready to serve. Whip cream until it forms soft peaks and fold into sauce. Serve with or pour over fresh fruit or molded salad.
YIELD: ABOUT 3 CUPS

 HONEY-FRUIT DRESSING

Although this is super for all fruits, it is especially great when poured over berries (wine-berries, blueberries, raspberries, and strawberries, in particular) and served in peeled fruit halves.

¾ **cup sour cream**
3 tablespoons honey
½ **teaspoon grated orange rind**
½ **teaspoon grated lime rind**
½ **teaspoon grated lemon rind**
1 tablespoon fresh orange juice
1 tablespoon fresh lime juice
1 tablespoon fresh lemon juice
⅛ **teaspoon ground nutmeg**
⅛ **teaspoon salt**
Fresh mint leaves for garnish

Combine all ingredients thoroughly and chill for at least an hour. Pour over top of fruit slices or berries, reserving little extra dressing to serve on side. Garnish with fresh mint sprigs.
YIELD: 1 CUP

HORSERADISH DRESSING

The secret to making your own horseradish is to grind it with a fan behind you to blow away the strong odor and prevent the eyes from watering. Today it is still available in the local farmers' markets and is well worth the money.

1½ **cups sour cream**
¼ **cup grated fresh horseradish**
2 tablespoons fresh lemon juice
1 tablespoon Worcestershire sauce
3 tablespoons granulated sugar
1 tablespoon chopped fresh chives
½ **teaspoon dry mustard**
½ **teaspoon coarsely ground black pepper**
1 teaspoon salt

Blend all ingredients thoroughly and chill. Will keep, in an airtight container, for at least one week.
YIELD: 2 CUPS

 CREAMY SWEET-SOUR DRESSING

Everyone asks for this recipe. It is so simple yet so great, you'll make lots at a time and store it in the refrigerator. Just shake it up when you are ready to serve and it will taste better than any "bought" dressing.

½ **cup cider vinegar or white wine vinegar**
⅔ **cup granulated sugar**
¾ **cup evaporated milk**
½ **teaspoon salt**
Several dashes of freshly ground black pepper
½ **teaspoon celery seed**
1 tablespoon chopped fresh or dried herbs (parsley, rosemary, chives, thyme, etc.)

Blend all ingredients thoroughly until sugar is dissolved. Cover and refrigerate at least 30 minutes. This will keep, tightly covered, for at least one week.
YIELD: ABOUT 2 CUPS

BEER BATTER

This batter is excellent for deep frying vegetables, fish, or edible flowers. It is very light.

¾ **cup all-purpose flour**
¼ **teaspoon salt**
1½ **teaspoons baking powder**
¼ **teaspoon ground white pepper**
2 tablespoons milk
½ **cup beer**
1 large egg

Mix all batter ingredients together in blender or mixer. Cover and chill for at least 30 minutes—it is even better if you can refrigerate it overnight.
YIELD: ABOUT 1½ CUPS

🦋 APPLE STUFFING 🦋

This stuffing is great with pork chops, lamb, or any type of fowl.

6 slices bacon
½ cup chopped celery
¼ cup chopped onion
¼ cup chopped fresh parsley
½ cup granulated sugar
4 cups cored and diced apples (peeled if desired)
1 cup finely crushed saltine crackers

Preheat oven to 350°F.
Fry bacon in large saucepan or skillet. Remove bacon when crisp and drain on paper towels. Break into bits. Saute celery, onion, and parsley for several minutes in bacon fat over medium heat, then remove to large bowl. Put sugar in skillet, add apples, and saute in bacon fat over medium heat until edges of apples are golden and nearly soft, about 3 minutes. Add bacon bits, celery mixture, and crackers and blend thoroughly. Stuff in meat or fowl or bake in 2-quart buttered baking dish for 30 minutes.
YIELD: ABOUT 7 CUPS OR ENOUGH TO STUFF AN 8-POUND BIRD, 6 PORK CHOPS, OR
CROWN ROAST OF LAMB.

🦋 ALMOND STUFFING 🦋

This is very rich and nutty–perfect with small birds or veal.

3 slices bacon
1 cup chopped celery
⅓ cup slivered almonds
½ teaspoon salt
½ teaspoon ground white pepper
1 tablespoon chopped fresh parsley
1 cup fresh bread crumbs
½ cup light cream or half and half

Preheat oven to 350°F.
Fry bacon in large, heavy skillet until crisp. Remove bacon, drain on paper towels, then crumble. Saute celery, almonds, salt, pepper, and parsley in bacon grease over medium heat until almonds are golden, about 5 minutes. Stir in bread crumbs and cream. Remove from heat and spoon into buttered 1-quart baking dish. Bake for 25 to 30 minutes or until it pulls away from sides of baking dish. If using some for stuffing birds, bake remainder in small baking dish for last 10 minutes.
YIELD: ABOUT 3 CUPS OR ENOUGH TO STUFF 1 CHICKEN, 2 GAME HENS, OR 4 QUAIL

🦃 OYSTER STUFFING 🦃

As a child, I would read the menu served at the White House on Thanksgiving Day. It always included oyster stuffing. When oysters are plentiful or you want to really celebrate, try this with turkey, chicken, or pheasant.

⅓ **cup chopped celery**
¼ **cup chopped onion**
¼ **cup water**
4 cups fresh bread cubes
2 large eggs, lightly beaten
1 teaspoon Old Bay (seafood) seasoning
½ **teaspoon ground white pepper**
1 cup shucked oysters with liquor (about 1½ dozen)
½ **cup half and half, milk, or evaporated milk**

Preheat oven to 350°F.

Cook celery, onion, and water in small saucepan over medium heat for 3 minutes, or until liquid has evaporated. Remove from heat. Check oysters for shells. Place bread, beaten eggs, celery mixture, seasonings, oysters, and cream in large mixing bowl and blend thoroughly. Pour into greased 2-quart baking dish or stuff into roast or fowl. If baking separately, bake lightly tented, with aluminum foil, for 30 minutes or until golden brown.

YIELD: ABOUT 6 CUPS OR ENOUGH TO STUFF A LARGE (12-POUND) TURKEY OR 2 CHICKENS OR 2 PHEASANTS

Variation:

Clam and Oyster Stuffing:
Add an additional cup of bread cubes or broken crackers and 1 cup chopped or whole shucked clams (be sure to check for shells).

🦗 SALSIFY STUFFING 🦗

Folks will be certain they are eating oysters, so don't tell them they're not! We usually serve this with roast duck or roast turkey. Why not try it with beef or pork roasts cut with pockets? Fill with the stuffing for an elegant dinner, or serve it as a side dish.

2 pounds salsify (oyster plant)
1 teaspoon salt
4 cups water
3 tablespoons butter or margarine
⅓ cup chopped celery
⅓ cup chopped onion
½ teaspoon Old Bay (seafood) seasoning
½ teaspoon dried dillweed
2 cups bread cubes
1 cup broken crackers or oyster crackers
2 large eggs, lightly beaten
¾ cup milk
½ teaspoon salt
½ teaspoon ground black pepper
1 tablespoon fresh lemon juice

Preheat oven to 350°F.

Scrub and boil salsify in salt and water, covered, over medium-high heat until tender, about 20 minutes. Drain, peel, and cut salsify into ½-inch thick slices. Melt butter in deep, heavy saucepan and saute celery and onion for 3 minutes 3 minutes over medium heat. Remove from heat and add all other ingredients. Toss lightly until completely blended. Pour into buttered 2-quart casserole or baking dish and bake for 35 to 40 minutes or until golden brown.
YIELD: ABOUT 4 CUPS OR 6 SERVINGS

🦅 CORNBREAD-BACON STUFFING 🦅

This stuffing will make you yearn for the country, or at least a vacation to the country. It tastes great with any kind of poultry or game or pork roast.

6 slices bacon
½ cup chopped onion
1 cup chopped celery
2 tablespoons chopped fresh parsley
1½ cups chicken broth
3 cups Cornbread cut into cubes (page 170)

Preheat oven to 350°F.

Fry bacon in large, heavy skillet until crisp. Remove bacon, drain on paper towels, and crumble. Drain all but 2 tablespoons of bacon grease. Saute onion, celery, and parsley in fat over medium heat until onion is clear, about 5 minutes. Add broth, cornbread cubes, and crumbled bacon, and mix thoroughly. Pour into buttered baking pan and bake for 35 minutes or until it pulls away from sides of baking pan.

YIELD: 4 SERVINGS OR ENOUGH TO STUFF A ROASTER CHICKEN OR 2 GAME HENS

🦅 CHESTNUT STUFFING 🦅

Chestnut trees were everywhere until the blight of the early 1900s. Since then they have become quite a delicacy. Available, canned, from France, they are expensive but worth every penny. If you are lucky enough to find them in the markets, enjoy them with any kind of poultry. To prepare raw ones, make a slit on side of shell, cover with water and boil for 15 minutes. Peel and remove paper-thin skin while warm.

3 cups boiled or canned chestnuts, drained
4 tablespoons (½ stick) butter, melted
¼ cup light cream or milk
½ cup finely broken saltine crackers
½ teaspoon salt
½ teaspoon coarsely ground white pepper

Preheat oven to 350°F.

Coarsely chop chestnuts in food processor or blender. Add all other ingredients and blend thoroughly. Pour into buttered 2-quart casserole and bake for 25 minutes or until it pulls away from sides of baking dish.

YIELD: 6 SERVINGS OR ENOUGH TO STUFF 10 TO 12 POUND TURKEY, 1 ROASTER CHICKEN, OR SEVERAL GAME HENS

RAISIN-PECAN STUFFING

4 tablespoons (½ stick) butter or margarine
1 cup chopped celery
1 cup chopped onion
6 cups fresh bread cubes
1 teaspoon salt
¼ teaspoon ground black pepper
1 teaspoon dried or fresh grated orange rind
1 cup raisins
1 cup broken pecans
½ cup chopped fresh parsley
½ cup white wine or apple juice

Preheat oven to 350°F.
Melt butter in large, heavy skillet and saute celery and onion over medium
heat until onion is clear, about 6 minutes. Add bread cubes, salt, pepper,
grated rind, raisins, pecans, parsley, and wine. Heat thoroughly, then pour
into buttered 2½-quart baking dish. Bake for 30 minutes or until golden
brown and pulls away from sides of baking dish.
YIELD: 6 SERVINGS, ABOUT 6 CUPS. ENOUGH TO STUFF SMALL TURKEY OR ROASTER
      CHICKEN, DUCK, OR SEVERAL GAME BIRDS.

DRIED FRUIT STUFFING

2 tablespoons (¼ stick) butter or margarine
1 cup chopped celery
½ cup chopped onion
1 teaspoon salt (optional)
1 teaspoon ground black pepper
1 teaspoon chopped fresh chervil
1 teaspoon chopped fresh parsley
1 cup chopped dried fruit
2 cups fresh bread crumbs
1⅓ cups apple wine or juice

Preheat oven to 350°F.
Melt butter in large, heavy skillet and saute celery and onion over medium
heat until clear, about 5 minutes. Add salt, pepper, chervil, parsley, dried
fruit, crumbs, and wine. Stir until blended thoroughly. Pour into buttered
2-quart baking dish and bake for about 30 minutes or until it pulls away from
sides of baking dish or pan.
YIELD: 4 SERVINGS, ABOUT 4 CUPS, OR ENOUGH TO STUFF A LARGE BIRD OR SEVERAL
      GAME HENS

 MOIST BREAD STUFFING

Whether you call it dressing, filling, or stuffing, this is the old stand-by.

6 cups fresh bread cubes, half brown bread, half white bread
3 large eggs, lightly beaten
Pinch of saffron threads
1 cup milk
½ cup chopped celery
⅓ cup chopped onion
1 teaspoon salt
½ teaspoon ground black pepper
4 tablespoons (½ stick) butter, melted

Preheat oven to 350°F.

Place bread cubes in large bowl. Pour beaten eggs over them. Crush saffron and sprinkle over bread. Add all other ingredients and toss gently as you would salad, not pressing cubes together. Spoon into greased baking pan or dish and bake for 30 to 35 minutes or until golden brown on top. This freezes well after baking and will keep at least 6 weeks if properly wrapped or covered.

YIELD: 6 SERVINGS, ENOUGH TO STUFF 10-POUND TURKEY, 2 PHEASANTS, 2 CHICKENS, OR
    4 GAME HENS.

 PECAN BREADING

This is an excellent breading for seafood or chicken. Make it ahead and store in an air-tight container in the refrigerator. It will keep for at least 4 weeks.

1 cup fresh bread crumbs
1 cup cornmeal
1 cup pecans

Place everything in food processor or blender and blend until pecans are finely ground. Store in refrigerator or freezer until needed.

YIELD: 3 CUPS

CHAPTER NINE

Breads, Biscuits, Buns, and Muffins

🪩 WHITE BREAD 🪩

Baking bread is one of the most satisfying and rewarding things you can do in the kitchen. It's fascinating to watch the rising, fun for children, and irresistible when taken from the oven. Better yet, the kitchen smells WONDERFUL!

2 packages dry granular yeast or 2 yeast cakes
¼ cup lukewarm water
Pinch of granulated sugar
2 cups milk, scalded
1½ tablespoons granulated sugar
2 teaspoons salt
3 tablespoons butter
2 large eggs, lightly beaten
7 cups sifted all-purpose flour
1 teaspoon butter

Preheat oven to 375°F.

Proof yeast by combining it with lukewarm water and pinch of sugar. If it foams, it is active and ready. Cool milk to lukewarm, place in large mixing bowl, and add sugar, salt, and butter. Slowly add yeast mixture, beaten eggs and about 2 cups of sifted flour. Cover with damp cloth and let rise until double, about 30 minutes, in warm, draft-free area. Then, punch down dough and add remaining flour, kneading until dough is smooth and elastic. Place in greased bowl and let rise again until double, about 30 minutes, in warm, draft-free place. Knead or punch down dough to remove all air bubbles. Cut into thirds and form into 3 loaves. Place loaves in greased 9 x 5 x 3-inch loaf pans. Cover and let rise again until double. Bake for 35 minutes. Loaves are fully baked when they sound hollow when tapped. Lightly butter tops, remove from pans immediately and serve warm or at room temperature. If freezing, place loaf in plastic bag while slightly warm to insure that it retains all its moisture when thawed.

YIELD: THREE 9 x 5 x 3-INCH LOAVES

🦚 OLD-FASHIONED OATMEAL BREAD 🦚

I receive letters from all over the country praising this bread recipe. A friend,
Blanche, shared this with me many years ago and it remains the best ever.

1¾ cups boiling water
1 cup rolled (quick-cooking) oats
5⅓ tablespoons (⅔ stick) butter or margarine
½ cup table molasses (golden, barrel, or King Syrup), do not use
    baking molasses
1 tablespoon salt
2 packages dry granular yeast or 2 yeast cakes
¼ cup lukewarm water
Pinch of granulated sugar
2 large eggs, lightly beaten
6 cups sifted all-purpose flour

Preheat oven to 375°F.

Combine boiling water, rolled oats, butter, molasses, and salt in large mixing
bowl. Cool to lukewarm. While cooling, proof yeast by adding it to lukewarm
water with sugar. If it foams, it is active. Add to lukewarm oat mixture
and blend well. Gradually stir in eggs and flour. Dough will be stickier than
regular bread dough. Pour into greased bowl, cover with damp cloth and
place in refrigerator for at least 2 hours or until needed. Remove chilled
dough and knead about 2 minutes to remove air bubbles. Divide into two and
shape into loaves on well-floured surface. Generously grease two 8½ x 4¼-
inch pans and sprinkle extra rolled oats around their bottoms and sides (extra
oats are optional but give bread special look). Place loaves into greased pans.
Cover with damp cloth and let rise in warm, draft-free place until double in
bulk, approximately 2 hours. Bake for 45 to 50 minutes or until done. Bread
should pull away from sides of pan. Remove from pans at once and serve
warm.
YIELD: TWO 8½ x 4½-INCH LOAVES

 POTATO BREAD

This bread is filled with nutrition and flavor.

2 packages dry granular yeast or 2 yeast cakes
¼ cup lukewarm water
Pinch of granulated sugar
2 cups cooked mashed potatoes (save the water they were cooked in)
1 cup potato water or lukewarm water
1 cup milk, scalded
1½ tablespoons salt (more or less as desired)
3 tablespoons butter
2 tablespoons light brown sugar
2 tablespoons granulated sugar
2 large eggs, lightly beaten
5½ to 6 cups sifted all-purpose flour
1½ tablespoons butter, melted

Preheat oven to 375°F.

Proof yeast by dissolving it in lukewarm water with pinch of sugar; if it foams, it is active. Combine mashed potatoes, potato water, milk, salt, butter, sugars, and beaten eggs in large mixing bowl. Stir in yeast mixture and 2 cups of flour. Knead on floured board or counter until smooth. Cover with damp cloth and place in warm, draft-free area until double in bulk, approximately 30 minutes. Punch down and add remaining flour. Knead until smooth and elastic. Put in well-greased bowl, turning dough so it is greased on both sides. Cover with damp cloth and let double again, approximately 30 minutes. Divide into three parts and form into loaves. Place loaves in 3 well-greased 8½ x 4½-inch loaf pans and bake for 45 to 50 minutes or until done. Bread should pull away from sides of pan and sound hollow when tapped with fingers. Brush tops of loaves with butter for soft, shiny look and remove from pans immediately.
YIELD: THREE 8½ x 4½-INCH LOAVES

CORNBREAD

My family often serves warm cornbread and fresh, pitted and sweetened sour cherries with milk or cream as a luncheon dish. When we bake it with floured fruit, we call it "corn-pone." So versatile, cornbread can be made in cake pans, muffin tins, or iron molds resembling ears of corn. After one day, cornbread makes an excellent stuffing, or when dried, crumbs are very flavorful for topping vegetables.

1½ cups cornmeal
1 cup all-purpose flour
¼ cup lightly packed light brown sugar
1 teaspoon salt
2 teaspoons baking soda
¼ pound (1 stick) butter, or half butter and half margarine, melted
2 large eggs, lightly beaten
1 cup milk
½ cup sour cream

Preheat oven to 375°F.

Sift cornmeal, flour, brown sugar, salt, and baking soda together. Place butter and eggs in large mixing bowl. Alternately mix in flour mixture, milk, and sour cream, beating until just blended. Do not over beat. Pour into greased 9-inch square cake pan or molds. Bake for about 30 minutes or until toothpick, when inserted into thickest part of bread, comes out clean. Cool slightly before removing from pans. If using cast-iron molds, invert on cooling rack.

YIELD: 9-INCH SQUARE PAN, 18 MUFFINS, OR 24 GEMS FROM IRON MOLDS

Variation:

For cornbread cubes, cut cornbread into 1-inch squares
and place on cookie sheets. Bake in preheated 275°F
oven for about 12 minutes. These freeze well.

 BUTTERMILK BISCUITS

These biscuits are as light as feathers. If you do not have buttermilk,
add 1 tablespoon cider vinegar to 1 cup milk.

2 cups all-purpose flour
1 tablespoon granulated sugar
4 teaspoons baking powder
½ teaspoon salt
½ cup vegetable shortening
1 large egg, lightly beaten
⅔ cup buttermilk

Preheat oven to 400°F.

Sift flour, sugar, baking powder, and salt together in large mixing bowl. Cut in shortening with fork or pastry blender. Stir in egg and buttermilk, mixing thoroughly. Knead lightly on floured surface and pat or roll to about ¾-inch thickness. Cut into desired shapes, flouring cutter each time after cutting. Place on an ungreased baking sheet and bake for 12 to 14 minutes or until golden brown. Serve warm.
YIELD: 16 BISCUITS

Variation:

Brush tops with melted butter and sprinkle with cinnamon sugar.

Cheese Biscuits:
Add 1 cup grated Cheddar to batter.

🦅 1-2-3-4 BISCUITS 🦅

My mother told me I could bake these as soon as I could count.
They are so easy and good, you'll try them, too.

2 cups all-purpose flour
4 teaspoons baking powder
½ teaspoon salt
3 tablespoons vegetable shortening
1 cup milk

Sift dry ingredients into large bowl. Cut shortening with pastry blender
or your hands until you have fine crumbs. Pour in milk and stir until well
blended. Turn dough onto floured surface, knead for one minute and roll or
pat to about ¾ inch thick. Cut with floured cutter and place on ungreased
baking sheet. Bake for 12 to 15 minutes or until lightly brown on top. Serve
warm. (Brush tops with butter if desired.)
YIELD: 16 BISCUITS

🦅 GRAHAM ICE BOX ROLL 🦅

A perfect dessert to make and store in refrigerator for "spur-of-the-moment" entertaining.

24 graham crackers (3-inch square)
1 cup coarsely chopped or broken nuts
1 cup chopped dates
¼ teaspoon salt
3 cups miniature marshmallows or 20 regular ones cut in small pieces
½ cup milk
1 cup Whipped Cream (page 213, optional)

Roll crackers between 2 sheets of wax paper to make fine crumbs (food
processor works well). Reason I use crackers instead of packaged crumbs
is because crumbs tend to be drier. Reserve about ⅓ of crumbs for coating
finished roll. Combine crumbs, nuts, dates, salt, and marshmallows in large
mixing bowl, moisten with milk and stir until blended. Form into roll about 3
to 3½ inches in diameter, packing firmly. Roll in reserved crumbs and wrap
tightly in plastic wrap. Chill in refrigerator for several hours or until needed.
To serve, cut into 1-inch slices and top with whipped cream.
YIELD: 6 TO 8 SERVINGS

 **MOTHER'S ICE BOX ROLLS**

Mother often served these instead of bread when she entertained. They're great!

1 package dry granular yeast or yeast cakes
2 tablespoons lukewarm water
Pinch of granulated sugar
1 cup boiling water
¼ cup granulated sugar
½ cup teaspoon salt (less if desired)
1 tablespoon vegetable shortening
1 large egg, lightly beaten
2½ cups all-purpose flour
1 tablespoon butter or vegetable shortening

Preheat oven to 400°F.

Proof yeast by dissolving it in lukewarm water and adding pinch of sugar. If it foams, it's active and ready. Mix boiling water with sugar, salt, and shortening in large mixing bowl. Let cool to lukewarm and add yeast mixture and beaten egg. Gradually stir in flour until well blended. Do not knead. Turn into large, greased bowl, cover with damp cloth and refrigerate overnight or for at least 4 hours. With buttered hands, mold dough into balls and place in greased muffin pans. Cover with damp cloth and let stand in warm, draft-free area until doubled, approximately 2 hours. Bake for 12 to 15 minutes. Brush tops with butter or shortening and remove from pans immediately. If freezing, place in heavy plastic bags and freeze while still warm.
YIELD: 15 TO 17 ROLLS

🦚 GRACE'S MUFFINS 🦚

*Grace Knepper of Somerset County, Pennsylvania, gave lots to her church
and community but she was best known for the food she prepared for family
and friends. These muffins were one of her favorites–the recipe was adapted
continuously to take advantage of the bounty of every season.*

2 cups sifted all-purpose flour
1 teaspoon salt
1 tablespoon granulated sugar
4 teaspoons baking powder
1 large egg, lightly beaten
1 cup milk or water
¼ cup vegetable shortening, melted

Preheat oven to 400°F.

Sift dry ingredients together and blend lightly with liquid and beaten egg. Fold
in melted shortening and stir until just blended, about 30 seconds. Do not
over blend. Fill well-greased muffin cups half full and bake for 20 minutes or
until lightly browned on top.
YIELD: 12 TO 16 REGULAR-SIZE MUFFINS OR 24 MINI MUFFINS

Variations:

Blueberry:
Add 1 scant cup of blueberries, washed, drained, and dredged in flour.
Sprinkle 1 tablespoon of sugar over berries if they are not sweet.
Cheese: Add 4 tablespoons grated Cheddar cheese and
dash of paprika. Top muffins with grated cheese.

Cranberry:
Add 1 cup cranberries, washed, stemmed, dredged in
2 tablespoons flour and 3 tablespoons granulated sugar.

Date:
Add ½ cup finely cut dates and 1 teaspoon vanilla extract.
Holiday: Add ½ cup mixed candied fruit, ¼ cup
currants, and ¼ cup chopped pecans.

🏮 BRAN MUFFINS 🏮

*These are popular everywhere and it seems each area has a special name
for them. Nevertheless, a cookbook shouldn't be without them.*

½ cup boiling water
½ cup 100% Natural Bran Cereal
¼ cup vegetable shortening
¾ cup granulated sugar
1 large egg, lightly beaten
1 cup buttermilk
1¼ cups unsifted all-purpose flour
1¼ teaspoons baking soda
¼ teaspoon salt
1 cup All Bran

Preheat oven to 400°F.

Pour boiling water over bran and let stand. In large mixing bowl, cream
shortening and sugar together. Add eggs, buttermilk, and then 100% Natural
Bran. Mix flour, soda, salt, and All Bran together in another large mixing
bowl. Next add 100% Natural Bran mixture all at once. Fold only until dry
ingredients are just moistened. Let stand for at least 30 minutes. Fill greased
muffin tins ⅔ full and bake for 15 to 20 minutes or until golden brown on top.
Bake only as many as you need for serving. Refrigerate the remainder of
batter and add your favorite extras. Batter keeps for weeks if tightly covered.
YIELD: 15 MUFFINS

Variations:

Add ⅓ cup raisins, chopped nuts, or dried fruits to batter before baking.

🦅 STICKY BUNS 🦅

These are beautiful and dainty if made very small, but most people go wild when they get the chance to sink their teeth into a great big one! The Pennsylvania Dutch call these Schneckenhaus'ln (little snail houses) because they look like little snails.

1 recipe Basic Sweet Dough (page 242)
4 tablespoons (½ stick) melted butter or margarine
½ cup lightly packed light brown sugar
1½ teaspoons ground cinnamon
2 tablespoons granulated sugar
⅓ cup light corn syrup (I use Karo)
½ cup coarsely chopped English walnuts or pecans
½ cup seedless raisins

Preheat oven to 350°F.

Divide dough in half and roll out into rectangles about 13 x 9-inches. Combine melted butter, brown sugar, cinnamon, granulated sugar, and corn syrup. Spread over dough and sprinkle with chopped nuts and raisins or have one with nuts and other with raisins. Roll up jelly-roll fashion and cut into 1½ x 2-inch thick slices. Place on greased baking pan or sheet or in greased muffin cups. Cover and let rise in warm, draft-free place until almost double, about 30 minutes. Bake for 25 minutes or until golden brown. Turn upside down onto wax paper immediately after removing from oven. This gives syrup a chance to run around sides of buns.
YIELD: 12 LARGE, 18 MEDIUM-SIZE, OR 24 TINY BUNS

HOT CROSS BUNS

Historic Donegal Presbyterian Church, founded before 1721, serves a lovely breakfast after the East Sunrise Service. We all look forward to the tasty hot cross buns served with the traditional baked ham and eggs and all the trimmings. The congregation enjoys sharing this day with visitors, so if you are in the area, do make plans to join us at Donegal. You are always welcome.

1 teaspoon ground cinnamon
¼ teaspoon ground cloves
1 cup dried currants
½ cup finely cut candied citron
1 recipe Basic Sweet Dough (page 242)
1 large egg, lightly beaten
2 cups sifted confectioner's sugar
¼ cup milk
1 teaspoon vanilla extract
Pinch of salt

Preheat oven to 400°F.

Mix cinnamon, cloves, currants, and citron together until blended, add to dough. After first rising, shape dough into round buns and place them in two well-greased 13 x 9 x 2-inch pans. Cover lightly and let rise until double, about 45 minutes. Brush tops with beaten egg. Make cross on each bun with sharp knife. Bake for 20 minutes. While buns are baking, combine sugar, milk, vanilla, and salt until well blended. Remove buns to cooling rack and brush cross markings with confectioner's sugar mixture. Serve warm.
Yield: 36 buns

🎀 SOFT PRETZELS 🎀

Making your own pretzels is a real labor of love. It can also be an excuse for a party. Why not have a get-together and let guests twist their own? There are many legends about the pretzel but I like the one that claims they were a monk's gift to the children for learning their prayers. They really taste best when taken right from the oven, or at least kept warm until served. Salted or unsalted, they're enjoyed by most folks with a mustard or cheese spread for dipping.

½ cup water (105°F to 115°F)
1 package (1 tablespoon) dry yeast
1 cup milk
¼ cup honey or granulated sugar
4 tablespoons (½ stick) butter or vegetable shortening, at room
    temperature
1 large egg, separated
1 teaspoon salt
4½ to 5 cups all-purpose flour
8 cups water
8 tablespoons baking soda
¼ cup coarse salt (optional)

Preheat oven to 425°F.

Place warm water in small bowl and add yeast. Let stand for about 10 minutes until it foams. Sir until dissolved and pour into large mixing bowl. Add milk, honey, butter, egg yolk, and salt. Slowly add flour until dough is stiff enough to knead. Place on floured surface and knead by pressing heel of your hand into dough and rolling it over again and again for about 5 minutes. Cover with towel and let dough rise on board for one hour. Pinch off dough size of golf balls. Roll with palms of your hands into strips about 18 inches long and ½ inch thick. Twist each into shape and place on tray. Bring water and baking soda to boil in large stainless steel saucepan or kettle (baking soda will stain an aluminum pan) over high heat. Drop three pretzels at time into boiling water, making sure they do not touch each other, boiling for about ½ minute over high heat—be careful, they will become soggy if overcooked. Remove pretzels with slotted spoon and place them on greased cookie sheets. When all are cooked, lightly beat egg white and 1 tablespoon water together with fork. With pastry brush, cover top of each pretzel with egg white mixture. Sprinkle with small amount of coarse salt, if desired, and bake for 13 to 15 minutes or until golden brown. Remove from oven and cool slightly on baking racks or linen towels. For reheating, tent with foil and warm in preheated oven for 375°F oven for 6 minutes.

YIELD: 18 FOUR-INCH PRETZELS OR 24 THREE-INCH PRETZELS

CHAPTER TEN

Cobblers, Pies, Cakes, and Icings

 APRICOT COBBLER

This is the kind of fruit cobbler I make most often. My family used this recipe for the first sour cherries and followed through the year with every kind of fresh fruit in season. We always served it in bowls with plenty of fresh sweetened milk.

Fruit mixture:
½ to ¾ cup granulated sugar
1 tablespoon cornstarch
1 cup boiling water or canned fruit juice, such as apricot, peach, or
    pineapple
3 cups apricot halves (canned or fresh)
1 tablespoon butter
¼ tablespoon butter
¼ teaspoon ground cinnamon
⅛ teaspoon ground nutmeg

Pastry:
1 cup all-purpose flour
1 tablespoon granulated sugar
1½ teaspoons baking powder
½ teaspoon salt
3 tablespoons butter, melted
½ cup milk

Preheat oven to 400°F

Mix sugar and cornstarch and add to water or juice in large, heavy saucepan. Bring to a boil and simmer over medium heat 1 minute. Add fruit, butter, and spices, stirring until heated through, about 5 minutes. Pour into buttered 1½ -quart baking dish. Sift flour, sugar, baking powder, and salt in large mixing bowl. Beat in butter and milk until well blended. Spoon batter over fruit and bake for 30 minutes or until golden on top. Serve hot or warm.
YIELD: 4 TO 6 SERVINGS

 PEACH COBBLER

Use any fruit you choose, but this is the old-fashioned style cobbler.

Pastry:
3½ cups all-purpose flour
1 teaspoon salt
1 teaspoon baking powder
¼ pound (1 stick) butter or margarine
½ cup vegetable shortening
½ cup cold water

Fruit mixture:
8 peaches, or 4 cups, halved, pitted, peeled, and sliced ⅓ inch thick
⅛ teaspoon ground cinnamon
⅛ teaspoon ground nutmeg
½ cup granulated sugar
½ cup lightly packed light brown sugar
2 tablespoons (¼ stick) butter, melted

Preheat oven to 350°F.

Cut, flour, salt, baking powder, butter, and shortening in large mixing bowl until it forms fine crumbs. Add water gradually until dough is moistened and can be formed into ball. Roll out ⅛ inch thick enough to top the cobbler and set aside. Roll out rest of dough about ¼ inch thick and place on an ungreased cookie sheet. Cut it into 2-inch squares and bake for 8 to 10 minutes. Do not let them brown.

In a greased 9 x 13-inch cake pan or baking dish, place several squares of dough. Combine peaches with cinnamon, nutmeg, and sugars. Layer peaches and dough squares, ending with peaches. Dribble melted butter and top with unbaked crust. Slit or cut a design into crust to allow steam to escape. Bake for 1 hour or until filling bubbles around edges. Serve warm with milk, sweetened if desired.
YIELD: 4 TO 6 SERVINGS

Variation:

Use any type of fruit, peeled or unpeeled, with pits removed.

🐉 BASIC PIE DOUGH 🐉

*I like to make a large quantity of these crumbs. I only use the amount I need
for the day by adding the water and refrigerate the rest. Usually the amount
of crumbs you can hold in both hands together is enough for one crust. These
crumbs will keep in the refrigerator for at least 4 weeks if tightly covered.*

**½ cup fresh lard or vegetable shortening
4 tablespoons (½ stick) butter
¾ teaspoon salt
2½ cups all-purpose flour
About ⅓ cup ice water**

Preheat oven to 350°F.
Put shortening, butter, salt, and flour into a large bowl. Cut with pastry
blender or rub with your hands until they are fine crumbs. Carefully dribble
water evenly over crumbs with one hand while tossing crumbs lightly with
other hand. Use only enough water to hold dough together. As dough
becomes moist, gently press it to side of bowl. The less it is handled, the
flakier it will be. If you are using a food processor, add water cautiously,
watching for the moment it starts to form a ball. Generously flour board
or counter, making sure top and bottom of dough are floured. Pat edges of
dough before rolling (this will prevent an uneven crust when baking). Roll
out dough about ⅛ inch thick, moving rolling pin lightly until round crust is
about an inch larger than pie pan. Place dough in pan, cutting off any excess
dough. Crimp edges with your fingers or a pastry crimper.

If making patty shells, roll out dough into large rectangle. Use a 3-inch round
cutter to cut circles of pastry. Press each circle gently into a muffin cup.
Crimp the edges in your favorite fashion.

If making pastry squares, roll out dough onto large cookie sheet. Cut dough
with a crinkle cutter in form of squares or diamonds.

Keep pieces of excess dough in plastic wrap, keeping it moist until you are
ready to roll it out. Do not use dough over and over again or it will become
dry and tough.

To bake pie or patty shells, prick dough four or five times with a fork to
prevent it from shrinking while baking. Bake for approximately 10 minutes
for a prebaked shell or 20 minutes for a fully baked shell. If pastry puffs
during baking, gently press bubbles with back of a soup or serving spoon.
Before removing baked shells from oven, check for any trace of fat bubbles.
If you find any, bake a bit longer or until they disappear. Fully baked shells
must be dry, light golden, and flaky.

To bake pastry squares, set in oven until they puff and are golden brown.
They should be crisp and flaky.
YIELD: ENOUGH DOUGH FOR TWO 9-INCH PIE SHELLS, ONE DOUBLE CRUST OR 10 PATTY
    SHELLS.

BAKING POWDER CRUST

This crust is really flaky and great for meat pies or apple dumplings.

2½ cups all-purpose flour
2 tablespoons baking powder
1 teaspoon salt
4 tablespoons (½ stick) butter or margarine
¼ cup lard or vegetable shortening
1 cup milk

Blend flour, baking powder, salt, butter, and shortening with pastry blender or with hands. Gradually add milk until it forms a soft ball. Roll out a bit thicker than regular pie dough on well-floured board.

YIELD: ENOUGH DOUGH FOR TWO 9-INCH PIE CRUSTS OR TO COVER A 9 X 13-INCH BAKING DISH.

MILK PIE

This pie was always eaten as a snack because it was made with dough left over from making several pies. Some called it sugar pie, Johnny pie, or, I suppose, the name of any child enjoying it.

½ cup all-purpose flour
¾ cup granulated sugar (less if desired)
1 cup milk
½ cup half and half
1 unbaked 9-inch pie shell
1 tablespoon butter, melted
Several dashes of ground cinnamon and nutmeg

Preheat oven to 350°F.

Combine flour and sugar. Gradually whip in milk and cream until smooth. Pour into pie shell, dribble top with melted butter and sprinkle with cinnamon and nutmeg. Bake for about one hour, or until center is set and doesn't shake when pie is jiggled. Serve warm.

YIELD: ONE 9-INCH

AMISH VANILLA PIE

Abe's mother, Elizabeth, makes the best vanilla pies. Even though they are Mennonites, the recipe is still the same. It is one of the dessert favorites here at Groff's Farm Restaurant because it is lighter than shoo-fly pie–more like pecan pie without the nuts. While you're at it, make two–they freeze well.

**1 cup table molasses (golden, barrel, or King Syrup), do not use
    baking molasses**
½ cup granulated sugar
1 large egg, slightly beaten
2 tablespoons all-purpose flour
½ teaspoon salt
2 cups hot water
1 teaspoon vanilla extract
2 unbaked 9-inch pie shells

Crumb topping:
1 cup granulated sugar
¼ pound (1 stick) butter
2 cups all-purpose flour
½ teaspoon baking soda
½ teaspoon cream of tartar

Preheat oven to 375°F.

Combine molasses, sugar, egg, flour and salt in 1-quart saucepan and mix well. Gradually add hot water and cook over medium heat until thickened, about 6 minutes, stirring constantly. Remove from heat and add vanilla. Cool and pour into unbaked pie shells.

To make crumb topping, mix all ingredients in large bowl, cutting with pastry blender or rubbing by hand until mixture forms fine crumbs. Divide them in half, spreading evenly over each pie. Bake for 10 minutes. Then reduce heat to 350°F and bake about 30 minutes or until center doesn't shake when jiggled. Serve warm or at room temperature.
YIELD: TWO 9-INCH PIES.

🦎 CHOCOLATE CREAM PIE 🦎

Cream fillings are great because you can put some in a bowl to serve separately, and fill a baked shell with the other half.

½ **cup unsweetened cocoa**
½ **cup boiling water**
4 tablespoons (½ stick) butter, melted
1 cup granulated sugar
⅓ **cup cornstarch**
¼ **teaspoon salt**
3 cups milk, warmed
1 large egg, lightly beaten
1 teaspoon vanilla extract
2 baked 9-inch pie shells
Whipped Cream (page 213) or shaved milk or dark chocolate for
   topping

Stir cocoa into boiling water until it's a smooth paste. Stir about 3 tablespoons of melted butter into cocoa mixture. Combine sugar, cornstarch, and salt in 2-quart saucepan. Slowly add warm milk and stir until blended. Add cocoa mixture and beaten egg. Cook over medium-low heat, stirring constantly until thick but not boiling. Remove and add rest of melted butter and vanilla. Pour into baked pie shells. When cool, pipe edge with whipped cream or top with shaved chocolate.

YIELD: TWO 9-INCH PIES OR 5 CUPS

🦎

Variation:

Chocolate Pudding:
Follow the above recipe but use ¼ cup cornstarch. When done, pour into dish and top with whipped cream or shaved chocolate.

APPLE PIE

There are so many ways to serve apple pie that I'll leave it up to your own creative mind. We enjoy deep-dish apple pie with milk as a summer meal, but who could refuse a piece of apple pie with coffee in the morning? It sure beats eating filled doughnuts for breakfast.

Unbaked top and bottom crust for 9-inch pie (page 181)
½ cup granulated sugar
3 tablespoons all-purpose flour
⅓ teaspoon salt
½ teaspoon ground cinnamon
¼ teaspoon ground nutmeg
3½ to 4 cups sliced tart apples (Stayman, Granny, or Smokehouse),
      cored, peeled, and sliced
½ teaspoon grated lemon rind
1 tablespoon fresh lemon juice
½ cup sour cream or milk
2 tablespoons (¼ stick) butter, melted

Preheat oven to 350°F.

Roll out bottom pie crust, fit into a 9-inch pie pan, and trim edges without crimping. Put in oven for 5 minutes or until dough puffs (do not fully bake!) to prevent a soggy crust. Remove from oven immediately. Combine sugar, flour, salt, cinnamon, and nutmeg and toss with sliced apples. Add lemon rind, lemon juice, and sour cream, stirring until well blended. Pour into shell, roll out top crust, and slit it with your own design to let steam escape. Moisten edges of bottom crust with milk or water. Place top crust over pie and crimp edges together to seal. Bake for 50 minutes. Increase heat to 375°F and let bake another 10 minutes or until golden on top. Some of juice should bubble through slits and around edges. Serve warm or cold.
Yield: One 9-inch pie.

🦢 LEMON MERINGUE PIE 🦢

This is my favorite pie. As a child I really thought the meringue was magic, as it always had a few drops of gold on top, formed by the sugar melting when baked in the meringue. Later I found out it was caused by the pie "weeping" and considered undesirable by professional bakers. You couldn't make me believe that, because I liked it when a bit of the sticky meringue would stick to the tip of my nose as I was eating a big, high piece of pie.

¼ **cup cornstarch**
2 cups water
1 cup granulated sugar
3 large eggs, separated
Grated rind and juice of 2 lemons
1 tablespoon butter
¼ **teaspoon salt**
1 baked 9-inch pie shell
1 recipe Great Meringue (page 213)

Dissolve cornstarch in ½ cup of water. Pour rest of water into top of double boiler and bring to a boil over boiling water. Add dissolved cornstarch and sugar, bring to a boil, and cook over medium heat until thickened, about 10 minutes, stirring constantly. Beat egg yolks lightly with fork, add in several tablespoons of cornstarch mixture, and beat until well blended. Then add beaten eggs to cornstarch mixture and cook together over medium heat for 2 minutes. Remove from heat and add lemon rind and juice, butter, and salt, blending well. Cool to lukewarm while making meringue and pour into baked pie shell. Spread meringue evenly over filling, touching all around edges. Swirl and peak with back of spoon. Place on middle rack under preheated boiler and broil for a few seconds, only enough to brown the peaks a light gold. Let cool to room temperature.

YIELD: ONE 9-INCH PIE

 **BANANA CREAM PIE**

*Abe can make one of these pies disappear in the blink of an eye–I guess
that's why our grandsons call the dessert cart "Pop's Cart."*

2 cups milk
⅔ cup granulated sugar
½ teaspoon salt
3 tablespoons cornstarch
3 large eggs, separated
1½ tablespoons butter
1 teaspoon vanilla extract
1½ cups sliced bananas
1 tablespoon fresh lemon juice
1 baked 9-inch pie shell
1 recipe Great Meringue (page 213)

Scald 1½ cups of milk on top of double boiler over simmering but not boiling
water. Combine sugar, salt, and cornstarch with remaining milk and stir
until dissolved. Add this to hot milk and bring to a boil over boiling water;
lower heat to medium and cook until thickened. Beat egg yolks lightly with
fork, then add several tablespoons of milk mixture and beat into yolks until
well blended. Add eggs to milk mixture and cook together over medium heat
for 2 minutes. Remove from heat and stir in butter and vanilla. Toss sliced
bananas with lemon juice to keep them from getting brown. Spread thin layer
of filling in bottom of pie shell, then sliced bananas. Top with rest of filling
and let cool while making meringue. Top with meringue and slip under a
preheated boiler until gold. Let cool and enjoy!
YIELD: ONE 9-INCH PIE

Variation:

Coconut Cream Pie:
Follow the above recipe but omit lemon juice and bananas. Use
1¼ cup shredded coconut instead, folding it in with butter and vanilla.

🦚 MONTGOMERY PIE 🦚

Historic Donegal Presbyterian Church could not have their traditional
"Donegal Day" without serving this pie. Now that Abe and I are members
of Donegal, we're often asked to bring some of them for the picnic. It's similar
to shoo-fly pie, but with a gooey lemon bottom and white cake top.

2 unbaked 9-inch pie shells

Bottom:
Grated rind and juice of 1 lemon
½ cup granulated sugar
½ cup table molasses (golden, barrel, or King Syrup), do not use
   baking molasses
1 large egg, lightly beaten
1 tablespoon all-purpose flour
1 cup boiling water

Top:
1 cup granulated sugar
¼ cup vegetable shortening
1 large egg
1½ cups all-purpose flour
2 teaspoons baking powder
½ teaspoon salt
½ cup milk

Preheat oven to 350°F.

Combine all ingredients for bottom part of pies in 1-quart saucepan and bring
to boil over medium heat, stirring until thickened, about 10 minutes. Cool
a bit, then pour into pie shells. For top part, cream sugar and shortening in
large mixing bowl until fluffy. Add egg and beat thoroughly. Sift flour, baking
powder, and salt in medium-size bowl and add to egg batter alternately with
milk until well blended. Spoon batter evenly over lemon filling and bake for
45 minutes or until center does not shake when pie is juggled. Serve warm or
at room temperature.
YIELD: TWO 9-INCH PIES

RAISIN PIE

Known as "funeral pie" because it was always served to the mourning family and friends after the church service, it most often was made with a latticed top or crumb topping which I thought was too sweet. This recipe is more like a custard, a bit tart and wonderful with a dollop of whipped cream.

1 cup red wine (white will do)
1½ cups seedless raisins
4 tablespoons (½ stick) butter
¾ cup granulated sugar (less if desired)
3 large eggs, lightly beaten
1 teaspoon grated lemon rind
1 tablespoon fresh lemon juice
¼ teaspoon salt
1 teaspoon vanilla extract
1 unbaked 9-inch pie shell

In saucepan, heat wine, then add raisins and let them soak until plump. Cream butter and sugar in mixing bowl. Beat in eggs, lemon rind and juice, salt, and vanilla. Batter may look a bit curdled, but don't worry. Add raisins and wine, mixing well. Puff unbaked pie shell by placing it in oven as you are preheating it to 325°F for approximately 6 minutes. As soon as it puffs, remove it (this will keep crust from getting soggy) and pour batter in. Bake in preheated oven for 50 minutes or until filling is set. Cool before serving, room temperature is best.

YIELD: ONE 9-INCH PIE

 CHERRY CRUMB PIE

Everyone loves our crumb pies and this one is no exception.

1 cup granulated sugar, less if desired
3 tablespoons arrowroot or cornstarch
½ cup water or liquid from canned cherries
1 teaspoon fresh lemon juice
½ teaspoon ground cinnamon
2½ cups pitted cherries, fresh, frozen or canned
1 unbaked 9-inch pie shell (puffed in the oven for a few minutes; see
**   page 181)**
1½ tablespoons butter, melted
½ recipe Crumb Topping (page 212)

Preheat oven to 350°F.

Combine sugar, arrowroot, and water in saucepan, stirring until dissolved.
Bring to a boil and stir over medium heat until slightly thickened, about
3 minutes. Remove from heat and add lemon juice, cinnamon, and cherries.
Pour into pie shell and dribble top with melted butter. Sprinkle filling with
crumb topping and bake for 45 to 50 minutes or until juice starts to bubble
through topping.
YIELD: ONE 9-INCH PIE

Variation:

Blueberry Crumb Pie:
Substitute blueberries for cherries and add ½ teaspoon ground nutmeg.

🐉 MINCEMEAT PIE 🐉

My family had mince pie fall, winter, and spring. We ate it hot for dessert and cold for breakfast. It makes sense to enjoy this as a snack, too, for it is very nutritious. I took the flavor for granted until I tried over people's mincemeat. This is mincemeat with lots of beef. You also must realize that the plain people do not believe in drinking socially, but many of them use liquor in cooking certain important dishes. It really isn't as good without the spirits. Also, making sure you use light table molasses, not baking molasses. Baking molasses is dark, nearly black, and has a strong sulphur taste. Mincemeat freezes well, so it's best to make a lot at a time.

To make a mincemeat pie:
Pastry for two 9-inch crusts (page 181)
2½ cups mincemeat
½ cup red wine or whiskey

Preheat oven to 350°F.

Fill unbaked crust with mincemeat, pour wine over it, and top with crust. Seal, slit vents in top crust, and bake for 45 minutes or until juice bubbles out of slits on top.

Mincemeat:
2½ pounds lean ground beef
4 cups dried apples, soaked in 3 cups water overnight
2½ pounds fresh apples (Stayman, Winesap, Smokehouse, or
   Jonathan), peeled, cored, and quartered
2 lemons, quartered and seeded
½ pound raisins
½ pound currants, or more raisins if unavailable
1½ cups lightly packed light brown sugar
2 cups table molasses (golden, barrel, or King Syrup), do not use
   baking molasses
½ cup cider vinegar
1½ cups heavy red wine
½ teaspoon ground cinnamon
½ teaspoon freshly grated nutmeg
½ teaspoon ground cloves
¼ teaspoon ground mace

Cook meat in large, heavy skillet over medium heat, break it up with wooden spoon, until all traces of pink are gone, but before it begins to brown. Drain off fat. Coarsely chop soaked apples, fresh apples, and lemons, rind and all, in a food processor or grinder. In large stock pot combine all ingredients and bring to a boil. Simmer for at least 30 minutes over low heat, stirring occasionally to prevent sticking. It should be the consistency of thick chutney. If you are canning some of this, ladle into hot, sterilized jars and seal immediately with new lids and seals. If you are freezing it, cool first then freeze.

🦋 SHOO-FLY PIE 🦋

This has got to be the best-known pie of the Pennsylvania Dutch.

1 9-inch unbaked pie shell

Crumb Topping:
1 cup unsifted flour
½ cup lightly packed light brown sugar
¼ cup vegetable shortening

Liquid Bottom:
1 teaspoon baking soda
1 cup boiling water
1 cup golden table molasses
¼ teaspoon salt

Preheat oven to 350°F.

Put unbaked pie shell in oven for about 5 minutes to prevent the bottom from getting soggy. Combine topping ingredients in bowl and cut together with pastry blender or rub with fingers until mixture forms fine crumbs. Set aside. Dissolve baking soda in water in large mixing bowl. Add molasses and salt and blend well. Pour this into pie shell and sprinkle evenly with crumb topping. Bake in preheated 375°F oven for 10 minutes, then reduce the temperature to 350°F and bake for another 30 minutes, or until set (when pie is given a gentle shake, the top remains firm). Serve warm with whipped cream or ice cream.

YIELD: ONE 9-INCH PIE

 # PUMPKIN CHIFFON PIE

This is a very light and mild-flavored pumpkin pie.

1 unbaked 10-inch pie shell
1¼ cups cooked pumpkin, drained
3 large eggs, separated
¾ cup lightly packed light brown sugar
1 tablespoon cornstarch
½ teaspoon salt
⅛ teaspoon ground ginger
⅛ teaspoon ground cloves
¼ teaspoon freshly grated nutmeg
¾ teaspoon ground cinnamon
1¼ cups milk, scalded
¼ cup granulated sugar

Put unbaked pie shell in preheated 350°F oven for 5 minutes or until dough puffs (do not fully bake it!) to prevent a soggy crust. Remove from oven immediately. Put pumpkin in large mixing bowl. Beat in egg yolks, brown sugar, cornstarch, salt, and spices. Gradually stir in scalded milk, mixing until blended. Whip egg whites with sugar in large mixing bowl until stiff then fold into pumpkin mixture. Pour into pie shell and bake in preheated 400°F oven for 10 minutes. Reduce heat to 350°F and continue baking 35 to 40 minutes longer or until center does not shake when pie is jiggled. Cool and serve with ice cream or whipped cream.

Yield: One 10-inch pie

 GOLD CAKE

*I often thought my mother made angel food cakes because we used yolks for noodles,
but looking back, I know she loved to bake and we loved to eat all her cakes,
especially her gold cake. Frosted with Sea Foam Frosting (page 210), it seems
light. When frosted with chocolate or caramel icing, it is especially rich.*

**8 tablespoons (1 stick) butter or half margarine and half vegetable
shortening
1½ cups granulated sugar
8 large egg yolks
2¼ cups cake flour
3 teaspoons baking powder
½ teaspoon salt
1 cup milk
½ teaspoon lemon extract
½ teaspoon vanilla extract
Frosting of your choice (see Index)**

Cream butter and sugar together in large mixing bowl until light and fluffy.
Add yolks and beat thoroughly. Sift flour, baking powder, and salt onto a
plate or sheet of wax paper. Return to sifter and sift again. Gradually add
flour mixture and milk alternately to egg batter and blend until smooth. Stir
in extracts and pour batter into two greased and floured 9-inch cake pans.
Bake for 25 to 30 minutes or until a toothpick inserted in middle of cake
comes out clean. Cool a few minutes before inverting on cooling racks. Frost
with your favorite frosting.
YIELD: TWO 9-INCH LAYERS OR ONE 9 X 13-INCH CAKE

Variation:

Orange or Mandarin Orange Cake:
Follow above recipe, using 2 teaspoons baking powder and
1 teaspoon baking soda and substituting ½ cup of orange juice
for the milk and ½ teaspoon grated orange rind for the vanilla
extract. Frost with: Orange Cream Frosting (see page 211).

CRUMB CAKE

To most folks, this would seem to be a coffee cake. To the Pennsylvania Dutch it is a dessert, served right from the oven with canned or poached peaches, pears, or apricots. The fruit is served on the side and the juice is poured over the cake–Wow!

4 cups all-purpose flour
12 tablespoons (1½ sticks) butter or vegetable shortening
2½ cups lightly packed light brown sugar
1 teaspoon ground cinnamon
1 teaspoon ground cloves
2 teaspoons baking soda
1½ cups buttermilk

Preheat oven to 350°F.

Blend flour, butter, sugar, and spices with a pastry blender or your hands in a large mixing bowl until it makes fine crumbs. Reserve 1½ cups of crumbs for topping. Dissolve soda in buttermilk and mix with remaining crumbs until well blended. Pour into 2 greased 9-inch cake pans or one 9 x 11-inch pan and top with reserved crumbs. Bake for 35 to 40 minutes. Do not overbake but it should not shake in the middle when jiggled. Remove and serve warm right from pan.

YIELD: TWO 9-INCH ROUND CAKES OR ONE 9 x 11-INCH CAKE

🦅 SAFFRON CAKE 🦅

Thelma and Bill Smith are special friends. Bill makes the nicest cookie cutters and Thelma gave me this recipe. She writes it this way: "We lived in a town that was mostly English and Welsh. The tradition at Christmas was to have and visit friends, neighbors, and relatives. Each visit you always served tea, cookies, and the special treat, Saffron Cake. At Christmas time the druggist would make sure he had plenty of saffron because at that time saffron was sold by weight. Today I can only buy saffron at one food store in our area (Wind Gap, Pa.) and believe it or not, Betty, I must go to the office and they have it in their safe. I also must depend on the spice company to put up enough to make it a delicious cake."

2 cups granulated sugar
½ pound (2 sticks) butter, at room temperature
3 large eggs, lightly beaten
2 tablespoons grated lemon rind
1 tablespoon baking powder
½ teaspoon salt
3 cups all-purpose flour
½ dram of saffron threads steeped in 1 scant cup of boiling water for 30 minutes
1 cup raisins
1 cup currants (If currants are not available, substitute white raisins.)

Preheat oven to 350°F.

In large mixing bowl, cream sugar and butter together until light and fluffy. Slowly add eggs until well blended. Add lemon rind. Sift baking powder, salt, and flour. Mix flour and saffron water alternately into creamed mixture until thoroughly combined. Fold in raisins and currants. Pour into two greased 9 x 5 x 2¾-inch loaf pans. Bake for 25 minutes. Reduce heat to 325°F and bake another 25 minutes or until skewer comes out clean when inserted into middle of cake. Cool and store in cool place, wrapped in wax paper, until ready to serve. Slice in very thin slices as this is a very flavorful cake.

YIELD: TWO 9 x 5 x 2¾-INCH LOAVES

 COCONUT CAKE

*This is the cake we looked forward to enjoying especially at
Easter. Grandma loved her sweets and so did we.*

**5⅓ tablespoons (⅔ stick) butter
⅓ cup vegetable shortening
1 cup granulated sugar
3 large eggs, separated
2½ cups sifted cake flour
2¼ teaspoons baking powder
½ teaspoon salt
⅓ cup milk
1 teaspoon vanilla extract
Boiled Frosting (page 210)
1½ cups shredded coconut**

Preheat oven to 375°F.

Cream butter and shortening in large mixing bowl. Gradually beat in sugar,
creaming until very light. Add egg yolks one by one, beating well after each
addition. In another bowl, sift flour, baking powder, and salt three times.
Alternately blend dry ingredients and milk into creamed mixture. Beat until
smooth, then add vanilla. Beat egg whites until stiff but not dry, then fold
them into cake batter, blending but not beating. Pour batter into two greased,
floured 9-inch layer cake pans and bake for approximately 30 minutes or until
a toothpick inserted into cake's center comes out clean. Remove and cool
a few minutes. Invert on racks until completely cooled. Cut each layer in
half horizontally and frost, generously adding coconut on top of each layer of
icing, making sure you have plenty of coconut for outside of cake.
YIELD: TWO 9-INCH ROUND LAYERS

🎴 MORAVIAN SUGAR CAKE 🎴

Well-kept secret recipes must be shared before they're lost. Thanks to several ladies of the church, this recipe has been saved for the enjoyment of future generations and those who may never have the opportunity to visit Bethlehem or Lititz, where it is traditional.

1 cup cooked mashed potatoes (save ¼ cup of the water the potatoes were cooked in)
1 cup granulated sugar
1 package active yeast
¼ pound (1 stick) butter
¼ cup lard or vegetable shortening
1 teaspoon salt
2 large eggs, lightly beaten
5 to 5½ cups sifted all-purpose flour

For the holes:
4 tablespoons (½ stick) butter
1 cup light brown sugar (do not pack down when measuring)

Preheat oven to 350°F.

If you start with raw potatoes, dice 3 medium potatoes and cook in just enough water to cover over medium heat until soft. Drain, reserving ¼ cup of water, and mash until lumps disappear. Add sugar to potatoes and beat until fluffy. Dissolve yeast in lukewarm potato water. To be sure yeast is active, add a pinch of sugar; if it foams, the yeast is good.

Slowly cream butter, lard, salt, eggs, yeast, and potato water until well blended. Gradually add flour, kneading with dough hook of a mixer, until dough is smooth and elastic. If kneading by hand, work dough by pressing down with the heel of your hand, pushing dough back and forth, folding it, and pressing it again and again until all air bubbles are removed and dough is smooth and elastic. It should pull away from sides of bowl and look like satin, it should not look dry. Turn dough into greased bowl, turning it so all sides are greased. Cover with a clean, damp cloth and let rise in warm, draft-free area until doubled in size. Knead for a minute, then divide evenly between four greased 6½ x 10-inch pans. Cover with same cloth and let rise again for one hour. Break butter into tiny pieces and punch them into cakes in rows with your fingertips. Press brown sugar into same holes, sprinkling remainder over tops. Bake for 20 to 25 minutes or until golden brown and crusty on top and cake pulls away from sides of pan. Serve warm.
YIELD: FOUR 6½ x 10-INCH CAKES

SHELLBARK (HICKORY NUT) CAKE

Shellbarks are so unique to this area that few people know how wonderful they are. Known as hickory nuts, these nuts are larger, the shell harder, than the small hickory variety. They grew wild, but the best varieties were nurtured by many who couldn't survive winter without them. Only folks that know their worth can find them in the farmers' market and are happy to pay the price.

4 large egg whites
¼ teaspoon cream of tartar
1 cup granulated sugar
5⅓ tablespoons (⅔ stick) butter or margarine
1¾ cups cake flour
½ teaspoon salt
3 teaspoons baking powder
½ cup milk
1 teaspoon vanilla extract
¼ cup all-purpose flour
½ cup chopped shellbarks (other nuts may be substituted)
Your favorite frosting, or dust with sifted confectioner's sugar
Extra shellbark halves for topping

Preheat oven to 350°F.

In large mixing bowl, beat egg whites until foamy, add cream of tartar, and beat until they start to form peaks. Gradually add ½ cup of sugar and beat until whites hold firm but not dry peaks. Set aside. Cream butter and remaining sugar until light in large mixing bowl. Sift 1½ cups flour, salt, and baking powder. Blend flour mixture and milk alternately with butter-sugar mixture. When thoroughly blended, add vanilla, then dredge nuts in remaining flour and add to batter, folding in gently. Fold in egg whites and pour batter into two greased and floured 8-inch cake pans. Bake for about 25 to 30 minutes. Insert toothpick in center of cake; if it comes out clean, it is done. Remove from oven and cool a few minutes before inverting on cooling racks. Frost with your favorite frosting, topping with extra nuts.
YIELD: TWO 8-INCH LAYER CAKES

Variation:

White Cake:
Use 1¾ cups cake flour and omit nuts. I recommend butter-cream frosting, chocolate, or cream cheese frosting.

❈ SPICE CAKE ❈

With Cream Cheese Frosting (page 214), this is hard to beat.

6 tablespoons vegetable shortening
6 tablespoons (¾ stick) margarine
¾ cup firmly packed light brown sugar
4 large eggs
2¼ cups cake flour
1 cup granulated sugar
1 teaspoon baking powder
1 teaspoon baking soda
½ teaspoon salt
½ teaspoon ground nutmeg
½ teaspoon ground cloves
1 teaspoon ground cinnamon
1 cup buttermilk or thick milk (add 1 tablespoon fresh lemon juice or
vinegar to whole milk)
1 teaspoon vanilla extract
Frosting or confectioner's sugar

Preheat oven to 350°F.

Cream shortening, margarine, and brown sugar in large mixing bowl. Beat until light and fluffy. Gradually add eggs and beat until light and smooth. Sift flour and sugar, baking powder, baking soda, salt, and spices. Add gradually, alternately with buttermilk to creamed mixture until well blended. Add vanilla, blend, and pour into one 9 x 13-inch or two 9-inch round greased and floured cake pans. Bake for 30 to 35 minutes for 2 pans or 40 to 45 minutes for one large pan. Cake is done when a toothpick, inserted in the middle of cake, comes out clean. Frost with your favorite frosting or sift confectioner's sugar over top.

YIELD: ONE 9 x 13-INCH CAKE OR TWO 9-INCH ROUND LAYERS

 BUTTER SPONGE CAKE

*Because it is so light, this cake is perfect for use as a shortcake with fresh
fruit. It is also great when iced with Caramel Icing (page 212).*

4 large eggs
1½ cups granulated sugar
1½ cups all-purpose flour
1 teaspoon baking powder
Pinch of salt
⅔ cup milk
2 tablespoons (¼ stick) butter
1 teaspoon vanilla extract

Preheat oven to 350°F.

Cream eggs and sugar in large mixing bowl until light and foamy. Sift flour,
baking powder, and salt in another bowl. In small saucepan, heat milk and
butter. Alternately mix hot milk and butter and sifted flour into creamed
mixture. Add vanilla and mix until well blended. Pour batter into greased
and floured 9 x 13-inch cake pan and bake for 45 minutes or until a toothpick
inserted into center of cake comes out clean. Remove from oven and cool a
few minutes before inverting onto rack.

YIELD: ONE 9 x 13-INCH CAKE OR TWO 8-INCH ROUND LAYERS

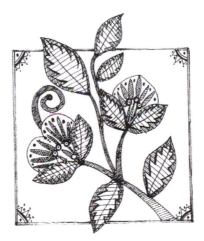

🦋 FLAME CAKE 🦋

Today this cake is known as red velvet, but years ago, it was called flame cake. No matter what name we give it, everyone loves it.

½ cup vegetable shortening
1½ cups granulated sugar
2 large eggs
1 teaspoon salt
1 teaspoon vanilla extract
2 teaspoons unsweetened cocoa
¼ cup red food coloring
1 teaspoon baking soda
1 teaspoon cider vinegar
2¼ cups flour, sifted
1 cup buttermilk
1 recipe Butter Frosting (page 209) or Cream Cheese Frosting (page 214)

Preheat oven to 350°F.

Cream shortening, sugar, and eggs in mixing bowl until fluffy. Blend in salt and vanilla. Slowly add cocoa and food coloring, mixing until well blended. Dissolve baking soda in vinegar, add to cake mixture. Alternately blend flour and buttermilk into cake mixture, beating until thoroughly mixed. Pour batter into greased 8½ x 11-inch cake pan and bake for 25 to 30 minutes or until a toothpick inserted in center of cake comes out clean. Remove from oven and let cool in pan for a few minutes before turning it onto cooling rack. If you are planning on icing cake and serving in pan, there is no need to invert. Ice with traditional butter frosting or cream cheese frosting.
YIELD: ONE 8½ X 11-INCH CAKE OR TWO 8-INCH ROUND LAYERS

 GINGERBREAD CAKE

I love this cake right from the oven with a nice lemon-rum sauce or warm Applesauce (see page 61).

6 tablespoons (¾ stick) butter or margarine
6 tablespoons vegetable shortening
1 cup lightly packed light brown sugar
3 large eggs, lightly beaten
**1 cup buttermilk or thick milk (add 1 tablespoon lemon juice or
 vinegar to whole milk)**
1 teaspoon salt
1 teaspoon baking soda
1 teaspoon ground cinnamon
1 teaspoon ground ginger
1 teaspoon ground nutmeg
3 cups all-purpose flour
**1 cup table molasses (golden, barrel, or King Syrup), do not use
 baking molasses**

Preheat oven to 350°F.

Cream butter and shortening and brown sugar in large mixing bowl until fluffy. Gradually add eggs and buttermilk, beating until well blended. Sift salt, soda, spices, and flour and add alternately with molasses to egg mixture. When batter is smooth, pour it into greased and floured 9 x 13-inch cake pan and bake for 50 minutes or until a toothpick, when inserted in center of cake, comes out clean. Let cool in pan, cutting into large squares for serving.
YIELD: ONE 9 x 13-INCH CAKE

🌿 LEMON CHIFFON CAKE 🌿

This is a great cake to serve plain with fresh fruit. For cooler weather,
serve this cake with a Lemon-Lime Sauce (see page 157).

2¼ cups sifted cake flour
1½ cups granulated sugar
1 tablespoon baking powder
1 teaspoon salt
½ cup vegetable oil
5 large eggs, separated
⅔ cup cold water
2 teaspoons vanilla extract
1 tablespoon fresh lemon juice
Grated rind of 1 lemon
½ teaspoon cream of tartar
Confectioner's sugar

Preheat oven to 375°F.

Sift flour, sugar, baking powder, and salt in large mixing bowl. Make well in center of dry ingredients with wooden spoon. Add, in following order, oil, egg yolks, water, vanilla, lemon juice, and rind. Stir with spoon until batter is smooth. In another large mixing bowl, beat egg whites with cream of tartar until stiff peaks form. Pour batter over egg whites in gentle stream, then fold in very gently with rubber spatula. Pour batter into ungreased, footed 10-inch tube pan 4 inches deep. Take a table knife and, starting center, by tube, cut several circles in batter around pan until you reach outer edge. This will puncture air bubbles and prevent holes in finished cake. Bake on middle rack for 55 minutes, then lower the temperature to 350°F and bake 12 minutes longer. Turn cake pan upside down to cool, but do not remove cake from pan for at least 1 hour. If pan does not have feet, place center tube over a funnel or catsup bottle. Dust top of cake with confectioner's sugar before serving.

YIELD: ONE 10-INCH CAKE

 PLUM-CHEESE SQUARES

Very rich, tart, and crunchy, these squares are perfect for dessert or tea.

For the pastry:
1½ cups all-purpose flour
½ cup granulated sugar
1 teaspoon salt
½ pound (2 sticks) butter or margarine
2 large egg yolks or 1 whole egg
1 teaspoon cider vinegar
¼ cup water

For the plum-cheese filling:
4 cups pitted plums
1 cup granulated sugar
½ teaspoon ground cinnamon
½ teaspoon ground nutmeg
8 ounces cream cheese, at room temperature
3 large eggs, lightly beaten
¾ cup sour cream
1 teaspoon vanilla extract
1 teaspoon fresh lemon juice
1 teaspoon grated lemon rind

Preheat oven to 350°F.

If you are using a food processor for pastry, combine all ingredients and pulse in processor until it forms a ball in bowl. Press gently into 9 x 13-inch cake pan. To make by hand, combine flour, sugar, and salt in large mixing bowl. Cut in butter with pastry blender or rub dry ingredients and butter with your hands until they form fine crumbs. Combine yolks, vinegar, and water in another bowl and gradually add to crumbs, tossing them lightly until fully moist. Press evenly into pan. Bake for 15 minutes. Cool a few minutes, then add plums. Combine ⅓ cup of sugar, cinnamon, and nutmeg in small bowl and sprinkle over plums. Bake another 15 minutes. Meanwhile, beat cream cheese, eggs, sour cream, the remaining sugar, vanilla, and lemon juice and rind in large mixing bowl until smooth and creamy. Pour cheese mixture over plums and bake 40 to 50 minutes longer. The cake is done when the center does not shake when pan is jiggled. Cut into small squares when cold.
YIELD: ONE 9 x 13-INCH CAKE

🦚 ANGEL FOOD CAKE 🦚

There seemed to be a contest among all our family bakers to see how high and fine-textured their angel food cakes could be. It has a lot to do with beating and blending of egg whites. When I gave this recipe to our son to make for the first time, he read it hurriedly; thinking 1 cup egg whites meant beaten, he used two egg whites and beat them until stiff, making one cup. Of course, the cake was one inch high and looked more like a torte shell. It also taught me the importance of writing precisely what I mean in recipes!

1 cup sifted cake flour
1 cup granulated sugar, less 1 tablespoon
1 cup egg whites (usually the whites of 10 large eggs), at room
temperature
¾ teaspoon cream of tartar
¼ teaspoon salt
1 teaspoon vanilla extract

Preheat oven to 375°F.

Sift flour and half the sugar together onto a plate or piece of wax paper. Gently pour it back into sifter and sift again. Place egg whites in large mixing bowl and whip until foamy, about 1 minute. Add cream of tartar and whip until they form moist, stiff peaks, about 4 minutes. The beaten egg whites should be very shiny and, when lifted, stand straight up. Using wire whip of mixer or a hand whisk, slowly fold in flour mixture alternately with rest of sugar, adding about 2 tablespoons at a time until it is all folded in. Scrape down sides of bowl, then add salt and vanilla, folding just until all traces of flour are gone. If you are folding in with a spatula or hand whisk, fold in slow circular motion—do not beat. Gently pour or spoon batter into ungreased 10-inch tube pan. Use a long knife to circle batter; starting in center, around tube, circle several times, ending at outside edge of pan to pop any large air bubbles. Place pan in middle rack of oven and bake for 40 to 45 minutes. Insert long wire or wooden skewer in center of cake; if it comes out clean cake is done. Remove and invert immediately. If pan does not have "feet", place center of pan over neck of a bottle or an upside-down funnel. Leave in pan until ready to frost. Frost with light icing or sprinkle with confectioner's sugar.

YIELD: ONE 10-INCH CAKE

 BLUEBERRY CAKE

This is a small cake; just enough for one meal, served with mounds of freshly picked berries.

½ cup vegetable shortening
1¼ cup granulated sugar
1 large egg
2½ cups all-purpose flour
2½ teaspoons baking powder
½ teaspoon salt
¾ cup milk
1¼ cups fresh blueberries

Preheat oven to 350°F.

Cream shortening and 1 cup of sugar in large mixing bowl. Add egg and beat well. Sift flour, baking powder, and salt in medium-size mixing bowl; reserve ½ cup to dredge blueberries. Alternately mix milk and flour mixture into creamed mixture gradually. Beat until batter is smooth. Dredge berries in remaining flour and fold into batter until all traces of flour are gone. Sprinkle top of batter with remaining ¼ cup sugar. Pour into greased and floured 9-inch square baking pan and bake for 40 to 45 minutes or until toothpick inserted in center comes out clean.

YIELD: ONE 9-INCH SQUARE CAKE.

BUTTERMILK CHOCOLATE CAKE

We've served this cake ever since we started serving meals in our home, now known as Groff's Farm Restaurant. We frost the cakes with butter cream or caramel icing and serve it in small pieces with cracker pudding at the beginning of the meal so everyone will make enough room for dessert later on.

2 cups lightly packed light brown sugar
8 tablespoons (1 stick) butter or half margarine or vegetable
    shortening
2 large eggs
¾ cup buttermilk
½ cup unsweetened cocoa
½ cup strong coffee, boiling hot
1 teaspoon baking soda
1 teaspoon cider vinegar
½ teaspoon salt
1 teaspoon vanilla extract
2½ cups sifted all-purpose flour

Preheat oven to 350°F.

Cream sugar and butter in large mixing bowl until fluffy. Add eggs one at a time, beat a minute, then add buttermilk. Put cocoa in small bowl and add coffee to it slowly, stirring constantly to prevent lumping. Add this to creamed mixture, beating until well blended. In small bowl, moisten baking soda with vinegar, add to creamed mixture. Stir in salt and vanilla. Gradually add flour, beating until smooth. Pour batter into greased and floured 9 x 13-inch cake pan. Bake for 45 minutes or until a toothpick, inserted in center of cake, comes out clean. Cool and frost with your favorite icing. I like caramel myself (see page 212).

YIELD: ONE 9x13-INCH CAKE OR TWO 9-INCH ROUND LAYERS

🦚 BUTTER FROSTING 🦚

*One of the quickest and easiest frostings, this can be prepared in minutes. It
keeps for a week or two in the refrigerator if it is tightly covered.*

3 tablespoons butter, at room temperature
1 tablespoon heavy cream
1½ cups confectioner's sugar
Pinch of salt
½ teaspoon vanilla extract

Cream all ingredients in large mixing bowl until light and fluffy. Spread on
cake.
YIELD: ENOUGH TO ICE ONE 9 X 13-INCH CAKE

Variations:

Add 1 ounce melted milk or dark chocolate or 1 tablespoon grated orange rind
and 1 tablespoon orange juice, omitting the vanilla, or 1 tablespoon grated
lemon rind and 1 tablespoon fresh lemon juice, again omitting the vanilla.

Hint:
This recipe should be doubled to frost a 3-layer 9-inch cake.

BOILED FROSTING
SEVEN-MINUTE ICING

Perfect, light, and airy, this is the one we used for coconut layer cakes.

1½ cups granulated sugar
½ cup water
⅛ teaspoon cream of tartar
2 large egg whites
½ teaspoon vanilla extract

Combine sugar, water, and cream of tartar in heavy saucepan. Stir, then bring to a boil over high heat without stirring again until it reaches 242°F on candy thermometer or spins a thread. Meanwhile beat egg whites in bowl until they hold soft peaks. Beat about 3 tablespoons of hot sugar syrup into whites until blended. Gradually add remainder of syrup, beating steadily until frosting stands in soft peaks, approximately 6 minutes. Add vanilla and continue to beat until stiff enough to frost cake. If frosting is too sugary, add a few drops of lemon juice.

YIELD: ENOUGH FROSTING FOR A TWO-LAYER CAKE

Variation:

Sea Foam Frosting:
Follow the above recipe, using ¾ cup granulated sugar and ¾ cup lightly packed light brown sugar instead of 1½ cups granulated sugar.

 MARSHMALLOW FROSTING

This is an excellent frosting for layer cakes.

1½ cups granulated sugar
½ cup water
1 cup marshmallows
3 large egg whites
Pinch of salt
¾ teaspoon vanilla extract

Combine sugar and water in heavy saucepan. Bring to a boil over high heat, not stirring, until syrup reaches 242°F on candy thermometer or spins a thread. Remove from heat and add marshmallows, stirring until melted. Beat egg whites until they form soft peaks, slowly pour syrup into whites, beating constantly until thoroughly blended. Add salt and vanilla and beat until cool enough to spread. Frost cake immediately.

YIELD: ENOUGH FROSTING FOR A TWO-LAYER CAKE

 ORANGE CREAM FROSTING

1 tablespoon grated orange rind
1 teaspoon grated lime or lemon rind
¼ cup fresh orange juice
1 tablespoon fresh lime or lemon juice
1 pound confectioner's sugar (about 3½ cups sifted)
4 tablespoons (½ stick) butter or margarine, at room temperature
1 large egg yolk
Pinch of salt

Combine orange and lime rinds with juices. Let stand while you sift confectioner's sugar. Cream butter until light and fluffy. Gradually add egg yolk and salt and blend thoroughly. Slowly add about one cup of sifted sugar, the rind and juice mixture, then slowly beat in remainder of sugar. When blended, beat vigorously until light and fluffy and easy to spread.

YIELD: ABOUT 2½ CUPS OR ENOUGH TO FROST A LARGE LAYER CAKE

CARAMEL ICING

This icing is especially good on chocolate cake but my mother always added milk to thin it enough to spread on her white layer cakes.

¼ pound (1 stick) butter
1 cup lightly packed light brown sugar
¼ cup evaporated milk
Pinch of salt
2 cups confectioner's sugar
½ teaspoon vanilla extract

Melt butter in saucepan, add brown sugar, and bring to a boil over medium heat. Reduce heat to medium-low for 2 minutes, stirring constantly. Remove from heat and add milk and salt. Return to stove and bring to a full boil over medium heat. Remove from heat and let cool until lukewarm. Gradually beat in confectioner's sugar and vanilla, beating until icing is thick enough to spread.

YIELD: ENOUGH ICING FOR A 13 X 9-INCH CAKE OR 2-LAYER CAKE. RECIPE SHOULD BE DOUBLED FOR A 3-LAYER 8-INCH CAKE.

BASIC CRUMB TOPPING

Make a lot of these crumbs (they're great for fruit pies, especially blueberry and cherry) and refrigerate them in an airtight container. It saves a lot of time later and they'll keep for at least 4 weeks.

3 cups all-purpose flour or 2 cups flour and 1 cup fresh bread crumbs
12 tablespoons (1½ sticks) butter or margarine, at room temperature
½ cup granulated sugar
½ teaspoon salt

Cut all ingredients with a pastry blender, by hand, or with a food processor until crumbs are very fine. Sprinkle evenly, ½ inch thick, over top of pie filling before baking.

YIELD: ENOUGH FOR FOUR 9-INCH PIES

WHIPPED CREAM

*It doesn't take long to whip cream if the bowl and beaters are
thoroughly chilled in the freezer before you start.*

1 cup heavy cream
2 tablespoons granulated sugar
½ teaspoon vanilla extract

Pour cream into large, chilled mixing bowl. Beat with electric mixer on
medium-high speed until it forms soft peaks, about 2 minutes. Gradually add
sugar and vanilla and continue beating until it forms firm peaks.
YIELD: 2 CUPS

Variation:

Maple Whipped Cream:
Add ¼ cup pure maple syrup to cream and omit sugar and vanilla.

Spiced Whipped Cream:
Place 1 teaspoon curry powder and ½ teaspoon ground nutmeg in small
skillet or saucepan and heat over low heat, stirring constantly with wooden
spoon until slightly dark, about 2 minutes. Cool. Fold into whipped cream.

GREAT MERINGUE

*This makes a fine, high meringue, thanks to my friend Marion
Cunningham and The Fannie Farmer Baking Book!*

⅔ cup egg whites (about 6 large egg whites)
½ cup granulated sugar
⅓ teaspoon cream of tartar
¼ teaspoon salt

Combine all ingredients in large mixing bowl. Place over pan of hot water
and stir briskly until mixture feels slightly warm to the back of your hand or
finger, about 15 seconds. Remove bowl from water and beat with mixer on
high speed until meringue holds firm peaks, about 1½ minutes.

Do no overbeat or the meringue will be dry and hard to spread.
YIELD: ENOUGH TO COVER A 9-INCH PIE.

 BOILED ICING

Mother Groff often broiled this icing on a yellow cake for quick entertaining.

4 tablespoons (½ stick) butter, melted
5 tablespoons evaporated milk
⅓ cup firmly packed light brown sugar
½ cup coconut (medium shred)

In small mixing bowl, combine all ingredients thoroughly. Spread on warm cake. Do not remove cake from pan. Place cake on medium rack of oven. Broil 6 minutes or until icing bubbles and is golden brown.

YIELD: ENOUGH TO ICE ONE 13 X 9-INCH CAKE.

CREAM CHEESE FROSTING

This is easy to make and especially good on fruit and nut cakes.

3 ounces cream cheese
6 tablespoons butter (¾ stick), at room temperature
1 cup confectioner's sugar
1 teaspoon vanilla extract

Beat all ingredients in large mixing bowl until satin smooth. Frost cake when cool.

YIELD: ENOUGH TO FROST ONE 9 X 13-INCH CAKE OR TWO 9-INCH LAYERS

Variation:

Chocolate Cream Frosting:
Add 1 square unsweetened chocolate (1 ounce) or
2 tablespoons unsweetened cocoa powder to above recipe.

CHAPTER ELEVEN

Puddings, Cookies, Candies, and Other Pennsylvania Dutch Treats

 **APPLE MERINGUE PUDDING**

This is not just another applesauce. It is a wonderfully light and airy pudding. Granny Smith, Greening, or summer Rambo apples are especially good.

12 tart cooking apples, peeled and cored
1 cup water
6 large eggs, separated
⅔ cup granulated sugar
2 tablespoons (¼ stick) butter
½ teaspoon ground nutmeg
½ teaspoon ground cinnamon
½ teaspoon lemon extract
½ teaspoon almond extract
⅓ teaspoon salt

Meringue:
⅓ teaspoon cream of tartar
¼ cup granulated sugar
½ teaspoon lemon extract
Ground nutmeg or cinnamon, or cinnamon sugar for garnish

Preheat oven to 375°F.
Place apples and water in large saucepan and cook covered, over medium heat until soft, about 10 minutes. Puree in food processor, food mill, or blender, then transfer to large mixing bowl. Beat egg yolks lightly with fork and add to apples, along with sugar, butter, nutmeg, cinnamon, extracts, and salt. Beat thoroughly and pour into buttered baking dish or pan. Bake for 12 minutes. While baking apples, whip egg whites and cream of tartar into soft peaks. Slowly add sugar and lemon extract and beat until it forms stiff peaks. Remove pan from oven only long enough to spread meringue on top. Cut through pudding with blade of table knife to make sure some of meringue gets into apples. Swirl meringue with tip of blade and place in oven until golden brown, about 15 minutes. Be careful not to burn top. Turn off oven and let stand for another 10 minutes. Remove from oven and cool before serving. Sprinkle with nutmeg or cinnamon or cinnamon sugar. This is good served warm or cold.
YIELD: ABOUT 3 CUPS

🦚 BREAD PUDDING 🦚

Everyone loves this bread pudding. It's delicious with a lemon sauce.

6 cups bread cubes or slices without crusts, cut into large pieces
¾ teaspoon ground nutmeg
½ teaspoon ground cinnamon
½ cup raisins
3 cups milk
3 tablespoons butter
3 large eggs, lightly beaten
½ cup granulated sugar
¼ teaspoon salt
1 teaspoon vanilla extract
¼ cup slivered blanched or toasted almonds (optional)

Preheat oven to 375°F.

Place bread cubes or pieces in buttered 7 x 11-inch or 9-inch square baking dish or pan. Combine nutmeg, cinnamon, and raisins, and sprinkle evenly over bread. Heat milk in 1½-quart saucepan over medium-high heat. Add butter. Combine eggs, sugar, and salt, and stir into milk until completely dissolved. Add vanilla, then slowly pour milk mixture over bread. Let stand for 15 minutes or until bread absorbs liquid. Top with almonds, if desired. Bake for 1 hour or until golden colored and knife, inserted in center, comes out clean. Serve warm with or without sauce.

YIELD: 6 SERVINGS

INDIAN PUDDING

The American Indian has given us so many wonderful corn dishes, this being one of them. It's great served with Whipped Cream (page 213) or Hard Sauce (page 156).

½ **cup cornmeal**
2 **cups milk, scalded**
1 **tablespoon butter**
¼ **cup table molasses (golden, barrel, or King Syrup), do not use**
   baking molasses
⅔ **cup raisins**
1 **large egg, lightly beaten**
2 **tablespoons granulated sugar**
½ **teaspoon salt**
¼ **teaspoon ground ginger**
¼ **teaspoon ground cinnamon**
2 **cups milk**

Preheat oven to 300°F.

Stir cornmeal into hot milk with whisk, stirring until smooth. Add butter, molasses, raisins, egg, sugar, salt, ginger, and cinnamon. Blend thoroughly and let stand until it thickens, about 5 minutes. Pour into buttered 1-quart baking dish. Top with 2 cups milk. Bake for 2 hours or until set. Serve warm.

YIELD: 6 SERVINGS

 VANILLA CREAM PUDDING

This is often served with fresh or canned fruit, layered if you wish, for a beautiful dessert. It also makes the perfect filling for Cream Puffs (see the recipe on page 240).

¾ cup granulated sugar
6 tablespoons all-purpose flour
¼ teaspoon salt
2 cups milk
2 tablespoons (¼ stick) butter
2 large eggs, lightly beaten
1 teaspoon vanilla extract

Combine sugar, flour, and salt in small bowl. Scald milk in large, heavy saucepan and gradually pour in sugar mixture, stirring constantly over medium heat until thickened, about 5 minutes. Add butter and stir. Remove small amount of thickened filling and pour it over beaten eggs. Mix together, then pour into filling, simmering over low for 5 more minutes. Remove from stove and add vanilla. Cool (place wax paper on top to prevent top from drying) and serve.

YIELD: ABOUT 3 CUPS OR ENOUGH TO FILL 1 DOZEN LARGE CREAM PUFFS

MARSHMALLOW PUDDING

Even though there aren't any marshmallows in this pudding, it tastes and looks as though there are. Children and adults alike love it.

1 quart milk
3 tablespoons cornstarch
½ cup milk
¼ teaspoon salt
¾ cup granulated sugar (less if desired)
1 teaspoon butter
2 large egg whites, stiffly beaten
1 teaspoon vanilla extract
2 ounces (2 squares) unsweetened chocolate
Whipped Cream for topping (page 213; optional)

Scald quart of milk in 2-quart saucepan. While heating it, combine cornstarch, milk, salt, and sugar. Add to scalded milk, reduce heat to low, and cook until thickened, about 10 minutes. Stir in butter and divide pudding into 2 equal parts. Cool for several minutes, then fold beaten egg whites and ½ teaspoon of vanilla into one part. Stir melted chocolate and remaining vanilla into other half. Spoon alternate spoonsful into chilled mold. Chill, covered with wax paper or plastic wrap, until firm, at least 2 hours. Unmold by dipping mold in warm water for about 15 seconds. Place serving plate on top of mold and quickly turn it upside down. Leave mold in place and refrigerate for few minutes to keep pudding from weeping. Remove mold and top pudding with whipped cream if desired.

YIELD: 6 SERVINGS

RHUBARB-ORANGE PUDDING

*This was one of the first fresh puddings of the season. Now
rhubarb is available almost all year round.*

**4 oranges, 3 cups peeled, seeded, sliced, and quartered with a sharp
 knife (about 3 cups)**
6 stems rhubarb, trimmed and cut in 1-inch cubes (about 4 cups)
Juice of 1 lemon
½ cup water
½ cup granulated sugar
¼ teaspoon salt
5 tablespoons tapioca
½ cup orange juice
1 cup apple wine or light white wine
Several drops of red food coloring (optional)
2 or 3 dashes of ground nutmeg
Grated orange rind for garnish

Place oranges and rhubarb in heavy 2-quart saucepan and add lemon juice,
water, sugar, salt, and tapioca. Bring to boil and simmer over low heat for
5 minutes, stirring occasionally. Add orange juice and apple wine. Cook till
thickened, approximately 6 minutes. Stir in food coloring and nutmeg, then
remove from stove and let cool for at least 10 minutes. Pour into serving
bowl. When ready to serve, garnish with curls of orange rind or fresh flowers.
YIELD: 6 SERVINGS

CARAMEL PUDDING

Most people think of this as butterscotch pudding. It's a far cry from the boxed kind. It is so smooth and creamy, I guess that's why it's Abe's favorite.

2 tablespoons (¼ stick) butter
1 cup lightly packed brown sugar
½ teaspoon salt
3 cups milk
1 tablespoon all-purpose flour
2½ tablespoons cornstarch
2 large eggs, lightly beaten
1 teaspoon vanilla extract

Melt butter in heavy skillet or large saucepan. Add brown sugar and salt, stirring constantly over medium-high heat until it caramelizes, about 5 minutes—be careful not to burn it. Remove from stove and slowly mix in 2 cups of milk. Return to stove and heat to near boiling over medium heat, stirring constantly. Combine flour and cornstarch and stir in; then slowly add remaining cup of milk. Reduce heat to low and cook until thickened and smooth. Remove few tablespoons of pudding, and stir them into beaten eggs; then return mixture to pudding. Cook another 2 minutes, being careful not to let it boil. Remove from heat and stir in vanilla. To prevent skin from forming on top, lay wax paper over it. Serve warm or cold.
YIELD: 6 SERVINGS

GLORIFIED RICE

Everyone's favorite pudding, this was often called heavenly rice. A special family dinner or church social was not complete without it. It's pretty, light, and always popular with all ages.

2 cups (20-ounce can) pineapple tidbits
¼ cup granulated sugar
2 cups cooked long-grain rice (soft but not mushy)
24 marshmallows or 2 cups of miniature marshmallows
1 cup heavy cream, whipped to form peaks
Maraschino cherries and pecan halves or chopped nuts for garnish

Drain pineapple and combine it with sugar. Stir until sugar dissolves and add to rice in large mixing bowl. Fold in marshmallows and let stand for at least 1 hour. Before serving, fold in whipped cream until blended. Garnish with cherries and nuts. Chill until ready to serve.
YIELD: 6 SERVINGS

🦚 RICE PUDDING 🦚

Everyone asks why my rice pudding is so creamy. When you start with natural rice and cook it slowly, you'll understand why the extra effort is worth it.

1 cup long-grain rice
2 cups water
½ teaspoon salt
6 cups milk
¼ pound (1 stick) butter or margarine
½ teaspoon salt
¼ cup granulated sugar
2 large eggs, beaten
1 teaspoon vanilla extract

Place rice, water, and salt in medium-size saucepan and boil over medium heat for 15 minutes. Drain. In heavy saucepan or on top of double boiler over simmering water, heat milk, butter, and salt until butter melts. Add rice and simmer over low heat, lightly covered, for 1½ hours, stirring often to prevent sticking. Then, combine sugar and beaten eggs thoroughly and slowly blend in with rice. Continue to simmer until thickened but not boiling, about 15 minutes. Remove from heat and add vanilla or any other flavorings you desire. Serve warm or chilled.

YIELD: 6 SERVINGS

Variations:

For different flavors, add in 1 tablespoon fresh lemon juice, 1 cup raisins, or several dashes of ground cinnamon at same time you add sugar and eggs.

CRANBERRY CRUMBLE

The apples keep this dessert from being too tart.

Bottom part:
1 cup uncooked oatmeal
1 cup lightly packed light brown sugar
½ cup all-purpose flour
1 teaspoon ground cinnamon
6 tablespoons (¾ stick) butter
¾ cup chopped English walnuts

Top:
8 ounces cream cheese
½ cup firmly packed light brown sugar
3 tablespoons cornstarch
¼ teaspoon salt
2½ cups cranberries, fresh or frozen
3 apples, cored, peeled, and sliced
¼ cup orange juice

Preheat oven to 350°F.
Blend all ingredients for bottom part together in large mixing bowl, rubbing with your hands until they form large crumbs. Reserve half and press other half of crumbs into buttered 9-inch baking pan or dish. Bake for 15 minutes. Set aside. Beat or stir cream cheese until smooth and creamy and spread in bottom of baked shell. Combine brown sugar, cornstarch, and salt together in large mixing bowl. Toss cranberries and sliced apples in orange juice, then add to brown sugar mixture. Mix thoroughly and spoon onto cream cheese. Top with reserved crumbs. Bake for 45 minutes or until golden brown. Cool and serve chilled.
YIELD: 6 SERVINGS

Variations:

Rhubarb-Strawberry Crumble:
3 cups coarsely chopped rhubarb and 2 cups sliced strawberries for cranberries and apples.

Blueberry Crumble:
Substitute 4 cups blueberries for cranberries and apples and add ½ teaspoon ground nutmeg, ½ teaspoon grated lemon rind, and 1 tablespoon fresh lemon juice to above recipe.

Peach Crumble:
Substitute 4 cups sliced peaches for cranberries and apples. Add ½ teaspoon ground cinnamon, ½ teaspoon ground nutmeg, 1 teaspoon each of grated orange and lemon rind, and 1 teaspoon fresh lemon juice to above recipe.

🦎 FRUIT AND NUT COOKIES 🦎

Barb's great-grandmother from Somerset County made these cookies for her friends and family, using their own homemade maple sugar. Today, her family enjoys these cookies most during the holidays.

1 cup lightly packed maple sugar or light brown sugar
¼ pound (1 stick) butter
3 large eggs, lightly beaten
½ cup table molasses (golden, barrel, or King Syrup), not baking molasses
2½ cups all-purpose flour
1 teaspoon ground nutmeg
½ teaspoon ground cloves
1 teaspoon ground cinnamon
½ teaspoon ground ginger
1 teaspoon baking soda dissolved in ½ cup boiling water
1 cup raisins
1 cup chopped dates
1 cup chopped nuts

Preheat oven to 350°F.

Cream sugar and butter together in large mixing bowl until light and fluffy. Gradually add eggs and molasses, beating thoroughly. Sift flour, nutmeg, cloves, cinnamon, and ginger together in another bowl. Add flour mixture to creamed mixture alternately with soda water until batter is smooth and creamy. Fold in raisins, dates, and nuts. Chill dough for at least one hour. Drop by spoonful onto greased cookie sheet about 2 inches apart. Bake for 10 to 12 minutes or until mark is not left in center of cookie when lightly touched with your finger. Cool on clean linen towel. Store in airtight container. They taste better if stored for day or two.

YIELD: ABOUT 4 DOZEN 2-INCH COOKIES

 ICE-BOX NUT COOKIES

Delicious and old-fashioned, these cookies are good anytime.

2 cups lightly packed light brown sugar
½ cup lard or vegetable shortening
¼ pound (1 stick) butter
2 large eggs, lightly beaten
3½ cups sifted all-purpose flour
1 teaspoon baking soda
½ teaspoon salt
1 teaspoon vanilla extract
1 cup broken or coarsely chopped nuts

Preheat oven to 350°F.

In large mixing bowl, cream brown sugar, lard, and butter together until light and fluffy. Gradually add beaten eggs, combined thoroughly. Sift flour, baking soda, and salt together in another bowl, then slowly add to creamed mixture. Add vanilla, beat thoroughly, then fold in nuts. Form dough into roll about 2 inches in diameter, wrap in plastic wrap, and freeze for at least 1 hour. When hard, slice about ¼-inch thick and place on greased cookie sheet. Bake for about 6 minutes or until golden brown—watch them carefully, they burn easily.

YIELD: ABOUT 5 DOZEN 2-INCH COOKIES

🪺 PEPPERNUTS OR SOFT SUGAR CAKES 🪺

We always put a raisin in the middle of these delightfully soft cookies. Those who liked to "dunk" their cookies left them on a plate overnight, uncovered, so they would get a bit dry. The next morning they would dunk them in hot chocolate or coffee.

¼ pound (1 stick) butter
2 tablespoons (¼ stick) margarine
1⅓ cups granulated sugar
2 large eggs
¾ cup buttermilk
1 teaspoon baking soda, dissolved in 1 tablespoon boiling water
1 teaspoon vanilla extract
3 cups all-purpose flour
1 teaspoon baking powder
½ teaspoon ground nutmeg
¼ teaspoon salt
¼ cup raisins

Preheat oven to 350°F.

Cream butter, margarine, and sugar together in large mixing bowl until light and fluffy. Beat in eggs, one at time, beating lightly. Add buttermilk, dissolved soda, and vanilla, mixing thoroughly. Sift together flour, baking powder, nutmeg, and salt in another bowl. Gradually add to creamed mixture and beat until well blended. Refrigerate dough for 30 minutes. Drop batter by teaspoonsful onto greased baking sheet, spacing them at least 2 inches apart. Place raisin in center of each and bake for 15 minutes or until light brown. Test bake only one at first; if it is too thin, add bit more flour to batter. They will spread out, but should not be really thin.

YIELD: ABOUT 36 2-INCH COOKIES

 RAISIN-FILLED COOKIES

A year-round favorite, these cookies are made in large quantities in order to have enough to dunk in coffee after they become a bit dry. During the holidays or for special occasions, dates and figs were used instead of raisins and they were cut into fancy shapes.

Dough:
¾ **cup granulated sugar**
½ **cup vegetable shortening, at room temperature**
1 **large egg**
2½ **cups sifted all-purpose flour**
¼ **teaspoon salt**
2 **teaspoons baking powder**
¼ **cup milk**
1 **teaspoon vanilla extract**

Filling:
2 **teaspoon all-purpose flour**
½ **cup granulated sugar (less if desired)**
1 **cup water (or part apple cider or sweet red or white wine)**
1½ **cups raisins, or part chopped dates and figs**
½ **teaspoon grated lemon rind**
1 **tablespoon fresh lemon juice**
½ **teaspoon ground nutmeg**

Preheat oven to 350°F.

Cream sugar and shortening together in large mixing bowl until light and fluffy. Beat in egg. Sift sifted flour, salt, and baking powder together in another bowl. Add to creamed mixture alternately with milk until well blended. Mix in vanilla and chill, covered, until cold, about 1 hour. For filling, combine all ingredients in large saucepan and bring to boil, cooking over medium heat, about 5 minutes or until thickened. Cool filling thoroughly. Roll chilled dough very thin on floured board. Cut in rounds (2½ to 3 inches) or fancy shapes and place on greased cookie sheet about 1 inch apart. Spoon small teaspoonful of filling in center of each cookie. Cut tops for each cookie with same cutter, only cut out center of each with small cutter or thimble to allow filling to show through. Before putting tops on each, moisten edges of bottom cookie with wet finger or pastry brush. Place top on each and crimp with prongs of fort to seal. Bake for 15 minutes.
YIELD: ABOUT 3 TO 4 DOZEN, DEPENDING ON SIZE OF CUTTER

🦋 SAND TARTS 🦋

Our friend Elwood Grimm makes the best sand tarts in the world, using his father's recipe. For over 60 years Elwood has been making the traditional family specialty. He claims the cookies taste better when the dough is mixed with warm hands instead of a mixer. I believe him—you may want to try it, too.

2 cups (1 pound) confectioner's sugar
½ pound (2 sticks) butter, at room temperature
3 large eggs, lightly beaten
4 cups all-purpose flour, sifted
1 teaspoon vanilla extract
1 large egg, well beaten
½ cup granulated sugar
1½ teaspoons ground cinnamon
½ cup finely chopped pecans or English walnuts

Preheat oven to 350°F.

Cream sugar and butter together in large mixing bowl, beating vigorously with one hand until smooth, light, and creamy. Stir in eggs, slowly, until well blended. Stir in flour with wooden spoon or by hand until thoroughly blended. Add vanilla and mix well. Chill, covered, for several hours. Roll small amount of dough at time, keeping remainder of dough cold. Roll dough very thin, ⅛ to ¼ inch thick, using very little flour on board. Cut out cookies with cutter and place on greased cookie sheet. Brush with bit of beaten egg, top with sugar, cinnamon and nuts. Bake on middle rack until golden brown, about 7 minutes. Watch them closely to make sure they don't burn. Grease sheet each time after removing baked cookies. Remove and cool on clean linen towels. These cookies taste better after being stored in airtight containers for day or two.

Yield: About 9 to 10 dozen 2-inch cookies

SPRITZ COOKIES

Children love to decorate these cookies. Whatever the occasion, these cookies are always appreciated.

1¼ cups confectioner's sugar
½ pound (2 sticks) butter, at room temperature
2 large egg yolks
2½ cups all-purpose flour
½ teaspoon baking powder
⅛ teaspoon salt
1 teaspoon almond extract
1 teaspoon vanilla extract
Few drops of food coloring (optional)
Various toppings, chopped nuts, sprinkles, colored sugar (see Hint below)

Preheat oven to 375°F.

Cream sugar and butter together in large mixing bowl until light and fluffy. Slowly add egg yolks, beating thoroughly. Sift flour, baking powder, and salt together in another bowl. Gradually add flour to creamed mixture, beating until smooth. Add extracts and blend. Remove amount of dough that you want for plain vanilla cookies if you plan on adding food colorings to some of dough. Add food colorings to remaining batches of dough. Wrap each color dough in plastic wrap and chill thoroughly, at least one hour. When chilled, shape ball of dough into size of cookie press tube. Fill tube and press into desired shapes. Press onto ungreased cookie sheet, at least one inch apart. Decorate with topping of choice. Bake for 8 to 10 minutes or until set but not brown. Remove from cookie sheet immediately and place on clean linen towels to cool.

YIELD: ABOUT 6 DOZEN COOKIES

Hint:
To make your own colored sugar, place ½ cup of granulated sugar in clear plastic bag. Add few drops of food coloring and shake vigorously until evenly colored. Place in dry, warm area to dry for about 10 minutes. Stir and store in airtight container.

🦋 BLACK WALNUT BARS 🦋

The Blum family of York County shared this recipe with my family when I was a little girl. Even though I hated gathering and shelling the walnuts (they make your hands really black), enjoying these walnut bars made it all worthwhile.

Bottom layer:
1 cup lightly packed light brown sugar
½ pound (2 sticks) butter or ½ margarine, ½ butter
1½ cups all-purpose flour

Top layer:
2 cups lightly packed light brown sugar
4 large eggs, well beaten
2 teaspoons vanilla extract
½ teaspoon salt
2 tablespoons all-purpose flour
½ teaspoon baking powder
3 cups chopped black walnuts (English walnuts or pecans may be substituted)

Preheat oven to 350°F.

Cream sugar and butter together in large mixing bowl until well blended. Stir in flour thoroughly. Spread evenly in greased 9 x 3-inch baking pan. Bake for 5 minutes. It will look bubbly with holes all over, but that is fine. Let cool while making top layer. For top, cream brown sugar and eggs together in large mixing bowl until light and fluffy. Add vanilla. Sift salt, flour, and baking powder together in another bowl and add to egg mixture. Fold in nuts and pour over baked bottom layer. Return to oven and bake for 20 minutes or until light brown on top and firm to touch. Cool and cut into bars. Do not cut them too thin or they will crumble. These keep well if stored in an airtight container.

YIELD: 3 TO 4 DOZEN 1 X 2-INCH BARS

 DATE-FIG BALLS

These are best if eaten within a day or two; otherwise, the cereal loses its crunchiness.

¼ **pound (1 stick) butter or margarine**
1 **cup granulated sugar, less if desired**
2 **large eggs, lightly beaten**
½ **cup chopped dates**
½ **cup chopped figs or raisins**
2½ **cups Rice Krispies**
⅓ **cup chopped nuts**
⅓ **cup shredded coconut**

Melt butter in large, heavy saucepan. Add sugar, eggs, dates, and figs. Bring to boil over medium heat, stirring constantly with wooden spoon to prevent scorching. Cook slowly until thickened, about 6 minutes. Remove from heat and let cool to lukewarm. Fold in Rice Krispies and nuts. Form into small balls and roll in coconut. Cool on wax paper and store in airtight container.
YIELD: ABOUT 5 DOZEN COOKIES

🦅 MERINGUES 🦅

Instead of filling pie shells with fruit, make light and fluffy meringues, any size, and fill them with fresh fruit, pudding, or fruit sauce. The meringues may be made the day before, stored in airtight containers, and filled at the last minute.

3 large egg whites (about ½ cup), at room temperature
⅓ teaspoon cream of tartar
¾ cup granulated sugar
⅛ teaspoon salt
½ teaspoon vanilla extract

Preheat oven to 275°F.

Place egg whites and cream of tartar in large mixing bowl and beat with wire whisk beater or regular beater until frothy. Gradually add sugar, by tablespoonsful, to egg whites while beating on high speed. Add salt and vanilla and beat until whites hold firm peaks, approximately 1½ minutes. Do not over beat or meringue will be dry and hard to work with. Line baking sheet with parchment paper. With tip of knife, draw size circles you prefer meringues to be when finished. Spoon meringue into large pastry bag fitted with large star tip. Starting in center of each circle, pipe meringue in continuous spiral, filling in each circle. Pipe ring of meringue on top edge of each circle. If you want meringue stars for topping, pipe them on parchment, too. Bake for 45 minutes or until very light gold and firm to touch. They may crack, but that makes them pretty. Peel off parchment and let cool completely before storing. If you live in dry climate, meringues will stay crisp and fresh longer at room temperature in airtight container. If it is damp or humid, it is best to freeze them and crisp them in warm 150°F oven for 10 minutes before filling. Fill with your favorite filling or fresh fruit with fruit glaze.
Yield: two 9-inch rounds or six 3½-inch rounds

 CARAMEL CORN

*I could eat popcorn every day, but this is my favorite way to make it. This
keeps well in an airtight container, so make a lot at a time.*

1 cup granulated sugar
¼ cup lightly packed light brown sugar
6 tablespoons light corn syrup (I use Karo)
1½ teaspoons cider vinegar
6 tablespoons water
½ teaspoon salt
2 tablespoons (¼ stick) butter
½ teaspoon baking soda
½ teaspoon vanilla extract
1 cup salted or dry roasted peanuts (optional)
14 cups popped corn

Preheat oven to 200°F.

Combine sugars, syrup, vinegar, and water in large, heavy saucepan. Bring
to boil and cook over medium heat, brushing sides of pan with wet pastry
brush, until syrup reaches 290°F on candy thermometer (soft-crack stage),
about 12 minutes. If you do not have candy thermometer, drop bit of syrup
in cold water. It should turn hard and crack into pieces. Stir in salt and
cook over medium-high heat until it reaches hard-crack stage or 300°F on
thermometer, about 3 minutes. If you do not have thermometer, drop few
drops of syrup in more ice water; it should turn brittle at once. Remove from
heat and stir in butter, baking soda, and vanilla until well blended. Add nuts
to popcorn if desired and spread popcorn evenly in two buttered 9 x
13-inch baking pans. Pour syrup over all popcorn and mix until all kernels
are coated. Bake for 1 hour, stirring every 15 minutes. Cool on sheets of wax
paper and store in airtight containers.
YIELD: OVER 14 CUPS

🐦 CANDIED APPLES 🐦

Red candied apples are usually sold at popcorn stands at fairs, carnivals, or any outdoor festival. The more familiar recipe is the caramel apple, plain or rolled in nuts or shredded coconut. This is easy to make since all you have to do is melt caramels and dip the apples in the mixture and add sticks. The candied apples take time and are most enjoyed by children who don't mind getting their faces sticky.

6 small apples, suitable for eating on a stick (McIntosh, Jonathan, Red Delicious, Stayman, Winesap, or Baldwin are best)
6 popsickle sticks
¾ cup red cinnamon candies (sometimes called red hots, imperials, or hearts)
¼ cup granulated sugar
½ cup boiling water
¼ teaspoon fresh lemon juice
Few drops of red food coloring (optional)

Wash and dry apples and insert sticks into stem end of each. Apples should be room temperature to prevent moisture from forming inside taffy. Mix rest of ingredients together and cook over medium heat in small saucepan until reaching 300°F on candy thermometer (softball edge) or when you drop few drops in cold water and syrup gets hard and cracks immediately, about 12 minutes. It takes awhile to reach this stage but it occurs quickly, so do not leave area while syrup is boiling. As it nears 280°F, watch closely as it may burn if you do not take it off heat. Quickly dip each apple into hot syrup, covering it completely, and place it on greased cookie sheet to dry. Store on wax paper in dry area. If they are stored in moist or refrigerated area, they will weep and become sticky.

YIELD: 6 CANDIED APPLES

 CLEAR TOY CANDIES

I remember the clear toys we made that were molded in many shapes, such as reindeer, trains, animals, ships, birds, and most of all, children with their favorite toys, standing proudly in clear or tinted colors on tables, plates, or centerpieces. We made the same candy during the rest of the year, but during the holidays, the molds were a very special part of the celebration. The rest of the year we called it hard candy, but during special occasions we molded it to represent the season. Today, the molds are very expensive and sought after because they are no longer available or are only found in antique shops. The funny thing is, the recipe was the same, just the addition of food coloring for the holidays made them look different. As children, we were sure they tasted different, too. To purchase reproduction molds, write to Albert C. Dudrear, 125 East Philadelphia Street, York, PA 17403.

2 cups granulated sugar
⅔ cup light corn syrup (I use Karo)
1 teaspoon cider vinegar
⅔ cup water
Few drops of yellow, red, or green food coloring
1 teaspoon oil of peppermint or spearmint extract (optional)

Oil molds or shallow cake pans or muffin tins with olive or vegetable oil. Combine sugar, corn syrup, vinegar, and water together in deep saucepan. Stir until sugar is completely dissolved. Bring to boil over high heat. Do not stir mixture during cooking. Place candy thermometer in syrup and boil until it reaches 290°F. Add food coloring and any flavoring. Remove from heat and pour into molds. Do not scrape sides of pan or you will get sugar crystals in candies. If you pour it into flat pans, score it before it cools or break into pieces after it is dry. Store in cool, dry place in airtight container.

YIELD: ABOUT 1½ POUNDS

⁂ BEST AND EASIEST CANDY ⁂

Everyone makes this candy and it is fun to see how each family presents it. Some cut it into bars, some into squares, but the taste is still the same–delicious!

Equal amounts of marshmallow, melted chocolate (milk or dark chocolate), and roasted almonds

Stir all ingredients together and pour into baking dish or onto cookie sheet about 1½ inches thick. When cooled, cut as desired and wrap in clear plastic wrap or wax paper.
YIELD: DEPENDS ON VOLUME OF INGREDIENTS

Hint:
Any type of roasted nut is good in this recipe.

⁂ MORAVIAN MINTS ⁂

These mints are an important traditional treat. They are not hard to make after you see someone make them, but try them the second time before you give up. They are crunchy, not creamy like butter cream mints. If you do not have the old molds, don't worry. Pour them into the new plastic molds or even drop them on a lightly oiled cookie sheet, using ½ teaspoon syrup per mint.

2 pounds confectioner's sugar
½ cup plus 2 tablespoons water
Few drops of red, yellow, or green food coloring
½ teaspoon oil of wintergreen, peppermint, or spearmint extract

Place some water in bottom of double boiler and bring to boil. Place sugar and water in top part of boiler and stir over medium-high heat every five minutes for approximately 30 minutes (it will develop crust on top between stirrings). When sugar is dissolved but still runny, and reaches 180°F on candy thermometer, pour ½ teaspoon of mixture onto plate. If it hardens and doesn't run all over plate, add coloring and flavoring, and cook till it reaches 190°F, about 5 minutes. Stir completely and remove from heat. Pour into molds or spoon about ½ teaspoonful for each mint onto buttered or oiled cookie sheets. Do not scrape mixture from sides of pan or mints will contain crystallized sugar. When dry, store in airtight container between sheets of wax paper. Mints will be thin and crunchy. They are best when stored in cool, dry place.
YIELD: 1½ POUNDS

 VANILLA PULL TAFFY

Pulling taffy is especially fun during the cold winter months. The main reason for making it during the cold weather is because the taffy is very warm during pulling. Although it can be done alone, it is much more fun when made with a friend. Our youth group at church often planned a "taffy pull" for at least thirty children. The real competition was to see who could get their taffy white and smooth first. The screams of pleasure were as exciting as the best of summer games.

1 cup water
1½ cups light corn syrup (I use Karo)
2½ cups granulated sugar
3 tablespoons butter
¼ teaspoon salt
1 tablespoon vanilla extract

Butter sides of 3-quart stainless steel saucepan or kettle. Add water, syrup, and sugar, stirring with wooden spoon until sugar is dissolved. Bring to boil over medium-high heat without stirring. Place candy thermometer in syrup and continue to boil until syrup reaches 256°F, approximately 25 minutes. Add butter and salt and continue cooking till it reaches 262°F, about 2 minutes. Remove from heat and pour into oiled or buttered shallow pan or buttered marble slab or counter. When cool enough to handle, butter or oil your hands and pull sides of taffy toward middle. Add some of vanilla, work taffy for about 1 minute, and add remaining vanilla. Continue pulling taffy until it is creamy white and lukewarm. Keep your hands buttered to prevent taffy from sticking to them. When cool, twist into strands of taffy. Place on buttered counter, cut into 1-inch pieces with oiled scissors, and let dry or wrap in wax paper or plastic wrap. Store in airtight containers.
YIELD: 2 POUNDS

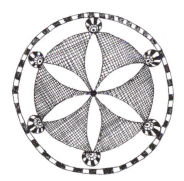

🪶 PEANUT BRITTLE 🪶

Everyone loves this brittle, and when wrapped in a fancy box, it's really special.

2 cups granulated sugar
3 cups light corn syrup (I use Karo)
¼ teaspoon salt
3 cups unroasted peanuts
1 teaspoon baking soda

In heavy 10-inch skillet (an iron skillet is best) pour sugar in circle. Add corn syrup and salt to center and place over medium heat. As syrup begins to boil, add raw peanuts and cook for an 8 additional minutes. Reduce heat to low and cook another 15 minutes or until syrup reaches 300°F on candy thermometer, stirring constantly. Then remove from stove and stir in baking soda. Butter cookie sheet or marble slab and pour out brittle evenly. As it begins to set, score it with sharp knife dipped in cold water. Break brittle into pieces when it is dry and cool. Store in dry, airtight container.
YIELD: ABOUT 2 POUNDS

Hint:
Any type of nut may be substituted for peanuts.

🪶 MAPLE FUDGE 🪶

The Pennsylvania Dutch of Somerset County always give this as their special treat for any occasion. We cannot include all the ways they use maple syrup, but they pour it over everything from waffles to ice cream. Making the syrup takes many hours and the final product is truly an act of love.

½ cup sweetened condensed milk diluted with ½ cup water or 1 cup
**   heavy cream or half and half**
1 cup lightly packed light brown sugar
¾ cup pure maple syrup
Pinch of salt
1 teaspoon butter
1 teaspoon vanilla extract
¾ cup pecans, broken into small pieces

Place diluted milk, sugar, syrup, and salt in heavy saucepan. Stir until blended and heat slowly till boiling, stirring constantly. Boil over high heat without stirring until syrup reaches 238°F, soft ball stage, when drop of syrup dropped in cold water forms soft ball. Remove pan from heat; add butter, but do not stir it in. Cool to lukewarm, then beat with mixer until creamy and thick. Add vanilla and nuts. Work with your hands (warm hands make fudge smoother) until very smooth and creamy. Spread in buttered 8-inch square pan, cut into small squares, and let cool.
YIELD: ABOUT 1 POUND

🌿 MARSHMALLOWS 🌿

Often known as "poor man's candy," this is fun to make and gets loads of raves.

6 tablespoons unflavored gelatin
⅔ cup water
3 cups granulated sugar
¾ cup light corn syrup (I use Karo)
¾ cup water
4 large egg whites
⅓ teaspoon cream of tartar
½ teaspoon salt
2 teaspoons vanilla extract
2 tablespoons cornstarch
1 cup confectioner's sugar or 2 to 3 cups toasted shredded coconut

Mix gelatin with ⅔ cup water in small bowl to soften. In heavy 3-quart saucepan combine sugar, syrup, and ¾ cup water. Bring to boil, stirring with spatula to get all crystals from sides of pan only one time. Continue to boil over medium-high heat, undisturbed, till syrup reaches 240°F on candy thermometer. Remove pan from heat and stir in gelatin (it will seem solid but will melt minute it hits hot syrup). Transfer mixture to bowl and beat with mixer until fluffy. Beat egg whites until nearly stiff in large mixing bowl. Gradually add cream of tartar and salt. Beat until very stiff. Slowly add gelatin mixture and continue beating until it is very thick and stringy, approximately 15 to 20 minutes. Beat in vanilla and cornstarch. Generously oil 11 by 13-inch baking pan and dust it with small amount of confectioner's sugar. Pour mixture into pan and dust with bit of confectioner's sugar. Let stand uncovered for several hours. Cut into 1-inch squares and roll in sifted confectioner's sugar or toasted coconut. (Dip knife in hot water first for easy, clean cutting).
YIELD: 2 POUNDS

 CREAMY NO-COOK FUDGE

You can make this one in a hurry.

8 ounces cream cheese
¼ cup condensed milk
2 tablespoons (¼ stick) butter
2 or 3 ounces (2 or 3 squares) unsweetened chocolate, melted,
**   or ½ cup unsweetened cocoa**
2 cups confectioner's sugar
1 teaspoon vanilla extract
½ teaspoon salt
1 cup chopped nuts (optional)

Combine all ingredients but nuts in large mixing bowl. Beat until creamy, about 15 minutes. If too dry, add small amount of milk to moisten. Remove from bowl, add nuts, work with your hands until very creamy, about 10 minutes. If you knead fudge on clean kitchen counter or marble slab, it will take longer, about 20 minutes. Press into lightly buttered 8-inch pan and score with an attractive pattern. Chill and cut when firm.
YIELD: ABOUT 1½ POUNDS

CREAM PUFFS

These are one of the best "fundraisers" for 4-H and high school band projects. I like them filled with Vanilla Cream Pudding (see page 218), but when they're made very small and filled with ham or chicken salad, they're great for parties.

1 cup water
¼ pound (1 stick) butter
¼ teaspoon salt
1 cup all-purpose flour
4 large eggs

Preheat oven to 425°F.
Put water in heavy saucepan and bring to boil over medium-high. Add butter and salt. When melted, add flour and stir briskly with wooden spoon. Reduce heat to medium-low and continue to cook, stirring constantly, until mixture leaves sides of pan, about 5 minutes. Remove from heat, cool for 5 minutes, then beat in eggs, one at time until batter is smooth and well mixed. Drop by spoonsful onto greased baking sheet or muffin pans, shaping batter to point. Place about 2 inches apart. Bake in oven for 15 minutes, reduce to 350°F and continue baking for 25 to 30 minutes longer. Cool and fill with your favorite filling. Pierce hole in side of cream puff and pipe filling in with large pastry tube or split half way around and fill with small spoon.
YIELD: 12 TO 15 CREAM PUFFS

❧ WHOOPIE PIES ❧

If you want these to last for any length of time, you have to wrap and freeze (or hide) them. They always seem to disappear before your eyes.

1 cup vegetable shortening or margarine
2 cups granulated sugar
2 large eggs
3½ cups all-purpose flour
1 cup unsweetened cocoa
2 teaspoons salt
2 teaspoons baking soda
1 cup buttermilk or milk soured with 1 tablespoon vinegar
1 cup hot coffee or water

Filling:
2 large egg whites
1 tablespoon vanilla extract
¼ cup milk
2 cups confectioner's sugar
¼ cup all-purpose flour
1 cup vegetable shortening
¼ pound (1 stick) butter

Preheat to 375°F.

Cream shortening and sugar together in large mixing bowl. Beat in eggs, one at time. In another bowl, sift flour with cocoa, salt, and baking soda. Gradually add this to creamed mixture alternating with buttermilk. Mix in hot coffee. Drop batter in teaspoonsful onto greased cookie sheets, space them about 3 inches apart. Bake in oven for 8 minutes. Store on wax paper until all cookies have been baked. For filling, beat egg whites until fluffy. Gradually beat in vanilla, milk, sugar, and flour. Add shortening and butter and beat until very fluffy. Take one cookie and place generous tablespoon of filling on flat side. Top with another cookie; they should look like yo-yos. These freeze well if wrapped individually.

YIELD: ABOUT 48 TO 60 WHOOPIE PIES

🐝 BASIC SWEET DOUGH 🐝

I love to use this recipe to make all kinds of party breads.

2 packages dry granular yeast or 2 yeast cakes
½ cup lukewarm water
Pinch of granulated sugar
1 cup milk, scalded
⅓ cup granulated sugar
1 teaspoon salt
2 large eggs, lightly beaten
4 tablespoons (½ stick) butter
4 tablespoons (½ stick) margarine
5 cups sifted all-purpose flour

Proof yeast by combining yeast with lukewarm water and pinch of sugar. If it foams, it is active and ready. Pour milk, sugar, and salt in large mixing bowl and stir until sugar is dissolved. Cool to lukewarm, then add yeast mixture, beaten eggs, butter, and margarine. Gradually add flour, kneading with dough hook of mixer or by hand on lightly floured surface for approximately 5 minutes or until dough is smooth and elastic; it should not stick to bowl or board. If it does, add more flour. Turn dough into greased bowl, turning it so all sides are greased. Cover with clean, damp cloth and let rise in warm, draft-free area until doubled in bulk, about 1 hour. Knead on lightly floured surface for minute to remove all air bubbles. When smooth, cover and let rise again until almost double, about 30 minutes. Shape as desired and bake as particular recipe indicates.

YIELD: 1 LARGE PAN OF ROLLS OR 1 COFFEE CAKE

 RAISED DOUGHNUTS

*Doughnuts are to Pennsylvania Dutch as bagels are to New Yorkers, and
they aren't just for breakfast anymore. The Dutch like to dunk them in
coffee or, for the children, hot chocolate after they are a day old.*

1 recipe of Basic Sweet Dough (page 242)
3 cups vegetable oil
½ cup confectioner's or granulated sugar

After second rising, knead and roll out dough ⅓-inch thick on well-floured
board. Cut with floured 3-inch doughnut cutter. Let rise on board until
almost doubled, approximately 40 minutes, uncovered. Heat oil in deep,
heavy skillet or pan to 375°F. Gently place doughnuts in oil, making sure
they do not touch one another. Turn them when golden brown on one side or
after about 3 minutes. Drain on paper towels. Place sugar in bag and shake
doughnuts in it until covered. If glazing them, use sugar icing used for hot
cross buns on page 177.
YIELD: 3 TO 4 DOZEN DOUGHNUTS

Variations:

Crullers:
Follow same instructions for raised doughnuts, but roll dough ½ inch
thick and cut into strips ½ inch wide and 8 inches long. Twirl or braid
two strips together and seal ends for each cruller. Let rise, then fry as for
doughnuts—they may take bit longer to fry because of double thickness
of cruller—about 4 minutes on each side. Shake in granulated sugar.
YIELD: ABOUT 2 DOZEN CRULLERS

Filled Doughnuts:
Follow same instructions as for raised doughnuts, but instead of cutting
dough into round doughnuts with hole in middle, cut dough in 3-inch
squares, prick them with fork several times on top, let rise, and then
fry as for raised doughnuts. Use pastry tube or cake decorator to fill
centers of doughnuts after they have fried with Vanilla Cream Pudding
(page 218), Apple Butter (page 251), or your favorite jelly by piercing
tip of tube into side of doughnut. Fill and shake in granulated sugar.
YIELD: 3 DOZEN FILLED DOUGHNUTS

Fried Dough:
Follow same instructions as for raised doughnuts, but cut dough
into strips ¾ inch wide and 8 inches long. Let rise, then fry as
for doughnuts. Serve plain or with sugar and molasses.
YIELD: 3 DOZEN STRIPS

🦅 FASTNACHTS 🦅

Better known as potato doughnuts, fastnachts are always baked
for Shrove Tuesday. A tradition with all the Christian churches,
this treat is very important to the Pennsylvania Dutch.

1 cup milk
1 cup cooked mashed potatoes
⅔ cup granulated sugar
½ teaspoon salt
3 tablespoons butter or vegetable shortening
3 tablespoons margarine
2 large or medium-size eggs, lightly beaten
1 package dry granular yeast or 1 yeast cake
¼ cup lukewarm water
6 cups all-purpose four
Vegetable oil for frying
Granulated or confectioner's sugar for coating

Scald milk and let cool to lukewarm while blending mashed potatoes, sugar, salt, butter, and margarine in large bowl. Gradually add beaten eggs and stir until creamy. Dissolve yeast in lukewarm water and add to potato mixture. Alternate adding in milk, flour, mixing or kneading with dough hook until dough is smooth and elastic, about 4 minutes. Turn into large greased bowl, turning until all sides are greased. Cover and set in warm, draft-free area. Let rise until double, about 45 minutes. Punch down or knead to remove all bubbles. Divide in half and roll out about ¾ inch thick. Cut dough in 3-inch squares, making 1-inch diagonal slit with greased knife. Cover squares and let sit until almost double. Fry them in 3 inches of oil heated to 370°F until they are golden brown on both sides. Drain on paper towels and shake in sugar while still warm.
Yield: 24 Fastnachts

Variation:

Cut and serve as regular doughnuts, frying the "holes" separately.

FUNNEL CAKES

*One of the oldest snacks or after-school treats, these are
becoming popular the world over. Great!*

**1 cup all-purpose flour
2 teaspoons granulated sugar
1 teaspoon baking powder
½ teaspoon salt
1 large or medium-size egg, lightly beaten
¾ cup milk
Vegetable oil for frying
Confectioner's sugar**

In large bowl, combine flour, sugar, baking powder, and salt. Gradually add
in beaten egg and milk until well blended. Let mixture stand for 15 minutes.
Heat ⅓ inch of vegetable oil in deep skillet to 390°F. When oil is hot, pour
batter into funnel, drizzling a thin stream of batter into hot oil. Start in center
of skillet, circling continuously until pan is filled or cake is desired size. Do
not stop pouring until cake is complete. Fry on each side until golden brown.
Drain on paper towels and serve warm with confectioner's sugar for dipping.
YIELD: 6 LARGE FUNNEL CAKES

Variation:

Add ⅓ cup semisweet chocolate mini-chips or morsels or
3 ounces semisweet grated chocolate to the batter.

 CHOCOLATE-COVERED PRETZELS

*Always served at Amish weddings and other special occasions, these treats
have become popular everywhere. They're fun and easy to make and keep
well in airtight containers to send to friends. Again, the secret is in the
combination of salty and sweet so familiar to the Pennsylvania Dutch.*

**1 pound chocolate of your choice (I prefer semisweet or any dark
sweet chocolate)**
1 pound thin pretzels, any size
Sprinkles (optional)

Melt chocolate in top of double boiler over simmering water. (Do not let any
steam or even drop of water make contact with chocolate or it will harden
and crumble.) Cool chocolate until, when touched to the upper lip, it feels
cool. This can be done by stirring chocolate with a silver spoon or working it
on marble or stainless steel surface by hand. Quickly dip pretzels in chocolate
and lightly cover with sprinkles while still moist. If you coat pretzels this way,
you do not have to refrigerate them, as it prevents chocolate from spotting at
room temperature.

YIELD: ABOUT 2 POUNDS

Variation:

Sprinkle with crushed nuts.

🎋 ICE CREAM 🎋

There's nothing like churning your own ice cream, adding in all the fresh fruits, and sitting down to a creamy bowl–especially on a hot day!

4 large eggs
2⅔ cups granulated sugar
⅓ teaspoon salt
2 (13-ounce) cans evaporated milk
1½ cups heavy cream
2½ cups milk
1½ tablespoons vanilla extract

Cream eggs, sugar, and salt together in large mixing bowl, blending until fluffy. Stir in evaporated milk, cream, milk, and vanilla. Pour into can of 4-quart freezer and cover with lid. Pack with crushed ice and rock salt, turning until ice cream is hard. (Using rock salt instead of iodized salt will reduce turning time.) Add more crushed ice, bit of water, and salt as ice melts, keeping ice to top of outside of freezer but not over lid. Be careful that salt does not seep into ice cream mixture inside freezer can.
YIELD: 4 QUARTS

Variation:

Add 2 cups any type of pureed fruit before you start turning freezer.

 FRIED ICE CREAM

Use any flavor ice cream for this delicious treat.

2 tablespoons vegetable oil
4 Crepes (page 60)
1⅓ cups ice cream
4 teaspoons butter, melted
4 teaspoons light brown sugar
¼ cup orange juice
Whipped Cream (page 213) or confectioner's sugar for garnish

Heat vegetable oil in large skillet over medium-high heat until it quickly fries cube of fresh bread, about 5 minutes. While heating skillet, place crepes on large serving dish and put ⅓ cup ice cream in center of each one. Quickly fold up sides of crepe into center. Brush tops of crepe with ½ teaspoon of butter and sprinkle with 1 teaspoon of brown sugar and 1 tablespoon of orange juice. Place crepes in heated skillet and fry over medium-high heat until they are golden brown, about 3 minutes. Turn and fry them on other side until butter, sugar, and juice caramelize, about 4 minutes. Serve immediately with whipped cream or sprinkled with confectioner's sugar, if desired.

YIELD: 4 SERVINGS

CHAPTER TWELVE

Preserves, Relishes, Pickles, and Vinegars

 CANNING OR PROCESSING METHODS

Canning—Cold-Pack Method

Home canning is really very simple. Although at first it may seem rather expensive to invest in all those jars and home canner, which is deep pot fitted with rack to hold 7 quart jars or 12 pint jars, remember that you will be using them over and over again for years. You only need to buy new replacement lids each time you fill jars. The rings, if washed and dried after each use, are usually good for at least 5 years. You can use big, deep pot and put rack inside, but canner is good investment. It doesn't cost much and you can also use it for cooking corn, steaming clams, or any kind of quantity cooking. Rack has handles so it is easy to lower or lift jars.

Technique for canning is simple, once you get used to it. First sterilize your jars for 15 minutes in boiling water, leaving them in water with heat off until you are ready to drain and use them. You can also sterilize them by leaving them in 250°F oven for 20 to 25 minutes. Be sure jars are hot when you pack them, as heat ensures that they seal properly. Best and safest jar to use is type with vacuum-seal flat lid and screw-on ring cover that fits over it. Don't boil lid, which has rubber seal around inside; just pour boiling water over it and leave in water until ready to use.

Drain, fill, and seal sterilized jars. Most home-canning booklets tell you to leave ½-inch head space for fruits and relishes, but I find it works best to fill jars to neck only. I also like to start canning from cool water, rather than putting jars into boiling water, as most booklets recommend. I lower jars on rack into canner, add enough water to come to neck of jars, bring this to boil, and boil for required time with cover on. This is known as cold-pack method.

For transferring fruits or relishes to jars, use glass or stainless steel measuring cups, slotted enamel, stainless steel, or wooden spoons, or enameled ladles, plus wide-mouthed funnel for filling jars with liquid.

(continued on next page)

(continued)

Fruits are canned in sugar or water syrup. I like to use thick syrup made from 1 cup granulated sugar and 1 cup water. You may reduce sugar by as much as ½ cup or use sugar substitute, following your own taste. Place it in saucepan and bring to boil over high heat. When sugar is completely dissolved, remove it from heat, keeping syrup warm until you are ready to pour it over fruit. Pack fruit in sterilized jars and add enough syrup to fill jar to neck. Before sealing, release any air that may be trapped in liquid by running long, thin, rubber spatula down between inside of jar and fruit, moving fruit around slightly to let air out. Wipe tops of jars, seal with vacuum lids and covers, and process by filling canner with lukewarm water up to necks of jars. Bring to full boil, covered, over medium-high heat. Start timing after water comes to full boil. Most fruits require 15 minutes for proper sterilization. Remove canner from heat and use metal tongs to secure jars as they are removed from water. If you have canner, basket is easily lifted up and rests on side of canner, making it very easy to remove jars. Place jars on linen towels away from drafts to cool. Let them stand at least 12 hours before storing them. Lid should be indented. If it is not, fruit inside should be discarded or consumed immediately. Before storing filled jars, wipe jars clean and make sure each one is sealed.

Canning—Open Kettle Method

Open kettle canning is usually done for jellies, jams, butters, and small amounts of fruit. Process means boiling jellies or fruit in syrup over medium heat until it is finished and ready to jar. When boiling fruit, it should give a bit when pressed. If fruit is halved, 12 minutes is adequate but if fruit has pits, such as apricots, they should be cooked 15 minutes. Transfer fruit into sterilized jars, fill to neck with hot syrup and seal with new lids and rings. Let them stand at last 12 hours before storing them. Store away from direct sunlight.

🦅 APPLE BUTTER 🦅

Traditionally, apple butter was made in a huge copper kettle and was an all-day affair. This recipe has been cut down and adapted to today's kitchen.

**15 pounds tart cooking apples (Winsap, Stayman, or Smokehouse
  varieties are best)**
2½ cups water
3½ cups granulated sugar
1½ cups cider vinegar
1 teaspoon ground cinnamon
½ teaspoon salt

Preheat oven to 375°F.

Wash, peel, core, and quarter apples. Put apples and water in large, heavy kettle and cook over low heat until fruit is soft, about 15 minutes. Drain extra liquid from apples and puree in food mill or food processor. Add sugar, vinegar, cinnamon, and salt to apple puree. Blend and pour mixture into heavy roasting pan. Bake, uncovered, for about 2½ hours, stirring every 15 minutes with wooden spoon to prevent sticking. This also keeps apple butter color even. It is ready to jar or serve when you can place 2 tablespoons of apple butter on saucer and turn it upside down without it dropping off. Ladle into hot sterilized jars and seal with new lids and rings.
YIELD: 10 PINTS

Variation:

Pear Butter is made by substituting an equal amount of pears
  for apples and adding 1 teaspoon ground nutmeg.

🐚 SPICED CANTALOUPE 🐚

Very delicately flavored, this unusual relish is excellent served with seafood.

2½ pounds firm, ripe cantaloupes (the better the fruit, the better the relish)
1 cup granulated sugar
¼ cup water
½ cup cider vinegar
Oil of cinnamon and oil of cloves; use 1 drop of each per pint
For canning instructions, see page 249.

Wash cantaloupe, and cut it in half to remove seeds; then cut into 1-inch slices and peel. Cut slices into 2-inch pieces or place slices whole into sterilized pint jars. Combine sugar, water, and vinegar in small, heavy saucepan and bring to boil over high heat. Reduce heat to medium and simmer for 2 minutes, then slowly pour some of syrup over cantaloupe. Add drops of oil on top of cantaloupe, fill to neck of jar with more. Place new self-sealing lid and cover on each jar and process in home canner for 15 minutes, timing from moment water comes to full boil.
YIELD: 5 PINTS

Variation:

Spiced Peaches:
Follow same recipe as spiced cantaloupe, but use peeled
peach halves instead of cantaloupe slices.

 BRANDIED APRICOTS

*There are so many ways to serve this recipe–let your imagination run wild! My
family enjoys them plain. We serve them with warm pudding or cake and pour
the syrup over the top, sometimes adding extra brandy to flambe. Try melting
your favorite chocolate bars and pouring it over the apricots right before serving.
Fill each apricot half with ice cream or sherbet or just use them for a fruit salad
topped with whipped cream flavored with 2 tablespoons of its syrup.*

2 cups granulated sugar
¾ cup water
¼ teaspoon salt
1½ teaspoons cider vinegar
2 pounds fresh apricots
1 cup brandy

In large enamel or stainless steel saucepan combine sugar, water, salt, and
vinegar. Bring to boil over high heat and add apricots. Reduce heat to
medium and simmer for 10 to 12 minutes, depending on size of apricots.
Remove fruit and let syrup boil over medium heat for 8 minutes more.
Remove pan from heat, add brandy and fruit and blend together. Ladle
apricots and syrup into hot sterilized jars and seal with new lids and rings.
Do not move jars for 12 hours to prevent seals from breaking. Store away
from direct sunlight for several weeks at least before serving.
YIELD: 4 PINTS

Variation:

Peaches, pears, and plums may be substituted. Peaches and
pears are best when peeled and plums should be pricked with
fork several times to prevent skins from bursting.

BASIC PICKLING SYRUP, SWEET

*The Pennsylvania Dutch love their pickles and relishes sweet,
thereby getting the tag line "Sweets and Sours."*

4 cups granulated sugar
2 cups cider vinegar
2 cups water
1 teaspoon salt
1 tablespoon celery seed
1 tablespoon mustard seed
1 tablespoon pickling spices (optional)

Combine all ingredients in large saucepan, stir, and bring to boil. Simmer
5 minutes over medium-high heat, adding any extra spices pickle recipe calls
for. Remove from heat and pour into sterilized jars. Seal with new lids if
you are not using it within day or two. Syrup will keep for several weeks in
refrigerator.
YIELD: 6 CUPS

Variation:

For semisweet pickling syrup that is somewhat
tart, decrease amount of sugar to 2 cups.

THREE-BEAN RELISH

*Many folks add oil and wine vinegar to this to create a beautiful
salad served on lettuce with hard-boiled eggs.*

3 cups green beans
3 cups yellow or wax beans
4 large onions
⅓ cup vegetable oil
6 cups Basic or Semi-sweet Pickling Syrup (page 254)
3 cups canned red kidney beans, rinsed and drained

Cut beans and onions into bite-size pieces. Put beans, onions, oil, and syrup
in 8-quart kettle. Bring to boil and simmer over medium heat until vegetables
are tender but not mushy, about 12 minutes. Add drained kidney beans
and simmer 5 more minutes over medium heat. Ladle into hot sterilized
jars, filling to neck of each jar and seal with new lids and rings. Let jars
stand 12 hours before moving to cool storage area to prevent breaking seals.
Refrigerate after opening.
YIELD: 10 PINTS

DILL BEANS

*It takes a long time to pack these beans but they are so good
to nibble on and enjoy anywhere, anytime.*

4 pounds whole, firm, young, green beans, trimmed
½ cup salt
4 fresh tarragon sprigs or 2 teaspoons dried
6 cups white vinegar
4 cups water
2 tablespoons dill seed
2 teaspoons dried dillweed

Soak beans for 1 hour in large pot with salt and enough water to cover. Rinse
and cover with fresh cold water. Bring to boil and cook over medium heat,
uncovered, for 2 minutes only. Drain into colander. When cool enough to
handle, pack trimmed whole beans lengthwise, carefully, into hot, sterilized
pint jars. Tuck sprig of tarragon (or put ½ teaspoon dried tarragon) in each
jar. Combine vinegar, water, dill seed, and dillweed in large saucepan, bring
to boil, and boil 2 minutes over medium heat. Pour over beans in jars and
seal with new lids and rings. Let stand 24 hours before moving to cool
storage area or shelves to prevent breaking seals. Refrigerate after opening
jar. They will keep at least 3 weeks if lid is closed properly.
Yield: 8 pints

🦚 CHOW CHOW 🦚

One of the most important and colorful of the relishes, chow chow is great served with any meal. The fun in making this relish is to see how many kinds of vegetables you can get in a jar.

1 cup each of lima beans, green beans (cut in 1-inch pieces),
  yellow beans (cut in 1-inch pieces),
  drained canned Great Northern beans,
  drained canned red kidney beans,
  drained canned navy beans,
  cauliflower buds,
  chopped celery,
  chopped red bell peppers,
  chopped green bell peppers,
  carrots (cut in ¼-inch pieces),
  corn kernels,
  pearl onions or chopped onions,
  grated cabbage,
  and sliced cucumbers or tiny pickles (1½ inches long)
5 cups Basic or Semi-sweet Pickling Syrup (page 254)
½ teaspoon ground turmeric
½ teaspoon salt

If frozen vegetables are used, they may be cooked together. For fresh vegetables, cook each vegetable separately in small amount of water over medium heat until tender but not mushy. Do not cook canned beans. Drain each and layer in large pan. Gently blend with your hands or wooden spoon to prevent breaking vegetables. Drain again. In large kettle bring syrup to boil, add turmeric, and salt, and gently spoon in vegetables with pierced spoon. When vegetables come to boil, simmer over medium heat for 5 minutes. Ladle into sterilized pint jars, filling to neck of each jar, and seal with new lids and rings. Let jars stand for at least 12 hours before moving them to cool storage area to prevent breaking seals. Refrigerate after opening.

YIELD: 7 PINTS

CORN RELISH

The cabbage in this relish is what makes the difference.

**6 cups Basic Pickling Syrup, using 4 cups white vinegar instead of
     cider vinegar and water (page 254)**
8 cups corn kernels, fresh or frozen
2 cups chopped cabbage
1 cup chopped onion
½ cup chopped green bell pepper
**½ cup chopped red bell pepper (substitute extra green pepper if red
     unavailable)**

Place everything in an 8-quart kettle. Bring to boil and simmer over medium
heat for 10 minutes. Ladle into hot sterilized jars, filling to neck of each jar,
and seal with new lids and rings. Let stand for 12 hours before moving them
to cool storage area to prevent breaking seals. Refrigerate after opening.
YIELD: 8 PINTS

RED PEPPER RELISH

Colorful, versatile, and tasty.

1 teaspoon salt
½ teaspoon dry mustard
4 cups Basic or Semi-sweet Pickling Syrup (page 254)
9 large red bell peppers, cored, seeded, and chopped
3 large onions, chopped
1 stem celery, chopped

Add salt and dry mustard to pickling syrup in 4-quart kettle. Stir and bring
to boil. Add peppers, onions, and celery, and bring to boil. Simmer over
medium heat for 10 minutes. Ladle into hot sterilized jars, filling to neck of
each jar, and seal with new lids and rings. Let stand 12 hours before moving
to cool storage area to prevent breaking seals. Refrigerate after opening.
YIELD: 6 PINTS

Variation:

Green bell peppers may be substituted for red. Add ½ teaspoon
     of cayenne pepper or Tabasco sauce if you like it hot.

 WATERMELON RIND PICKLES

So beautiful to serve, but truly an act of love to make, these are gifts of food that are treasured with every bite.

¼ **cup salt**
4½ **cups water**
2½ **pounds watermelon rind, peeled (leave ¼ inch of the pink flesh for color) and cut into 2-inch pieces**
2½ **cups granulated sugar**
1 **cup cider vinegar**
1 **cup water**
⅛ **teaspoon oil of cinnamon**
⅛ **teaspoon oil of cloves**
(The oils prevent the fruit from getting dark. If the oils are not available, use 1 teaspoon each of whole cloves and broken cinnamon sticks, placed in tea infuser.)

Mix salt and 4 cups of water until dissolved and pour over rind in an enamel, plastic, or stainless steel container. Cover and soak overnight. Next day drain and rinse rind in cold water. Drain again. Cook over high heat in enough fresh water to cover rind until rind is tender and translucent, about 30 minutes. Drain. Combine sugar, vinegar, ½ cup water, and oils in large enamel or stainless steel kettle and bring to full boil. Remove from heat and add rind. Let stand, lightly covered, overnight. Next day, drain syrup into large saucepan and bring to boil. Simmer over medium heat for several minutes and pour over rind again. Repeat this process for 3 days to make rind clear. Over last day, cook rind and syrup together over high heat for 3 minutes. Ladle into hot sterilized jars and seal with new lids and rings. Let jars stand for 12 hours before moving to cool storage area to prevent breaking seals. Refrigerate after opening.

YIELD: 6 PINTS

Variation:

Add ½ teaspoon peeled, sliced ginger root for added flavor.

🗒 DILL PICKLES 🗒

*These are so tasty, easy to prepare, and beautiful in the jars, it is
certainly worth the few minutes it takes to prepare them.*

**3 large cucumbers
1½ teaspoons dill seed
½ teaspoon dried dillweed
¾ teaspoon mustard seed
½ teaspoon minced garlic
½ cup cider vinegar
6 tablespoons water
2¼ teaspoons salt**

Wash cucumbers and cut into quarters lengthwise. If they have wax on the
shell, run hot water over them until you can wipe it off with paper towels.
Arrange in sterilized pint jars and add dill seed and dillweed, mustard seed,
and garlic. In large enamel or stainless steel kettle, combine vinegar, water,
and salt, and bring to boil over medium-high heat. Pour over cucumbers.
Seal jars with new lids, cover with rings, and process in canner for 5 to
6 minutes, timing from moment water comes to boil.
YIELD: 3 TO 4 PINTS, DEPENDING ON THE SIZE OF THE CUCUMBERS

🗒 BREAD-AND-BUTTER PICKLES 🗒

*These are the old standby because they go with everything—no
hamburger should be without them, sliced razor thin.*

**4 large, unwaxed cucumbers, sliced ¼ inch thick
3 large onions, sliced ¼ inch thick
½ large green bell pepper, chopped
½ large red bell pepper, chopped
2 tablespoons salt
4 cups ice cubes
3 cups Basic or Semisweet Pickling Syrup (page 254)
½ teaspoon ground turmeric
¼ teaspoon dried dillweed**

Toss cucumbers, onions, and peppers with salt in large bowl. Cover with ice
cubes and let stand three to four hours. Add turmeric and dillweed to pickling
syrup and bring to boil over high heat in large enamel or stainless steel kettle.
Rinse vegetables in cold water and add to boiling syrup. Boil over medium
heat for 3 minutes. Ladle into sterilized pint jars, filling to neck of each jar,
and seal.
YIELD: 5 PINTS

 SEVEN-DAY PICKLES

These pickles are so good, they definitely are worth the effort.

5 pounds medium-size cucumbers, 3 to 4 inches long
4 cups cider vinegar
4 cups granulated sugar
1 cup water
1 tablespoon salt
4½ teaspoons mixed whole pickling spices
Several drops of green food coloring (optional)

Wash cucumbers, holding them under hot water if they are waxed until you can wipe wax off with paper towel. Put them in large stock pot. Cover them with boiling water, cover with lid and allow to stand for 1 day. Drain and repeat process every day for four days, using fresh boiling water each time. On fifth day slice or quarter cucumbers. Combine vinegar, sugar, water, salt, and spices in large enamel or stainless steel kettle. Bring to boil over high heat and add cucumbers. Remove from heat and let stand, covered, till next day, then drain off syrup, add coloring, and bring syrup to boil in large saucepan. Pour over cucumber in kettle and bring to full boil. Pack in hot, sterilized, pint jars and seal. For canning instructions see "open kettle" method on page 250.

Yield: 6 pints

Variation:

Two-Day Sweet Pickles:
Dissolve 1 cup salt in 16 cups cold water. Let cucumbers stand in salt water brine for 24 hours. Drain and puncture each cucumber several times with fork. Bring vinegar, sugar, water, salt, and spices to boil in large enamel or stainless steel kettle, add cucumbers, and simmer over medium heat for 30 minutes. Remove from heat and let stand, covered, for 1 day. Drain syrup into large saucepan and add 1 cup vinegar and 1 cup granulated sugar. Stir until dissolved, then simmer over medium heat for 5 minutes. Pour over whole cucumbers in kettle and bring to full boil. Arrange cucumbers in hot, sterilized pint jars and seal, using new seals. Process according to "open kettle" canning method, explained on page 250.

Yield: 6 pints

 HERB VINEGAR

Use any fresh herb, blossom and all. If you like to combine herbs, put a sprig of tarragon with a sprig of thyme. Chives and chive blossoms look and taste nice with parsley. Rosemary is best with mint. A sprig of oregano or basil with its blossoms is delightful or combine them for a full-flavored vinegar. You can use small bottles as long as you can find corks that fit them–and don't forget to label them!

Handful of the fresh herbs of your choice
2 cups cider vinegar
2 cups white vinegar
1 tablespoon granulated sugar

Wash herbs and place several sprigs in each sterilized bottle. Bring vinegars and sugar to boil in large saucepan and pour over herbs. Cork tightly. Store at room temperature away from direct sunlight. Refrigerate after opening.
YIELD: 2 PINTS

CELERY VINEGAR

Mild and wonderful with fresh cutting lettuce.

1 large bunch fresh celery with leaves, chopped
2 tablespoons celery seed
2 cups cider vinegar
3 cups white vinegar
1 teaspoon salt
1½ tablespoons granulated sugar

Place celery in gallon jar or crock and add celery seed. Bring vinegars to boil in medium-size saucepan, add salt and sugar and stir until dissolved. Pour over chopped celery and cover. Let stand in cool place for at least two weeks. Strain through double thickness of cheesecloth, let stand, covered, overnight and bottle in sterilized containers. Cork tightly. Store away from direct sunlight. Refrigerate after opening.
YIELD: 3 TO 4 PINTS

ONION VINEGAR

Fun to make for gifts, it looks extra special when a few tiny onions are placed in the bottles before corking. This tastes great on burgers, fish, fillets, or in salad dressings!

6 large onions, chopped
1 tablespoon salt
3 cups white vinegar
2 cups cider vinegar
2 tablespoons granulated sugar

Sprinkle onions with salt and let stand, covered, overnight or at least 5 hours. Put onions in gallon crock or glass jar. Bring vinegars to boil and stir in sugar. Pour vinegar over onions and cover lightly. This will foam for few days, so be sure to use jar that is large enough to prevent exploding. Steep for two weeks in cool place. Then strain through double thickness of cheesecloth, bottle in sterilized containers, and cork. Store away from direct sunlight. Refrigerate after opening.

YIELD: 3 TO 4 PINTS

PEPPER VINEGAR

A splash of this will liven up any recipe that calls for vinegar. It is particularly delicious splashed on raw oysters, crab, or fish.

2 teaspoons whole black peppercorns
2 cups cider vinegar
2 cups white vinegar
½ teaspoon Tabasco sauce
2 tablespoons granulated sugar

Crush peppercorns with wooden mallet and place in crock or glass container. Bring vinegars and Tabasco to boil. Add hot vinegar and sugar to peppercorns, stirring until sugar is dissolved. Cover and let stand at least two weeks. Strain through double thickness of cheesecloth and bottle in sterilized containers. Cork tightly. Store away from direct sunlight. Refrigerate after opening.

YIELD: 2 PINTS

 # SUPERB VINEGAR

A very old recipe, this proves that light salad dressings always existed. It also makes a wonderful seasoning for gravies, sauces, and stews.

2 teaspoons allspice
1 teaspoon whole black peppercorns
1 tablespoon freshly grated nutmeg
2 tablespoons grated fresh horseradish
Pinch of red (cayenne) pepper
1 tablespoon salt
1 tablespoon granulated sugar
4 cups white vinegar

Crush allspice and peppercorns with wooden mallet. Place everything but vinegar in large, heavy saucepan. Then pour in vinegar and bring to boil. Remove from heat, pour into covered container, and let stand for at least two weeks. Strain through double thickness of cheesecloth and bottle in sterilized containers. Cork tightly. Store away from direct sunlight. Refrigerate after opening.

YIELD: 2 PINTS

❧ INDEX ❧

C

W

Cookbooks Published
by Cookbook Resources, LLC

Bringing Family and Friends to the Table

The Best 1001 Short, Easy Recipes

The Best 1001 Short, Easy Recipes

1001 Slow Cooker Recipes

1001 Short, Easy, Inexpensive Recipes

1001 Fast Easy Recipes

1001 America's Favorite Recipes

Easy Slow Cooker Cookbook

Busy Woman's Slow Cooker Recipes

Busy Woman's Quick & Easy Recipes

365 Easy Soups and Stews

365 Easy Chicken Recipes

365 Easy One-Dish Recipes

365 Easy Soup Recipes

365 Easy Vegetarian Recipes

365 Easy Casserole Recipes

365 Easy Pasta Recipes

365 Easy Slow Cooker Recipes

Super Simple Cupcake Recipes

Leaving Home Cookbook and Survival Guide

Essential 3-4-5 Ingredient Recipes

Ultimate 4 Ingredient Cookbook

Easy Cooking with 5 Ingredients

The Best of Cooking with 3 Ingredients

Easy Diabetic Recipes

Ultimate 4 Ingredient Diabetic Cookbook

4-Ingredient Recipes for 30-Minute Meals

Cooking with Beer

The Washington Cookbook

The Pennsylvania Cookbook

The California Cookbook

Best-Loved New England Recipes

Best-Loved Canadian Recipes

Best-Loved Recipes from the Pacific Northwest

Easy Slow Cooker Recipes (Handbook with Photos)
Cool Smoothies (Handbook with Photos)
Easy Cupcake Recipes (Handbook with Photos)
Easy Soup Recipes (Handbook with Photos)
Classic Tex-Mex and Texas Cooking
Best-Loved Southern Recipes
Classic Southwest Cooking
Miss Sadie's Southern Cooking
Classic Pennsylvania Dutch Cooking
The Quilters' Cookbook
Healthy Cooking with 4 Ingredients
Trophy Hunters' Wild Game Cookbook
Recipe Keeper
Simple Old-Fashioned Baking
Quick Fixes with Cake Mixes
Kitchen Keepsakes & More Kitchen Keepsakes
Cookbook 25 Years
Texas Longhorn Cookbook
Gifts for the Cookie Jar
All New Gifts for the Cookie Jar
The Big Bake Sale Cookbook
Easy One-Dish Meals
Easy Potluck Recipes
Easy Casseroles Cookbook
Easy Desserts
Sunday Night Suppers
Easy Church Suppers
365 Easy Meals
Gourmet Cooking with 5 Ingredients
Muffins In A Jar
A Little Taste of Texas
A Little Taste of Texas II
Ultimate Gifts for the Cookie Jar

cookbook resources LLC

www.cookbookresources.com
Toll-Free 866-229-2665
Your Ultimate Source for Easy Cookbooks

Classic **Pennsylvania Dutch** COOKING

300 Classic, Homemade, Hand-Me-Down Favorites

cookbook resources LLC

www.cookbookresources.com

Toll free 1-866-229-2665

Your Ultimate Source for Easy Cookbooks